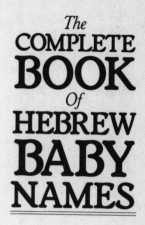

*The*
COMPLETE
BOOK
*Of*
HEBREW
BABY
NAMES

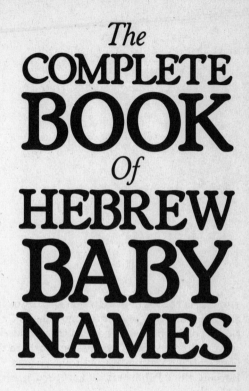

# The
# COMPLETE
# BOOK
## Of
# HEBREW
# BABY
# NAMES

## SMADAR SHIR SIDI

HarperSanFrancisco
*A Division of* HarperCollins*Publishers*

**Library of Congress Cataloging-in-Publication Data**

Sidi, Smadar Shir.
    The complete book of Hebrew baby names.

    1. Names, Personal—Jewish.    2. Names, Personal—Hebrew.
I. Title.
CS3010.S5    1989    929.4'4'089924    88-45679
ISBN 0-06-254850-6 (pbk.)

99 00 01 02  RRD(H)  20 19 18 17 16 15 14 13 12

# Contents

# Preface

"Could you please help me find a nice Hebrew name for my baby?"

If I could get a penny for each time I have heard this question, I would be a millionaire. And if I could get a dollar for each time I have helped to choose a Hebrew name....

Many people turned to me for names when I lived in Israel, where I worked as a journalist and wrote children's books. They were familiar with my writing, they knew I liked to give modern names to my heroes, and although they knew Hebrew as well as I did, they came to me for special names.

I was happy to share my ideas with them. Why not? At that time, I didn't have any children of my own, but whenever my suggestion for a name was accepted, I felt almost like a second mother to the baby.

In 1982, when my family and I moved to Minnesota, I faced a new name dilemma. Nice people shook my hand, saying, "It's good to meet you," but they couldn't pronounce my name—Smadar. It was a real tongue twister! Soon after, when people in the Twin Cities started to know me as a Hebrew teacher and a writer, they repeated the same old question: "Could you please help me find a nice Hebrew name?"

This book is an attempt to answer that question for contemporary Jewish parents. I have attempted to provide a complete directory of traditional and contemporary Hebrew names, plus advice and information on choosing a name. I can't consult with you in person, but I hope that *The Complete Book of Hebrew Baby Names* is the next best thing.

# Acknowledgments

Lots of friends deserve warm thanks for the endless lists of Hebrew names they gave me, and I thank them all.

In addition, I would like to take this opportunity to thank two very special people: Anna Marie Gardner, from Excelsior, Minnesota, my editor, without whose help this book would never have been written; and Vicki Lansky of The Book Peddlers, from Deephaven, Minnesota, my agent, without whose work this book would never have been published.

# Introduction:
# Why a Jewish Baby
# Has a Hebrew Name

The Hebrew name is an important part of the personality of every Jewish child. In Israel, of course, all children have Hebrew names. Many Jewish people in the United States and Canada, even those who don't plan to move to Israel, want their children to have names in Hebrew, the language of the Bible.

Religious Jewish people give their children Hebrew names (mainly from the Bible) as first names. In other families the Hebrew name is used as a second name, but it still has a special significance. It's more than an ordinary English middle name. It's part of the Jewish identity of the child.

Jewish people who do not live in Israel use their Hebrew names in several different ways. Some of them identify themselves with their Hebrew names only among other Jewish people, in their homes, and at synagogue. Others decide to use their Hebrew names all the time, in every place, even among non-Jewish people. There are no rules. Each person has the right to choose how and when to use his or her Hebrew name. A person may even choose not to use it at all.

The Hebrew name is given to the child at birth, often at a special naming ceremony. (See pages 11 to 12.) It is printed on the birth certificate. If parents send their children to a Jewish school (a full program or a Sunday school), the teachers will call them by their Hebrew names. If parents celebrate the bar mitzvahs or bat mitzvahs of their children, they will be called by their Hebrew names to read the Torah.

The Hebrew names of the bride and groom will appear in the Ketubah (as well as the Hebrew names of the parents and their witnesses). The Hebrew name will accompany the Jewish person until his or her last day on Earth and will be engraved on the tombstone.

When the baby who is given a Hebrew name grows up, he or she can choose how to use the Hebrew name. If you choose not to give your baby a Hebrew name, you keep this choice from your offspring.

I hope that this book will be a guide and resource for expectant parents and grandparents, for adult North American Jews who never received Hebrew names and would like to adopt them, and for those who would like to change their Yiddish names or their out-of-date Hebrew names to popular, modern Hebrew names.

# PART ONE

# 1.

# Choosing a Hebrew Name
# for Your Baby

Almost every Jewish child in the United States and Canada gets two names—one in English and one in Hebrew—and equal effort is made in searching for both names.

In some cases, of course, you may not have a choice—you want to name the baby after a relative and want to give your baby that relative's exact Hebrew or Yiddish name, even if it is out of date and unpopular. Or you may choose a modern Hebrew name that has the same meaning or initial sound as the name of your relative. But there are lots of other options too. You may want to give your newborn a name from the Bible, even though the variety of biblical names seems limited. Or you may have visited Israel or dream of moving there someday and are looking for the name of an Israeli flower or lake, a historical hero, or a beautiful spot you enjoyed in the Holy Land. Whatever your needs and desires for your child's name are, you should find help, advice, and thousands of possibilities in the pages that follow. Remember that good names are based not on whim or fancy, but on the true meaning and translation of the name.

You can name your baby after:

1. *A relative.* If you don't insist on giving the baby the exact Hebrew or Yiddish name of the relative, you can remember the late relative with a modern Hebrew equivalent. Because so many parents choose to name their newborns after relatives, Chapter 2 is devoted to this topic.
2. *An event.* You can give your baby a Hebrew name that commemorates a special event in the family's life, or is a symbol of something important that happened in Israel or in the United States or Canada.
3. *Relationships.* The Hebrew name can represent emotional relationships in the family or the baby's place in the family.
4. *The parashah.* You might want to choose a name that appears

in the weekly Torah portion, according to your baby's birthdate.

5. *A holiday, a month, or a season.* You can give your baby a name that reflects the season or the month of the birthday, or find a meaningful name for a baby who is born on one of the Jewish holidays, such as Passover, Hanukkah, Purim, or Sukkoth.

6. *Plants.* You can name the baby after trees or flowers that grow in Israel.

7. *Animals.* You can choose a name that means an animal, such as a deer or a bird.

8. *Places in Israel.* Lots of modern Hebrew names are also the names of cities, kibbutzim, lakes, or mountains.

9. *Historical heroes.* Children are named after both biblical heroes and those from current Israeli history.

10. *Current celebrities.* Many children are named after Israeli singers, actors, or musicians.

Hebrew names are selected by parents according to all of these categories, and each category has its advantages. There are also parents, of course, who invent a name, or those who adopt a suggestion of a relative or friend, but despite the category parents, even if they don't speak Hebrew fluently, *must* understand the meaning and the translation of the name. North American Jews might have difficulty expressing their feelings toward the baby in an unfamiliar language, and even Israeli natives might make serious mistakes by choosing a Hebrew name without giving it deep thought. The following story proves it:

A baby girl was born in Tel Aviv after the victory of Israel in the Sinai Campaign in 1956. In Israel this war was also known as the Kadesh Operation, because Kadesh is the name in the Bible for the Sinai peninsula. The happy father, coming home from the war, decided to name his daughter after this event, and he called her Kdesha, the feminine version of Kadesh. He didn't know that the word *kdesha* was used in the Bible to describe a prostitute. When he discovered the ancient meaning of this word, he changed his daughter's name, of course, but this anecdote shows that in some cases it's better not to be too original. Hebrew names, as well as English ones, that are given by parents with wild imaginations or wild ignorance might not be the perfect names for those who will have to carry them.

Therefore, when you search for the best Hebrew name for yourself or for a newborn, you may want to consider all of the following factors.

1. *Meaning.* Don't choose a Hebrew name just because it is pretty

or harmonious with the surname. Try to express yourself or your emotions through a meaningful name.

2. *The religious point of view.* The Torah doesn't dictate any rules about names that should not be used, but Jewish tradition suggests avoiding certain names. Most people choose to avoid names of wicked characters from the Bible or history, such as Pharaoh or Haman. Others also avoid using names of those who didn't respect God's will. Still others also avoid giving names that appear in the Bible before the time of Abraham, such as Adam or Noah. The customs vary from one community to the other. The fact is that today in Israel, Hagar is one of the most popular names for girls, in spite of the fact that in the Bible, she was the mother of Ishmael, who is classed in the Bible among the wicked, considered in rabbinic literature to be a symbol of impiety, and seen in modern Hebrew as the father of the Arab nations.

3. *Description.* You can choose a Hebrew name that describes the newborn's appearance or behavior, but nobody can guarantee that the descriptive name will always fit him or her. The Hebrew name Tamir, meaning "tall like the palm tree," might embarrass a short boy; the Hebrew name Yaffa, meaning "beautiful," might embarrass a girl who is not a beauty queen.

4. *Pronunciation.* Don't choose a Hebrew name that would be hard for you, your child, or your child's friends to pronounce.

5. *Sound.* Avoid giving your child a Hebrew name that doesn't sound good in English too. For example, Shai is a popular name in Israel for boys. It means "a gift, a present." In English-speaking countries, however, a young child might not feel comfortable with the name because it sounds like the word *shy.*

6. *Spelling.* Don't choose a name that is difficult to spell.

7. *Popularity.* You may not want to give your baby a standard, traditional name from the Bible, but you also may not want a modern name that is too unique or esoteric. See pages 9 to 10 for lists of the most popular Hebrew names today.

8. *Stereotypes.* Many Hebrew names suggest certain images you may or may not want for your child. For example, Yoram (a form of Yehoram) is a nice boy's name. It appears in the Bible as the name of a king, and in Hebrew it means "God is exalted." But in the past ten years this name among Israeli children has come to mean "an unpopular boy." Therefore, it's good to ask people who are familiar with the Israeli culture for possible stereotypes the name may suggest.

9. *Nicknames.* If the Hebrew name is long, you might want the child to have a nice, easy nickname.

10. *Double name.* Even if right now you don't have plans to visit or move to Israel, you might want a modern Hebrew name that will sound fine in both English and Hebrew. In this case the child gets only one name (it's less confusing!), which is used as both the English name and the Hebrew name.

Naming your child would be much easier if you could wait with both the English name and the Hebrew name until your child could talk, understand the meanings, and choose a name for himself or herself. If this were possible, your child wouldn't be able to blame you in the future for not choosing the right name. But the decision is yours, so it's important that you take the time and effort to open the Bible, look at a map of Israel, or use this book to explain to your child the meaning or the root of his or her Hebrew name. Understanding its meaning and the intentions and motives behind the name will encourage the child to use the Hebrew name and to be proud of it.

# 2.

# Naming Your Baby
# After a Relative

In naming their children, many parents remember relatives who are no longer living. They want to perpetuate their memories by naming their babies after them.

Different customs exist in different Jewish communities. Jews from Central or Eastern Europe, known as Ashkenazim, name newborns only after deceased relatives. They believe that naming a newborn after a living relative might shorten the life of the older person. On the other hand Jews from Spain, Portugal, Italy, North Africa, or the Middle East—known as Sephardim—believe that naming a newborn after a living relative will lengthen the life of the older person. They do not hesitate to name a newborn after a living grandparent or even parent.

If you wish to name your baby after a deceased relative, and you don't insist on giving the baby the exact Hebrew or Yiddish name of the relative, you have three choices:

1. You can look for a modern Hebrew name that has the same initial sound as the name of the relative. For example, the masculine name Zalman was common in the past, but it is not popular in Israel nowadays, and even carries an unfavorable stereotype. Instead of giving the baby an out-of-date name with bad connotations, you can look for modern Hebrew names beginning with the letter Z, such as Ze'ev (meaning "wolf"), or Zohar (meaning "light, brilliant"), and so on. You can even look for a modern Hebrew name that consists of a few letters from the name Zalman, such as Zemer (meaning "song") or Zivan (meaning "shining").

2. You can look for a modern Hebrew name that has the same meaning as the name of the relative. For example, the girl's name Gitele, which was so common in the past, is no longer popular in Israel, especially because it's not a Hebrew name. Gitele in Yiddish means "good" or "good person," and you can find lots of modern Hebrew names that express the same meaning, such as Tovah, Tovit, or Naamah.

3. You can look for a modern Hebrew name that is an abbreviation

for several names of relatives. For example, the boys' names Reuben and Nathan together create a beautiful modern name for a boy—Ron means "joy" or "song." The girls' names Rachel and Nechama create a few beautiful modern names for a girl, such as Rona, Ronit, Roni, or Renana—all meaning "joy."

You can create an original Hebrew name based on the abbreviations of several names, but if you don't speak Hebrew fluently, you should discuss your ideas with someone who does. There's a joke in Israel about a mother who wanted to name her daughter after her two late grandmothers, Shula and Chanah, so she named her baby Shulchanah. What's so funny about this name? Well, in Hebrew, Shulchan means "a table."

Another possibility for naming a baby after a deceased relative is not using the relative's name but choosing a modern Hebrew name that reflects your relationship with that person. For example, LeeAv means "I have a father," to remember the late grandfather, or Achi, which means "my brother," to remember the late brother. Unfortunately, the variety of names in this category is limited.

### SWITCHING NAMES FROM MALE TO FEMALE AND FEMALE TO MALE

If you want to name a newborn after a relative of the opposite sex, you again have three choices:

1. Look for a name that begins with the same initial sound as the name of the relative.

2. Look for a name that has the same meaning as the name of the relative.

3. Switch the name from male to female or vice versa by changing the suffix. Some names can be switched from male to female by adding the suffix "a" or "ah." For example: Meir—Meira; Ofer—Ofra; Dan—Dana. Other names can be switched from male to female by adding the suffix "it." For example: Ilan—Ilanit; Ori—Orit; Shalom—Shlomit. There are a few names that can be switched by adding the suffix "ina," such as Yona—Yonina, but the switching makes the new name too complicated, even awkward. Trying to switch Yaakov to Yaakovina simply doesn't sound good. Therefore the best way is to either stick to the initial sound or look for a name with the same meaning.

Don't forget that every name is only a combination of sounds and letters. The most important thing is the meaning behind it. When the right time comes, you will tell your child about the late relative he or she is named after, and the memory will live through your child.

# 3.

# The Most Popular Hebrew Names

Parents' preferences in baby names change because of times and tastes, but in North America, as in Israel, there are people who use only biblical names, no matter how popular or modern they are.

*Top Ten Biblical Boys' Names in the 1980s (with the Anglicized Forms)*

| | | |
|---|---|---|
| 1. | Avraham (Abraham) | אברהם |
| 2. | Yitzchak (Isaac) | יצחק |
| 3. | Yaakov (Jacob) | יעקב |
| 4. | Moshe (Moses) | משה |
| 5. | Aharon (Aaron) | אהרון |
| 6. | Yisrael (Israel) | ישראל |
| 7. | David | דויד |
| 8. | Yosef (Joseph) | יוסף |
| 9. | Shlomo (Solomon) | שלמה |
| 10. | Yehuda(h) (Judah) | יהודה |

*Top Twenty Boys' Names in the 1980s*

| | | |
|---|---|---|
| 1. | Sharon | שרון |
| 2. | Ron | רון |
| 3. | Uri | אורי |
| 4. | Gal | גל |
| 5. | Tomer | תומר |
| 6. | Asaf | אסף |
| 7. | Dan | דן |
| 8. | Yonatan | יונתן |
| 9. | Ofer | עופר |
| 10. | Noam | נועם |
| 11. | Ariel | אריאל |
| 12. | Michael | מיכאל |
| 13. | LeeOr (Lior) | ליאור |
| 14. | Doron | דורון |

15. Adi   עדי
16. Hadar   הדר
17. Boaz   בועז
18. Eran   ערן
19. Barak   ברק
20. Ben   בן

## Top Ten Biblical Girls' Names in the 1980s (with the Anglicized Forms)

1. Sara(h)   שרה
2. Rivka (Rebecca)   רבקה
3. Rachel   רחל
4. Leah   לאה
5. Miryam (Miriam)   מרים
6. Chana(h) (Hannah)   חנה
7. Dvora(h) (Debora(h))   דבורה
8. Ester (Esther)   אסתר
9. Dina(h)   דינה
10. Tzipora(h) (Zipporah)   ציפורה

## Top Twenty Girls' Names in the 1980s

1. Gali   גלי
2. Ofra   עופרה
3. Yardena   ירדנה
4. Rotem   רותם
5. Vered   ורד
6. Nili   נילי
7. Ruth   רות
8. Tali   טלי
9. LeeRon (Liron)   לירון
10. LeeMor (Limor)   לימור
11. Shiri   שירי
12. Keren   קרן
13. Roni   רוני
14. Hila   הילה
15. Michal   מיכל
16. Noa   נועה
17. Anat   ענת
18. Tamar   תמר
19. Yael   יעל
20. Dana   דנה

# The Naming Ceremony

The naming ceremony for a Jewish child is not described in the Bible; children in the Bible were named at the time of birth. For many years, however, it has been traditional to name a baby boy at his brith (circumcision) and to name a baby girl on the Sabbath following her birth.

Some parents insist on not announcing the baby's name until the naming ceremony, fearing that announcing it before the ritual might bring bad luck. In this case only the closest relatives of the newborn take part in choosing the name, and the final decision is kept a secret until the actual ceremony.

In the naming ceremony of both boys and girls, the name of the newborn is mentioned in the blessing, along with the name of the father. Some congregations today have adopted the custom of also including the mother's name in the blessing.

### THE NAMING CEREMONY FOR A BOY

On the eighth day after birth, upon completing the circumcision, the mohel (circumciser) holds up a cup of wine, pronounces the blessing for the wine, and recites this prayer for the child in Hebrew.

"Our God and God of our fathers, preserve this child to his father and to his mother, and let his name be called in Israel as _____, the son of _____. Let his father rejoice in his offspring and his mother be glad with the fruit of her body."

This prayer concludes with the words: "This little child named _____, may he grow to be great! Even as he now enters into the Covenant (of Abraham), so may he enter into the world of Torah, the nuptial canopy, and into good deeds."

The father and the sandak (godfather), who holds the baby during the circumcision, drink of the wine. A few drops are given to the infant, and the cup of blessing is sent to the mother, who also drinks from it.

### THE NAMING CEREMONY FOR A GIRL

The naming ceremony for a baby girl takes place in the synagogue. On the first Sabbath service after her birth or on other occasions when the Torah is read (at the morning service on a Monday, Thursday, or on Rosh Hodesh—the new moon), the father is honored with an aliya (called to the Torah). After the portion of the Torah is read, the father recites the final Torah blessing and the sexton or the rabbi recites a special prayer called Mi Shebayrach (meaning "May He who blessed") for the health of the mother and her daughter. A second Mi Shebayrach is then recited for naming the baby.

"May He who blessed our fathers, Abraham, Isaac, and Jacob, bless _____ and his daughter just born to him. May her name be known in Israel as _____, daughter of _____. O, guard and protect her father and mother, and may they live to rear her in the fear of God for the nuptial canopy and for a life of good deeds."

The naming ceremony is the first religious event in the life of a newborn boy or girl. The Hebrew name given to the child in this happy celebration will be an integral part of his or her life.

# PART TWO

# How to Use
# the Name Dictionary

Boys' names and girls' names are arranged alphabetically in two different sections. The boys' section is larger than the girls'—that's the nature of the language. Many of the girls' names are female versions of the boys'. Popular girls' names get a full explanation. Girls' names which are not very popular refer the reader to the explanation that appears in the boys' section.

On the first page of each English letter, there is a note of the equivalent Hebrew letter(s). Because some Hebrew letters have more than one English spelling, I have followed these two rules in alphabetizing the names:

1. All the names that start with the Hebrew letter 'ח and can be spelled using either Ch or H appear under the letter C.

2. All the names that start with the Hebrew letter 'צ and can be spelled using either Tz or Z appear under the letter T.

Each name is printed three times: in English letters, in English transliteration, and in Hebrew letters. The Hebrew name is spelled in full, writing without vowels. The Hebrew spelling is not repeated when the name has different forms which are spelled exactly the same because the changes in the forms of the name are only in the vowels. Biblical names are followed by the letter B and the name of the book(s) in which they appear.

In the explanation of each name the word *Hebrew* will be indicated by *H*, and the word *Yiddish* will be indicated by *Y*. When the name has a definite meaning in Hebrew, it says "in H." When the name is derived from the Hebrew, it says "from the H." Each name is also followed by one or more asterisks (*).

*     One asterisk for an old name
**    Two asterisks for a common name
***    Three asterisks for a very popular name
****    Four asterisks for a unique name.

At the end of the book you will find several appendixes. The first lists names that are related to the Jewish calendar; the second includes names that work in both Hebrew and English; the third offers names for multiple births.

In the appendixes each name is printed only in English. To understand its root or meaning, look for it in the alphabetical lists.

The last pages are empty, waiting for you to write down which names you liked, which names you considered, and how and why you decided to give a certain name to your baby.

# 6.

# Boys' Names

## A

**Abba** (Ah' bah) אבא
In H., "father."*

**Abir** (Ah beer') אביר
In H., "strong, mighty, courageous."* Another form is *Abiri* (Ah bee ree') אבירי, in H., "gallant, chivalrous."* Abirim is the name of a place (community settlement) in Israel in Galilee.

**Ach** (Ahch) אח
In H., "brother."* Other forms are *Acha* (Ah' cha) אחא;* *Achai* (Ah chahy') אחאי;* *Achi* (Ah chee') אחי, in H., "my brother";* and *Achina* (Ah chee' nah) אחינא.*

**Achan** (Ah chahn') עכן
From the H., "snake"; in the B. (Joshua).*

**Achav** (Ahch ahv') אחאב
In H., "father's brother; uncle"; in the B. (I Kings), a king.* Another form is *Achiav* (Ah chee ahv') אחיאב, in H., "my uncle."****

**Achaz** (Ah chahz') אחז
In H., "he held, grasped, detained"; in the B. (II Kings), a king. Also spelled Ahaz.* Other forms are *Achazia(h)* (Ah chahz yah') אחזיה, in H., "God has grasped"; in the B. (I Kings), a king. Also spelled Ahazia(h).* *Achazyahu* (Ah chahz yah' hoo) אחזיהו;* and *Achzai* (Ahch zahy') אחזי.*

**Achiam** (Ah chee ahm') אחיעם
In H., "brother of my nation"; in the B. (II Samuel), a warrior. Also spelled Achi-Am.* Another form is *Aviam* (Ah vee ahm') אביעם, in H., "the father of a nation," referring to God; in the B. (I Kings). Also spelled Avi-Am.**

**Achiasaf** (Ah chee ah sahf') אחיאסף
In H., "my brother gathered in." Also spelled Achiasaph.** Other

forms are *Amiasaf* (Ah mee ah sahf') עמיאסף, from the H., "my people were reunited," also spelled Amiasaph;** and *Aviasaf* (Ah vee ah sahf') אביאסף,* in H., "my father has collected, gathered in," referring to God; in the B. (Exodus). Also spelled Aviasaph.**

**Achida** (Ah chee dah') אחידע
From the H., "my brother knows much."**** Another form is *Avida* (Ah vee dah') אבידע, in H., "my brother knows"; in the B. (Genesis), a grandson of Abraham. Also the name of a place (kibbutz) in Israel in the Arava.**

**Achidan** (Ah chee dahn') אחידן
From the H., "my brother judged."**** Other forms are *Avidan* (Ah vee dahn') אבידן, in H., "my father judged" or "my father is a judge"; in the B. (Numbers), a leader. Also spelled Abidan;** and *Amidan* (Ah mee dahn') עמידן, from the H., "my nation is righteous" or "my people judged."****

**Achidod** (Ah chee dohd') אחידוד
In H., "my brother is an uncle" or "my brother is a friend."****

**Achiem** (Ah chee ehm') אחיאם
In H., "the brother of my mother, my uncle."****

**Achiezer** (Ah chee eh' zehr) אחיעזר
From the H., "my brother is my helper." In the B. (Numbers), a leader. Also the name of a place (moshav) in central Israel.* Another form is *Amiezer* (Ah mee eh' zehr) עמיעזר, from the H., "my nation is my support."*

**Achihud** (Ah chee hood') אחיהוד
From the H., "my brother is majestic"; in the B. (Numbers), a leader. Also the name of a place (moshav) in Israel in Galilee.**

**Achikam** (Ah chee kahm') אחיקם
In H., "my brother was established" or "my brother was resurrected," referring to the nation of Israel; in the B. (Jeremiah), the father of Gedaliah.*

**Achikar** (Ah chee kahr') אחיקר
From the H., "my brother is precious."* Other forms are *Amikar* (Ah mee kahr') עמיקר, from the H., "my nation is precious";* and *Avikar* (Ah vee kahr') אביקר, from the H., "my father is precious."*

**Achimaatz** (Ah chee mah' ahtz) אחימעץ
From the H., "brother of anger". In the B. (II Samuel), a son of Zadok.* Another form is *Avimaatz* (Ah vee mah' ahtz) אבימעץ, from the H., "father of anger."*

**Achiman** (Ah chee mahn') אחימן
From the H., "my brother is a gift"; in the B. (Numbers), a son of Anak.*

**Achimelech** (Ah chee meh' lech) אחימלך
In H., "my brother is a king," meaning "God is my brother"; in the B. (I Samuel), a priest.* Another form is *Avimelech* (Ah vee meh' lech) אבימלך, in H., "my father is a king," referring to God, in the B. (Judges). Also spelled Abimelech.*

**Achinadav** (Ah chee nah dahv') אחינדב
From the H., "my brother is noble"; in the B. (II Kings), an officer.* Another form is *Avinadav* (Ah vee nah dahv') אבינדב, from the H., "princely father"; in the B. (I Samuel), a son of King Saul.**

**Achiner** (Ah chee nehr') אחינר
In H., "my brother is a candle," meaning "my brother is a light." A symbolic name for boys born on Hanukkah.**** Another form is *Aviner* (Ah vee nehr') אבינר, in H., "my father is a candle," meaning "my father shows me the right way to go."****

**Achinoam** (Ah chee noh' ahm) אחינועם
In H., "my brother is charming, loveliness." Used also as a girl's name.**

**Achipelet** (Ah chee peh' leht) אחיפלט
From the H., "my brother is my deliverer."* Another form is *Avifelet* (Ah vee feh' leht) אביפלט, in H., "my father is my savior."*

**Achiram** (Ah chee rahm') אחירם
In H., "my brother is noble, lofty"; in the B. (Numbers), a son of Benjamin.*

**Achisamach** (Ah chee sah mahch') אחיסמך
From the H., "my brother is my support"; in the B. (Exodus). Also the name of a place (moshav) in central Israel.*

**Achisar** (Ah chee sahr') אחישר
In H., "my brother is a ruler, a prince, or angel."**** Another form is *Avisar* (Ah vee sahr') אבישר, in H., "my father is a prince, a ruler."****

**Achishachar** (Ah chee shah' chahr) אחישחר
From the H., "my brother is the dawn," as a symbol of hope; in the B. (I Chronicles).**** Another form is *Avishachar* (Ah vee shah' chahr) אבישחר, in H., "father of dawn."****

**Achishai** (Ah chee shahy') אחישי
In H., "my brother is a gift."**** Another form is *Amishai* (Ah mee shahy') עמישי, in H., "the gift of my nation."****

**Achishalom** (Ah chee shah lohm') אחישלום
In H., "my brother is peace," meaning "my brother will bring peace."****

**Achishar** (Ah chee shahr') אֲחִישַׁר
In H., "my brother is singing," meaning "my brother brings joy"; in the
B. (I Kings), an officer.**** Other forms are *Amishar* (Ah mee shahr')
עֲמִישַׁר, in H., "my people sing, rejoice";**** and *Avishar* (Ah vee shahr')
אֲבִישַׁר, in H., "my father sings."**

**Achitov** (Ah chee tohv') אֲחִיטוֹב
In H., "my brother is goodness."** Other forms are *Achituv* (Ah chee
toov'), same meaning, also the name of a place (moshav) in Israel in
the Sharon;** and *Avituv* (Ah vee toov') אֲבִיטוֹב, in H., "father of
goodness"; in the B. (I Chronicles).*

**Achitzedek** (Ah chee tzeh' dehk) אֲחִיצֶדֶק
In H., "my brother is justice."* Other forms are *Amitzedek* (Ah mee
tzeh' dehk) עֲמִיצֶדֶק, in H., "my nation is righteous" or "my nation is
justice";** and *Avitzdek* (Ah vee tzeh' dehk) אֲבִיצֶדֶק, in H., "my father
is justice."**

**Achitzur** (Ah chee tzoor') אֲחִיצוּר
In H., "my brother is a rock," meaning "strong."* Other forms are
*Amitzur* (Ah mee tzoor') עֲמִיצוּר, in H., "my nation is a rock," meaning
"strong" or "my support";** and *Avitzur* (Ah vee tzoor') אֲבִיצוּר, in H.,
"my father is a rock."**

**Achiya** (Ah chee yah') אֲחִיָּה
In H., "God is my brother"; in the B. (I Chronicles), a warrior, and
(I Kings) a prophet. Also spelled Ahia(h).* Another form is *Achiyahu*
(Ah chee yah' hoo) אֲחִיָּהוּ, same meaning.*

**Achlee** (Ahch lee') אֲחֵלִי, אַח־לִי
In H., "I've got a brother" or "my brother." Also spelled Achli.****

**Achva** (Ahch vah') אַחֲוָה
In H., "brotherhood, friendship." Used also as a girl's name. See
Achava.****

**Adael** (Ah dah ehl') עֲדָאֵל
From the H., "God is witness."****

**Adam** (Ah dahm') אָדָם
From the H. word *adama*, meaning "earth"; in H., "man, human
being, mankind"; in the B. (Genesis), the name of the first man God
created. As a pet form it is pronounced Ah' dahm.**

**Adar, Addar** (Ah dahr') אֲדָר
From the H., "exalted, praised"; in the B. (I Chronicles). The name of
the twelfth month in the Jewish calendar, when Purim is celebrated.**

**Adaya** (Ah dah' yah) עדיה
From the H., "God's jewel" or "God's witness"; in the B. (I Chronicles), a leader. Also spelled Adaia(h). Used also as a girl's name.****

**Adi** (Ah dee') עדי
In H., "a jewel" or "my adornment." Also the name of a place in Israel in Galilee. Also spelled Addi or Addie. Used also as a girl's name.*** Another form is *Adiel* (Ah dee ehl') עדיאל, from the H., "God's ornament"; in the B. (I Chronicles). Used also as a girl's name.***

**Adir** (Ah deer') אדיר
In H., "powerful, mighty, glorious, splendid." Adirim is the name of a place (moshav) in north Israel.*

**Adiv** (Ah deev') אדיב
In H., "gentle, polite, well-mannered."*

**Admon** (Ahd mohn') אדמון
From the H., "red." Admonit in H. is the name of a plant, peony.**

**Adoniya** (Ah doh nee yah') אדוניה
From the H., "God is my lord"; in the B. (II Samuel), one of David's sons. Also spelled Adonia(h).* Other forms with the same meaning are *Adoniyahu* (Ah doh nee yah' hoo) אדוניהו;* and *Adon* (Ah dohn') אדון, in H., "Mr., sir, ruler, owner."*

**Adoram** (Ah doh rahm') אדורם
From the H., "my God is mighty"; in the B. (II Samuel), an official.** Another form is *Adoniram* (Ah doh nee rahm') אדונירם.*

**Adriel** (Ahd ree ehl') עדריאל
From the H., "we are the crowd, mob of God"; in the B. (I Samuel).****

**Afik** (Ah feek') אפיק
In H., "riverbed, channel." Also the name of a place (kibbutz) in north Israel.**

**Agel** (Ah gehl') אגל
In H., "I will rejoice."**** Another form is *Agil* (Ah geel') אגיל**** or עגיל, in H., "an earring."****

**Agur** (Ah goor') אגור
From the H., "accumulated," referring to wisdom,* or עגור, in H., "crane bird." Also the name of a place (moshav) in central Israel.**

**Aharon** (Ah hah rohn') אהרון
From the H., "teaching" or "singing" or "shining"; in the B. (Exodus), the older brother of Moshe (Moses). The English forms are Aaron and Aron.**

**Ahud** (Ah hood') אהוד
In H., "sympathetic, lovely."***

**Ahuv** (Ah hoov') אהוב
In H., "beloved, sweetheart."* Other forms are *Ahuvam* (Ah hoov ahm') אהובעם, from the H., "beloved by the nation";**** *Ahuvya* (Ah hoov yah') אהוביה, from the H., "beloved by God," also spelled Ahuvia(h);* and *Ahuviya* (Ah hoo vee yah'), same meaning.*

**Akiva** (Ah kee' vah) עקיבא
From the H., "to hold by the heel," a form of the name Yaakov (Jacob). Rabbi Akiva was a Talmudic scholar in the first century who helped fight the Romans. Therefore this name is used especially for boys born on Lag b'Omer. The English form is Akiba.** Other forms with the same meaning are Akavya (Ah kahv yah') עקביא;* and *Akavel* (Ah kahv ehl') עקבאל.*

**Aldema(h)** (Ahl deh' mah) אלדמע
From the H., "no tears," meaning "we wish you a happy life." Used also as a girl's name.****

**Alexander** (Ah lex ahn' dehr) אלכסנדר
From the Greek name meaning "protector of men." Nickname is Alex.*

**Almog** (Ahl mohg') אלמוג
In H., "coral." Also the name of a tree that grows in India, sandalwood. Also the name of a place (kibbutz) in Israel, north of the Dead Sea.***

**Alon** (Ah lohn') אלון
In H., "oak tree"; in the B. (I Chronicles). Also spelled Allon. Several names of places in Israel start with this word.***

**Alter** (Ahl' ter) אלתר
From the Y., "old one."*

**Aluf** (Ah loof') אלוף
In H., "leader, champion, master, or loyal friend." Also the title in the Israeli army equivalent to brigadier. Also spelled Aluph.*

**Amal** (Ah mahl') עמל
In H., "work, labor, toil"; in the B. (I Chronicles), a member of Asher's tribe.* Other forms with the same meaning are *Amali* (Ah mah lee') עמלי, in H., "my work, my toil";* and *Amel* (Ah mehl').*

**Amarya** (Ah mahr yah') אמריה
From the H., "the word of God," meaning "decision"; in the B. (I Chronicles), a priest. Also spelled Amaria(h).* Another form is *Amaryahu* (Ah mahr yah' hoo) אמריהו, same meaning.*

**Amasya** (Ah mahs yah') עמסיה
From the H., "burden of God"; in the B. (II Chronicles), a military
leader. Also spelled Amasia(h).*

**Amatzya** (Ah mahtz yah') אמציה.
From the H., "strength of God" or "God will strengthen"; in the B.
(II Kings), a king. Also the name of a place (moshav) in south Israel.
Also spelled Amatzia(h).* Another form is *Amatzyahu* (Ah mahtz
yah' hoo) אמציהו, same meaning.*

**Amdiel** (Ahm dee ehl') עמדיאל
From the H., "God is my pillar," meaning "God is my support."*

**Ami** (Ah mee') עמי
In H., "my people, my nation"; in the B. (Ezra), a servant of King
Solomon. As a pet form it is pronounced Ah' mee.***

**Amiad** (Ah mee ahd') עמיעד
In H., "my nation is eternal." Also the name of a place (kibbutz) in
Israel in Galilee. Also spelled AmiAd.*** Another form is *Aviad* (Ah
vee ahd') אביעד, in H., "my father is eternal." Also spelled AviAd.***

**Amiaz** (Ah mee ahz') עמיעז
In H., "my nation is strong, mighty."** Other forms are *Amioz* (Ah
mee ohz') עמיעוז, same meaning, also the name of a place (moshav)
in Israel in the Negev;** and *Aviaz* (Ah vee ahz') אביעז, in H., "father
of strength" or "my father is strong."**

**Amichai** (Ah mee chahy') עמיחי
In H., "my nation lives."*** Another form is *Avichai* (Ah vee chahy')
אביחי, in H., "my father lives" or "my father will live" or "father of all
living things."**

**Amichen** (Ah mee chehn') עמיחן
In H., "my nation is gracious, lovely."**** Another form is *Avichen*
(Ah vee chehn') אביחן, in H., "father of grace."**

**Amichur** (Ah mee choor') עמיחור
From the H., "my nation is free."****

**Amidar** (Ah mee dahr') עמידר
From the H., "my nation is alive."*

**Amidor** (Ah mee dohr') עמידור
From the H., "the generation of my nation."** Another form is *Avidor*
(Ah vee dohr') אבידור, in H., "father of a generation."**

**Amidror** (Ah mee drohr') עמידרור
From the H., "my nation is free."** Another form is *Avidror* (Ah vee
drohr') אבידרור, in H., "father of freedom."**

**Amiel** (Ah mee ehl') עמיאל
From the H., "my nation belongs to God" or "God is with my nation";
in the B. (II Samuel). Also spelled Ammiel.**

**Amihud** (Ah mee hood') עמיהוד
From the H., "my nation is glorious"; in the B. (II Samuel), a member
of Simeon's tribe. Also the name of a place in Israel in Samaria
(Shomron).*** Other forms are *Amihod* (Ah mee hohd'), same
meaning;**** and *Avihud* (Ah vee hood') אביהוד, in H., "my father is
majestic"; in the B. (I Chronicles), a grandson of Benjamin. Also
spelled Abihud.*

**Amikam** (Ah mee kahm') עמיקם
In H., "my nation has been resurrected." Also the name of a place
(moshav) in Israel in the Negev.** Another form is *Avikam* (Ah vee
kahm') אביקם, in H., "my father is established" or "my father is
resurrected."*

**Aminadav** (Ah mee nah dahv') עמינדב
From the H., "my nation is noble"; in the B. (Exodus), a leader. Also
the name of a place (moshav) in Israel near Jerusalem.**

**Amior** (Ah mee ohr') עמיאור
In H., "my nation is a light."** Other forms are *Avior* (Ah vee ohr')
אביאור, in H., "father of light";* and *Aviur* (Ah vee oor') same
meaning.*

**Amir** (Ah meer') אמיר
In H., "treetop." Amirim is the name of a place (moshav) in Israel in
the Galilee.*** Or עמיר, in H., "sheaf of corn." Popular name for boys
born on Shavuot, known as the Feast of the Harvest. Also the name
of a place (kibbutz) in north Israel.***

**Amiram** (Ah mee rahm') עמירם
In H., "my nation is mighty, exalted."***

**Amiran** (Ah mee rahn') עמירן
In H., "my nation is joyful." Used also as a girl's name.*** Other
forms are *Amiron* (Ah mee rohn') עמירון;* *Amron* (Ahm rohn') עמרון,
in H., "my nation is joyful";* and *Avron* (Ahv rohn') אברון, in H.,
"father of joy."*

**Amishalom** (Ah mee shah lohm') עמישלום
In H., "my people are peaceful" or "my nation will have peace."*
Another form is *Avishalom* (Ah vee shah lohm') אבישלום, in H.,
"father of peace"; in the B. (I Kings).*

**Amishav** (Ah mee shahv') עמישב
In H., "my people return." This name is especially popular in Israel
after a war. Also the name of a place in Israel near Tel Aviv.**

**Amit** (Ah meet') עמית
In H., "friend" or "colleague." Used also as a girl's name.***

**Amitai** (Ah mee tahy') אמיתי
From the H., "truth" or "friend"; in the B. (Jonah), Jonah's father.
Also the name of a place (kibbutz) in south Israel.*** Another form
is *Amitan* (Ah mee tahn') אמיתן.*

**Amituv** (Ah mee toov') עמיטוב
In H., "my nation is good."**** Another form is *Avituv* (Ah vee toov')
אביטוב, in H., "father of goodness"; in the B. (I Chronicles).****

**Amnon** (Ahm nohn') אמנון
From the H., "faithful"; in the B. (II Samuel), the eldest son of King
David. Also a flower's name, amnon ve tamar, viola tricolor.***

**Amon** (Ah mohn') אמון
In H., "apprentice, educator, builder, architect"; in the B. (II Kings), a
king. Also the name of the Egyptian god of the sun. Also spelled
Ammon.****

**Amos** (Ah mohs') עמוס
From the H., "to be burdened, laden"; in the B. (Amos), a prophet.**

**Amotz** (Ah mohtz') אמוץ
From the H., "strong"; in the B. (Isaiah), Isaiah's father. Also spelled
Amoz.***

**Amram** (Ahm rahm') עמרם
In H., "mighty nation"; in the B. (Exodus), the father of Moshe
(Moses).***

**Anan** (Ah nahn') ענן
In H., "cloud"; in ancient H., "soothsayer"; in the B. (Nehemiah).*

**Aner** (Ah nehr') ענר
In the B. (Genesis), an ally of Abraham.****

**Aniam** (Ah nee ahm') אניעם
From the H., "I am a part of the nation"; in the B. (I Chronicles). Also
the name of a place (moshav) in Israel in Ramat Hagolan.* Or עניעם,
from the H., "God, answer the nation."****

**Arad** (Ah rahd') ארד
In H., "bronze."** Or ערד, the name of a place (city) in south Israel in
the Negev; in the B. (I Chronicles).** Other forms are *Ardi* (Ahr dee')

ארדי;* and *Arod* (Ah rohd') ארוד; in H., "bronze," in the B. (Numbers), Gad's son.*

**Arbel** (Ahr behl') ארבל
The name of a mountain and a place (moshav) in Israel in Galilee.***

**Arel** (Ahr ehl') אראל
In H., "lion of God," meaning "strong, brave" or "angel, messenger."** Other forms are *Areli* (Ahr eh lee') אראלי, same meaning, in the B. (Genesis), one of Jacob's grandsons;**** and *Ariel* (Ah ree ehl') אריאל, same meaning, in the B. (Ezra), a leader. The prophets used this name in referring to Jerusalem. Also the name of a place in Israel in Samaria (Shomron). Used also as a girl's name. Also spelled Aryel or Aryell.***

**Argaman** (Ahr gah mahn') ארגמן
In H., "purple." Also the name of a place (moshav) in Israel in the Jordan Valley.*

**Ari** (Ah ree') ארי
In H., "lion." Also a pet form of Arye. Also spelled Arie.***

**Ariav** (Ah ree ahv') אריאב
From the H., "father is a lion," meaning "strong, brave as a lion" or referring to God.****

**Aricha** (Ah ree' chah) אריכא
From the Aramaic, "long."*

**Arik** (Ah' reek) אריק
A nickname of Arye or Ariel. Arik Sharon is presently one of the most famous Israeli leaders.***

**Armon** (Ahr mohn') ערמון
In H., "chestnut" (tree, fruit).** Another form is *Armoni* (Ahr moh nee') ערמוני, in H., "reddish brown";** or ארמון, in H., "castle, palace."*

**Arnon** (Ahr nohn') ארנון
From the H., "roaring stream"; in the B. (Numbers), a stream.*** Other forms with the same meaning are *Arnan* (Ahr nahn') ארנן, in the B. (I Chronicles);* and *Arnoni* (Ahr noh nee') ארנוני.****

**Artzi** (Ahr tzee') ארצי
In H., "my land, my country," also "earthly." Especially popular among families who immigrate to Israel or for boys born on Israeli Independence Day. As a pet form it is pronounced Ahr' tzee.** Another form is *Artziel* (Ahr tzee ehl') ארציאל, from the H., "my country belongs to God" or "God is with my country."**

**Arye(h)** (Ahr yeh') אריה
In H., "lion"; in the B. (II Kings), an officer.**

**Arzi** (Ahr' zee) ארזי
In H., "my cedar."*

**Asa** (Ah' sah) אסא
From the Aramaic, "to heal" or "healer"; in the B. (I Kings), a king.*

**Asael** (Ah sah ehl') עשהאל
In H., "God has created"; in the B. (II Samuel). Also the name of a place in Israel near Jerusalem.* Other forms are *Asaya* (Ah sah yah') עשיה, in H., "God's creation"; in the B. (II Kings), a servant;* and *Asiel* (Ah see ehl') עשיאל, same meaning, in the B. (I Chronicles).*

**Asaf** (Ah sahf') אסף
In H., "he collected, gathered"; in the B. (II Kings), a Levite. A symbolic name for boys born on Sukkoth, known as the Feast of Ingathering. Also spelled Asaph. Nickname is *Assi* (Ah' see) אסי.*** Another form is *Asif* (Ah seef') אסיף, in H., "harvest." A symbolic name for boys born on Sukkoth or on Shavuot, known as the Feast of the Harvest. Also spelled Asiph.**

**Asarel** (Ah sahr ehl') אשראל
From the H., "prince of God"; in the B. (I Chronicles).* Another form is *Asriel* (Ahs ree ehl') אשריאל, same meaning, in the B. (Numbers).*

**Asher** (Ah shehr') אשר
From the H., "blessed, fortunate, happy"; in the B. (Genesis), one of Jacob's sons. Also spelled Asser.*

**Ashir** (Ah sheer') עשיר
In H., "rich"* or אשיר, in H., "I will sing."****

**Asis** (Ah sees') עסיס
In H., "fruit juice" or "new wine."*

**Atar** (Ah tahr') עתר
In H., "he prayed, he pleaded";* or אתר, in H., "place, site, location."**

**Atid** (Ah teed') עתיד
In H., "future, future tense" or "finally, ready."*

**Atir** (Ah teer') עטיר
From the H., "I will place a crown, a wreath."****

**Atzal** (Ah tzahl') אצל
In H., "he gave, inspired, blessed," referring to God.* Other forms with the same meaning are *Atzalya* (Ah tzahl yah') אצליה, from the H., "God gave, inspired, blessed";* and *Atzalyahu* (Ah tzahl yah' hoo) אצליהו, in the B. (II Kings).*

**Atzmon** (Ahtz mohn') עצמון
From the H., "strength." An ancient town in South Canaan.**

**Av** (Ahv) אב

In H., "father." The name of the fifth month in the Jewish calendar.*
Other forms are *Avi* (Ah vee') אבי, in H., "my father" or nickname of
Avraham, as a pet form pronounced Ah' vee;** *Avihu* (Ah vee' hoo)
אביהו, in H., "he is my father"; in the B. (Exodus), the second son of
Aaron, also spelled Abihu;* and *Aviya* (Ah vee yah') אביה, in H., "God
is my father"; in the B. (I Samuel), a son of Samuel, and (I Chronicles)
a king. Also spelled Avia(h). Used also as a girl's name.*

**Avdiel** (Ahv dee ehl') עבדיאל

From the H., "servant of God"; in the B. (I Chronicles), a leader.
Also spelled Abdiel.* Other forms with the same meaning are *Avdel*
(Ahv dehl') עבדל, in the B. (Jeremiah), an officer;* *Avda* (Ahv dah')
עבדא, in the B. (I Kings), a Levite;* and *Avdon* (Ahv dohn') עבדון, in
the B. (Judges), a judge.*

**Avgar** (Ahv gahr') אבגר

From the H., "father's house" or "dwelling of the father," referring to
God.****

**Aviav** (Ah vee ahv') אביאב

In H., "the father of my father, grandfather." Also spelled AviAv.**

**Avichayil** (Ah vee chah' yeel) אביחיל

In H., "my father is strong" or "father of strength"; in the B. (Esther),
the father of Queen Esther, and therefore a symbolic name for boys
born on Purim. Also the name of a place in Israel in the Sharon.**

**Aviel** (Ah vee ehl') אביאל

In H., "my father is God"; in the B. (I Samuel), the grandfather of
King Saul. Also the name of a place (moshav) in Israel in Samaria
(Shomron).***

**Aviezer** (Ah vee eh' zehr) אביעזר

In H., "my father is salvation," referring to God. Also the name of a
place (moshav) in central Israel.* Another form is *Aviezri* (Ah vee
ehz' ree) אביעזרי, in H., "my father is my help."*

**Avigal** (Ah vee gahl') אביגל

In H., "father of waves," meaning "father of the sea" or "father of joy,"
referring to God. Used also as a girl's name (see Avigayil).**

**Avigdor** (Ah veeg dohr') אביגדור

From the H., "father, protector." Also the name of a place (moshav) in
south Israel.**

**Avinatan** (Ah vee nah tahn') אבינתן

In H., "my father has given," referring to God. Used especially for
boys born after many years of barrenness.**

**Avinoam** (Ah vee noh' ahm) אבינועם
In H., "father of delight"; in the B. (Judges). Also the name of a place in Israel in Galilee. Used infrequently as a girl's name.*** Another form is *Avinaim* (Ah vee nah eem') אבינעים, same meaning.*

**Aviram** (Ah vee rahm') אבירם
In H., "my father is mighty"; in the B. (Numbers), Datan and Aviram were scandal-mongers. Also a modern form of Avraham.***

**Avishai** (Ah vee shahy') אבישי
In H., "gift of father," referring to God, or "my father is a gift for me" in case the boy's father is coming back from a war or recovering from a sickness; in the B. (I Samuel).*** Another form is *Avshai* (Ahv shahy') אבשי.****

**Avishama** (Ah vee shah mah') אבישמע
In H., "my father heard," referring to God.*

**Avishav** (Ah vee shahv') אבישב
In H., "my father came back." In Israel, used after a father's return from war. Used also as a girl's name.**

**Avishua** (Ah vee shoo' ah) אבישוע
From the H., "my father is salvation"; in the B. (Ezra).*

**Avital** (Ah vee tahl') אביטל
In H., "father of dew," referring to God; in the B. (I Chronicles), one of King David's sons. Also the name of a place (moshav) in north Israel in the Valley of Esdraelon (Jezreel). Also spelled Abital. Used also as a girl's name.*** Another form is *Amital* (Ah mee tahl') עמיטל, in H., "my nation is dew," meaning "my nation has hope." Used also as a girl's name.**

**Aviv** (Ah veev') אביב
In H., "spring." Avivim is the name of a place (moshav) in north Israel.*** Other forms are *Avivi* (Ah vee vee') אביבי, in H., "spring-time" or "springlike, fresh";* and *Avivya* (Ah veev yah') אביביה, in H., "God's spring."*

**Aviyam** (Ah vee yahm') אבי־ים
In H., "father of the sea"; in the B. (I Kings), a king.*

**Avizemer** (Ah vee zeh' mehr) אביזמר
In H., "my father is a song."*

**Avner** (Ahv nehr') אבנר
In H., "father of light" or "father's candle," meaning "Father is strong" or "Father shows the right way to go"; in the B. (I Samuel), the uncle of King Saul and commander of his army. The English form is Abner.***

**Avniel** (Ahv nee ehl′) אבניאל
In H., "God is my rock," meaning "strength."**

**Avraham** (Ahv rah hahm′) אברהם
From the H., "father of a mighty nation" or "father of a multitude." In the B. (Genesis), the first Hebrew man. His original name was Avram. The English form is Abraham. Nickname is Avi (Ah′ vee) אבי.**

**Avshalom** (Ahv shah lohm′) אבשלום
In H., "father is peace"; in the B. (II Samuel), the rebellious son of King David. Yad Avshalom (Avshalom's tomb) is the name of a place near Jerusalem. The English form is Absalom.***

**Avtalyon** (Ahv tahl yohn′) אבטליון
From the H., "father of dew"; in the Talmud, a scholar. Also the name of a place (moshav) in Israel in Galilee.*

**Ayal** (Ah yahl′) אייל
In H., "deer" or "ram."*** Another form is *Ayalon* (Ah yah lohn′) איילון. Also the name of a valley in Israel.**

**Az** (Ahz) עז
In H., "strong."* Other forms with the same meaning are *Azaz* (Ah zahz′) עזז;* *Azazyahu* (Ah zahz yah′ hoo) עזזיהו;* *Azi* (Ah zee′) עזי;* *Aziel* (Ah zee ehl′) עזיאל;* and *Aziz* (Ah zeez′) עזיז.*

**Azanya** (Ah zahn yah′) אזניה
From the H., "the hearing of God"; in the B. (Nehemiah). Also spelled Azania(h).* Another form is *Azanyahu* (Ah zahn yah′ hoo) אזניהו, same meaning.*

**Azarel** (Ah zahr ehl′) עזראל
In H., "God helped"; in the B. (I Chronicles), a warrior.* Other forms that mean, in H., "the help of God" are *Azarya* (Ah zahr yah′) עזריה; in the B. (II Kings), a king, also the name of a place (moshav) in Israel in the shefelah (coastal plain), also spelled Azaria(h);* *Azaryahu* (Ah zahr yah′ hoo) עזריהו, in the B. (II Kings), a king, also spelled Azariahu;* *Azriel* (Ahz ree ehl′) עזריאל, in H., "God is my help"; in the B. (I Chronicles), also the name of a place (moshav) in Israel in the Sharon.*

**Azrikam** (Ahz ree kahm′) עזריקם
From the H., "my help is established"; in the B. (I Chronicles). Also the name of a place (moshav) in Israel in the shefelah (coastal plain).*

# B

## THE HEBREW LETTER 'ב

**Bachan** (Bah' chahn) בחן
In H., "watchtower." Also the name of a place (kibbutz) in Israel in
the mountain of Samaria (Shomron).****

**Bahat** (Bah' haht) בהט
In H., "alabaster" or "porphyry." Used also as a girl's name.**

**Balak** (Bah lahk') בלק
From the H., "to destroy"; in the B. (Numbers).*

**Balfour** (Bahl' foor) בלפור
An English name, adopted into Israeli culture after Lord Balfour and
the Balfour Declaration (1917), which announced the decision of
England to help the Jewish people to establish a Jewish state in
Palestine.*

**Bar** (Bahr) בר
In H., "wheat, grain, corn." A popular name for boys born on Shavuot,
known as the Feast of the Harvest. Also means "pure, clean." Used
also as a girl's name.***

**Barak** (Bah rahk') ברק
In H., "lightning" or "glitter, splendor, glare, flash, gleam, shine"; in
the B. (Judges), an army officer. Also the name of a place (moshav)
in north Israel in the Valley of Edraelon (Jezreel); used also as a girl's
name.***

**Baram** (Bahr ahm') ברעם
From the H., "son of the nation." Also the name of a place (kibbutz)
in Israel in the Galilee.** Another form is *Barami* (Bahr ah mee')
ברעמי, from the H., "son of my nation."*

**Bareket** (Bah reh' keht) ברקת
In H., "emerald" or "agate." Also the name of a place (moshav) in
central Israel. Used also as a girl's name.**

**Bar-El** (Bahr Ehl') בר-אל
In H., "son of God."**

**Bar-Ilan** (Bahr' Ee lahn') בר-אילן
In H., "fruit of the tree." The name of a religious university in Israel.*

**Barkai** (Bahr kahy') ברקאי
In H., "morning star, announcement of dawn." Also the name of a
place (kibbutz) in central Israel in the Sharon.****

**Barkan** (Bahr kahn') ברקן
In H., "briar, thorn."****

**Bar-Kochva** (Bahr Kohch vah') בר־כוכבא
From the H., "son of a star." In the Jewish history the name of a
military leader who conquered Jerusalem from the Romans. This
name is used especially for babies born on Lag b'Omer.*

**Baruch** (Bah rooch') ברוך
From the H., "blessed"; in the B. (Jeremiah).** Another form is
*Baruchi* (Bah roo' chee) ברוכי, same meaning.**

**Bazak** (Bah zahk') בזק
In H., "lightning," meaning "as quick as lightning."**** Another form
is *Besek* (Beh' zehk).****

**Bdolach** (Bdoh' lahch) בדולח
In H., "crystal." Also the name of a place (moshav) in Israel in the
Gaza Strip. Used also as a girl's name.****

**Bechor** (Beh chohr') בכור
In H., "firstborn, eldest son." Popular among Sephardic families for
firstborn sons.* Other forms with the same meaning are *Becher*
(Beh' chehr) בכר; *Bachir* (Bah cheer') בכיר; and *Bichri* (Bech ree')
ביכרי.*

**Ben** (Behn) בן
In H., "son"; in the B. (I Chronicles.)***

**Ben-Ad** (Behn Ahd') בן־עד
From the H., "eternal, forever."**

**Ben-Ami** (Behn' Ah mee') בן־עמי
In H., "son of my people"; in the B. (Genesis). Also the name of a place
(moshav) in Israel in the Galilee.** Another form is *Ben-Am* (Behn
Ahm') בן־עם, בנעם.*

**Ben-Baruch** (Behn' Bah rooch') בן־ברוך
In H., "son of Baruch" or "a blessed one."*

**Ben-Chai** (Behn Chahy') בן־חי
In H., "son of life" or "son is alive." Used especially for boys who are
born sick.*

**Ben-Chanan** (Behn' Chah nahn') בן־חנן
From the H., "son of grace"; in the B. (I Chronicles). Also spelled
Ben-Hanan. Used to name a boy after a female relative, Chana.*

**Ben-Chayil** (Behn' Chah' yeel) בן־חייל
In H., "son of valor"; in the B. (II Chronicles).*

**Ben-Chorin** (Behn' Choh reen') בן־חורין
In H., "a free man." Used especially among Jews from Russia for the
first boy who is born in a free country, or for a boy born on Passover.*

**Ben-Shachar** (Behn Shah' chahr) 'בן־שחר
In H., "son of the dawn."****

**Ben-Tziyon** (Behn' Tzee yohn') בן־ציון
In H., "son of Zion." Also spelled Ben-Zion. A pet form is *Bentzi*
(Behn' tzee) בנצי.*

**Ben-Yishai** (Behn' Yee shahy') בן־ישי
In H., "son of Yishai." Yishai was the father of King David.*

**Berechya** (Beh rehch yah') ברכיה
In H., "blessed by God"; in the B. (I Chronicles, Zechariah). Also the
name of a place (moshav) in south Israel.* Other forms with the
same meaning are *Berechyahu* (Beh rehch yah' hoo) ברכיהו; *Brachya*
(Brahch yah') ברכיה; *Bruchel* (Brooch ehl') ברוכאל; and *Bruchiel*
(Broo chee ehl') ברוכיאל.*

**B'eri** (Beh eh ree') בארי
In H., "my well," meaning "my source of wisdom"; in the B. (Hosea),
the father of the prophet Hosea. Also a name of a place (kibbutz) in
Israel in the Negev.*

**Betuel** (Beh too ehl') בתואל
From the H., "house of God"; in the B. (Genesis), the father of Rivka
(Rebecca).*

**Betzalel** (Beh tzahl ehl') בצלאל
From the H., "under God's shadow," meaning "under God's protection";
in the B. (Exodus). Also spelled Bezalel.*

**Betzer** (Beh' tzehr) בצר
In H., "strength" or "ore."****

**Bilu** (Bee' loo) בילו
An acronym from the H. words "בית יעקב לכו ונלכה," or "Beyth Yaacov
lechu venelcha," meaning "Let us arise and go, O house of Jacob,"
(taken from Isaiah). The motto and the name of an organization of
young Russian Jews who immigrated to Palestine in 1882. Kfar Bilu is
the name of a place (moshav) in Israel in the shefelah (coastal plain).*

**Binyamin** (Been yah meen') בנימין
From the H., "son of my right hand," referring to strength; in the B.
(Genesis), the youngest of Jacob's twelve sons, so this name is often
used for the last son in the family. Pet name is *Beni* (Beh' nee) בני.
The English form is Benjamin.**

**Binyamin-Ze'ev** (Been yah meen' Zee ehv') בנימין־זאב
See Binyamin, see Ze'ev. The H. name of Theodor Herzl, the father
of political Zionism, who predicted the establishment of the Jewish
state. Used for boys born on Israeli Independence Day.*

**Bitzaron** (Bee tzah rohn') ביצרון
In H., "fortress, stronghold, a safe refuge or shelter." Also the name of
a place (moshav) in south Israel.*

**Bnaya** (Bnah yah') בניה
From the H., "son of God" or "God has built." Also the name of a
place (moshav) in Israel in the shefelah (coastal plain).** Another
form is *Bnayahu* (Bnah yah' hoo) בניהו, same meaning, in the B.
(II Samuel).*

**Boaz** (Boh ahz') בועז
From the H., "strength"; in the B. (Ruth), the second husband of
Ruth. A popular name for boys born on Shavuot, when the Bible
story of Ruth is read in the synagogue.***

**Brit(t)** (Breet) ברית
In H., "covenant." Used also as a girl's name.** Another form is *Britel*
(Breet ehl') בריתאל, in H., "covenant with God."****

**Brosh** (Brohsh) ברוש
In H., "cypress."****

**Bustan** (Boos tahn') בוסתן
In H., "garden." Bustan-Hagalil is the name of a place (moshav) in
Israel in the Galilee. Used also as a girl's name.****

# C

THE HEBREW LETTERS ח, כ'

**Carmel** (Cahr mehl') כרמל
From the H., "vineyard" or in H., "boiled green grain." The name of a
mountain in north Israel. Also spelled Karmel. Used also as a girl's
name.*** Another form is *Carmeli* (Cahr meh lee') כרמלי, from the H.,
"my vineyard" or after Mount Carmel. Also spelled Karmeli.****

**Carmi** (Cahr mee') כרמי
In H., "my vineyard"; in the B. (Genesis), a son of Reuven. Also spelled
Karmi. Used also as a girl's name.**

**Carmiel** (Cahr mee ehl') כרמיאל
From the H., "God is my vineyard," meaning "God is my source of wisdom." Also the name of a place in Israel, in Galilee. Also spelled Karmiel.** Another form is *Carmiya* (Cahr mee yah') כרמיה, with the same meaning. Also the name of a place (kibbutz) in Israel in the shefelah (coastal plain). Also spelled Karmiya. Used also as a girl's name.*

**Chagai** (Chah gahy') חגי
From the H., "my feast, holiday, celebration"; in the B. (Haggai), one of the twelve Minor Prophets. A popular name for babies who are born on one of the Jewish holidays. Also the name of a place near Jerusalem. Also spelled Hagai and Haggai.*** Another form with the same meaning is *Chagi* (Chah gee') חגי, in the B. (Genesis), a son of Gad. Also spelled Hagi.* Other forms are *Chagya* (Chahg yah') and *Chagiya* (Chah gee yah') חגיה, from the H., "festival of God"; in the B. (I Chronicles), also spelled Hagya and Hagiya.****

**Chai** (Chahy) חי
In H., "living, alive, lively, strong, healthy." Used especially for boys who are born sick. Also spelled Hai.*

**Chalamish** (Chah lah meesh') חלמיש
In H., "flint, rock."*

**Chalil** (Chah leel') חליל
In H., "flute." Also spelled Halil and Hallil.****

**Chalutz** (Chah lootz') חלוץ
In H., "pioneer." Also spelled Halutz.* Other forms are *Chalutzel* (Chah lootz ehl') חלוצאל, in H., "pioneer of God"; and *Chalutziel* (Chah loo tzee ehl') חלוציאל, same meaning.*

**Chamadya** (Chah mahd yah') חמדיה
In H., "desired, loved by God." Also the name of a place (kibbutz) in north Israel.** Another form is *Chamadel* (Chah mahd ehl') חמדאל, same meaning.*

**Chanan** (Chah nahn') חנן
In H., "he endowed" or "he was compassionate," referring to God; in the B. (I Chronicles), a leader. Also spelled Hanan.** Other forms are *Chananel* (Chah nahn ehl') חננאל, in H., "God was compassionate";* *Chananya* (Chah nahn yah') חנניה, same meaning, in the B. (Jeremiah), a prophet;** *Chananyahu* (Chah nahn yah' hoo) חנניהו, same meaning, in the B. (II Chronicles), an officer;* and *Chaniel* (Chah nee ehl') חניאל, from the H., "graciousness of God." Also the name of a place (moshav) in Israel, in the Sharon.*

**Chanoch** (Chah nohch') חנוך
From the H., "to educate" or "to inaugurate"; in the B. (Genesis). A symbolic name for boys born on Hanukkah. Also spelled Hanoch and Hanokh. The English form is Enoch.**

**Chasadia(h)** (Chah sahd yah') חסדיה
From the H., "mercy of God"; in the B. (I Chronicles). Also spelled Chasadya and Hasadia(h).* Another form is *Chasdiel* (Chahs dee ehl') חסדיאל, same meaning.*

**Chason** (Chah sohn') חסון
In H., "strong, powerful." Also spelled Hason.** Another form is *Chasin* (Chah seen') חסין, same meaning.*

**Chatzav** (Chah tzahv') חצב
In H., the name of a plant, squill. Also the name of a place (moshav) in Israel in the shefelah (coastal plain). Used also as a girl's name.****

**Chavakuk** (Chah vah kook') חבקוק
From the H., "to wrestle" or "to embrace"; in the B. (Habbakuk), a prophet. Also spelled Havakuk and Habakuk.*

**Chaviv** (Chah veev') חביב
In H., "lovely, beloved." Also spelled Haviv and Habib.*

**Chavivam** (Chah veev ahm') חביבעם
In H., "beloved by the nation."*

**Chavivel** (Chah veev ehl') חביבאל
In H., "beloved by God." Also spelled Havivel.* Another form is Chavivya (Chah veev yah') חביביה, same meaning.*

**Chayil** (Chah' yeel) חייל
In H., "power, strength, valor, wealth."****

**Chayim** (Chah' yeem) חיים
In H., "life." It's a custom to give this name as a middle name to a very ill man in hopes he will recover. Also spelled Chaim, Chayyim, Haim, and Hayyim.**

**Chazaya** (Chah zah yah') חזיה
In H., "God had seen, predicted"; in the B. (Nehemiah). Also spelled Hazaia(h).* Another form is *Chaziel* (Chah zee ehl') חזיאל, from the H., "vision of God"; in the B. (I Chronicles). Also spelled Haziel.*

**Chazon** (Chah zohn') חזון
In H., "prophecy, vision, revelation." Also the name of a place (moshav) in Israel in Galilee. Also spelled Hazon.* Another form is *Chezyon* (Chehz yohn') חזיון, same meaning, in the B. (I Kings).*

**Cheled** (Cheh' lehd) חלד
In H., "world, duration of life, lifetime"; in the B. (I Chronicles), a warrior. Also spelled Heled.****

**Chemed** (Cheh' mehd) חמד
In H., "grace, charm, delight, loveliness." Also the name of a place (moshav) in Israel in the shefelah (coastal plain). Used also as a girl's name.** Another form is *Chemdai* (Chehm dahy') חמדאי, same meaning.*

**Chen** (Chehn) חן
In H., "grace, charm, loveliness"; in the B. (Zechariah). Also spelled Hen. Used also as a girl's name.***

**Chermon** (Chehr mohn') חרמון
The name of the highest mountain in Israel. This mountain is in north Israel, on the border of Lebanon and Syria. Conquered by Israel in the Six-Day War. Also spelled Hermon.** Another form is *Chermoni* (Chehr moh nee') חרמוני.*

**Cherut** (Cheh root') חירות
In H., "freedom, liberty." Also the name of a political party in Israel. Also the name of a place (moshav) in Israel in the Sharon. A symbolic name for both boys and girls who are born on Passover, known as the Feast of Liberation. Also spelled Herut.**

**Cheshvan** (Chehsh vahn') חשוון
The eighth month in the Jewish calendar. Also spelled Heshvan.****

**Chetz** (Chehtz) חץ
In H., "arrow." Used especially for boys born on Lag b'Omer, when Israeli children play with bows and arrows.****

**Chevron** (Chehv rohn') חברון
The name of an ancient holy city near Jerusalem. The Cave of Machpelah is there. Also spelled Hevron and Hebron.*

**Chiddekel** (Chee deh' kehl) חידקל
The name of a river, Tigris. Also spelled Hiddekel.****

**Chilkiya** (Cheel kee yah') חילקיה
From the H., "God gave me a portion"; in the B. (II Kings). Also spelled Chilkia(h) and Hilkiah.* Another form is *Chilkiyahu* (Cheel kee yah' hoo) חילקיהו, same meaning.* Nickname for both names is *Chilik* (Chee' leek) חיליק.

**Chisdai** (Chees dahy') חיסדאי
From the H., "gracious."* Other forms are *Chisda* (Chees dah') חיסדא; and *Chesed* (Cheh' sehd) חסד, in H., "goodness."*

**Chizki** (Cheez' kee) חיזקי
From the H., "my strength"; in the B. (I Chronicles), a leader. Also
spelled Hizki.*

**Chizkiya** (Cheez kee yah') חיזקיה
From the H., "God is my strength"; in the B. (II Kings), a king of
Judah. Also spelled Chizkia(h). The English form is Hezekiah.*
Another form is *Chizkiyahu* (Cheez kee yah' hoo) חיזקיהו,
same meaning.*

**Chof** (Chohf) חוף
In H., "coast, shore, bank, beach."**** Another form is *Chofi* (Choh'
fee) חופי, in H., "my coast."****

**Choni** (Choh' nee) חוני
From the H., "gracious." Also spelled Honi. In the Talmud, Honi
Hamaggel, a kind of Rip Van Winkle, "the circle drawer."*

**Choresh** (Choh' rehsh) חורש
In H., "thicket, grove."****

**Chorin** (Choh reen') חורין
See Ben-Chorin.

**Chosen** (Choh' sehn) חוסן
In H., "riches, wealth, strength, power, immunity." Also the name of a
place (moshav) in Israel in the Galilee.**

**Chotam** (Choh tahm') חותם
In H., "seal, signet ring"; in the B. (I Chronicles).

**Choter** (Choh' tehr) חוטר
In H., "shoots, branch, twig, rod."****

**Chovav** (Choh vahv') חובב
In H., "beloved" or "friend"; in the B. (Judges), the father-in-law of
Moshe (Moses). Also spelled Hovav and Hobab.** Another form is
*Chovev* (Choh vehv'), same meaning, also spelled Hovev and Hobeb.*

# D

## The Hebrew Letter 'ד

**Dagan** (Dah gahn') דגן
In H., "corn, grain"; popular for babies, both boys and girls, born on Shavuot, known as the Feast of the Harvest. Beyth Dagan is the name of a place in Israel, south of Tel Aviv.**

**Dan** (Dahn) דן
From the H., "to judge"; in the B. (Genesis), the fifth of the twelve sons of Jacob. Also the name of a place (kibbutz) and a river in Israel in the Galilee. Pet name is *Dani* (Dah' nee) דני. The English pet form is Danny.***

**Daniel** (Dah nee ehl') דניאל
From the H., "God is my judge"; in the B. (Daniel), the hero who was cast into the lions' den. Used also as a girl's name. Pet form is *Dani* (Dah' nee) דני. The English pet form is Danny.*** Another form is *Danel* (Dahn ehl') דנאל, same meaning.****

**Datan** (Dah tahn') דתן
From the H., "faith, law"; in the B. (Numbers), Datan and his brother Aviram were scandalmongers.*

**David** (Dah veed') דויד
From the H., "beloved"; in the B. (I Samuel), the second king of Israel. Also spelled Davyd. Pet forms are *Dudu* (Doo' doo) דודו and *Dudi* (Doo' dee) דודי.**

**Dedan** (Deh dahn') דדן
In the B. (Genesis), a descendant of Abraham.****

**Dekel** (Deh' kehl) דקל
In H., "palm tree." Very popular for boys born on Sukkoth or on Tu b'Shvat. Also the name of a place (moshav) in south Israel.***

**Deuel** (Deh oo ehl') דעואל
From the H., "knowledge of God"; in the B. (Numbers).* Another form is *Dael* (Dah ehl') דעאל.****

**Din** (Deen) דין
In H., "law, verdict, justice." Used especially by those who like a Hebrew name with an English sound.*** Another form is *Dinya* (Deen yah') דיניה, in H., "judgment of God."****

**Dodi** (Doh dee') דודי
In H., "my beloved" or "my uncle."*

**Dolev** (Doh lehv') דולב
In H., "plane tree," a tree that grows in Israel in the Galilee. Also the
name of a place near Jerusalem.****

**Dolphin** (Dohl feen') דולפין
In H., the name of a large water-dwelling mammal.****

**Don** (Dohn) דון
In Spanish, "master." Used especially by those who like a H. name
with an English sound.**

**Dor** (Dohr) דור
In H., "generation, era." Also the name of a place (moshav) in Israel
in the shefelah (coastal plain).*** Other forms are *Dori* (Doh' ree) דורי,
in H., "my generation,"*** *Doriel* (Doh ree ehl') דוריאל, from the H.,
"generation of God,"**** *Dorli* (Dohr' lee) דורלי, in H., "my generation,"
used also as a girl's name,**** and *Doram* (Dohr ahm') דורעם,
in H., "generation of a nation."*****

**Doron** (Doh rohn') דורון
In H., "gift."*** Other forms are *Doran* (Doh rahn') דורן, same
meaning;**** and *Doroni* (Doh roh nee') דורוני, in H., "my gift."****

**Dotan** (Doh tahn') דותן
The name of a valley and a place in Israel in Samaria (Shomron). The
valley is mentioned in the B. (Genesis), in the story of Jacob's sons
selling Joseph. This name was especially popular after the Six-Day
War, in remembrance of the heavily armored battle between Israel
and Jordan. Used also as a girl's name.***

**Dov** (Dohv) דוב
In H., "bear." Pet form is *Dubi* (Doo' bee) דובי.**

**Dovev** (Doh vehv') דובב
From the H., "to cause to speak" or "to whisper." Also the name of a
place (moshav) in Israel in the Galilee near the border of Lebanon.****

**Dror** (Drohr) דרור
In H., "freedom, liberty, release from servitude." A symbolic name
for babies born on Passover. Also the name of a bird, swallow.***
Other forms are *Drori* (Droh ree') דרורי, in H., "my freedom";**** and
*Drorli* (Drohr' lee) דרורלי, in H., "I have freedom."*****

**Dvir** (Dveer) דביר
In H., "sanctuary, holy place." The name of the hinder or western
part of a temple.****

# E

**Eden** (Eh' dehn) עדן
In H., "pleasure, delicacy"; in the B. (Genesis), the Garden of Eden, the place where Adam and Eve lived, also known as Paradise, and (II Chronicles) a Levite. Also the name of a singing bird, paradise bird.** Another form is *Ednan* (Ehd nahn') עדנן.****

**Edi** (Eh dee') עדי
In H., "my witness," popular especially among those who like a H. name with an English sound.****

**Efrayim** (Ehf rah' yeem) אפריים
In the B. (Genesis), the son of Joseph (Yosef). Also spelled Efraim or Ephraim. Nickname is *Efi* (Eh' fee) אפי. **

**Efron** (Ehf rohn') עפרון
From the H., the name of a singing bird, lark (the exact H. name is efroni); in the B. (Genesis). Also spelled Ephron.****

**Ehud** (Eh hood') אהוד
From the H., "love"; in the B. (Judges), a judge. Nickname is *Udi* (Oo' dee) אודי.***

**Eilam** (Ehy lahm') עילם
From the H., "world, eternal"; in the B. (Genesis), one of Noah's grandsons. Also spelled Elam.****

**Eilon** (Ehy lohn') אילון
From the H., "oak tree" (the exact H. word is alon); in the B. (Genesis), one of Jacob's grandsons and (Judges) a judge. Also the name of a place (kibbutz) in Israel in the Galilee named after the oak trees growing in this area.*** Another form is *Elon* (Eh lohn') אלון. Elon Moreh is the name of a place in the Samaria (Shomron) named after the ancient city mentioned in the B. (Genesis).***

**Eitan** (Ehy tahn') איתן
In H., "strong, firm, mighty, permanent, steadfast"; in the B. (I Chronicles). Also the name of a place (moshav) in south Israel. Also spelled Etan, Ethan, and Eytan.***

**Elad** (Ehl ahd') אלעד
In H., "God is eternal"; in the B. (I Chronicles).*** Another form is *Eliad* (Eh lee ahd') אליעד, in H., "my God is eternal."**

**Elasa** (Ehl ah sah') אלעשה
In H., "God has created"; in the B. (I Chronicles).****

**Elazar** (Ehl ah zahr') אלעזר
In H., "God has helped"; in the B. (Exodus), a son of Aaron (Aharon).
Also the name of a place (moshav) in central Israel.** Other forms
are *Elezri* (Ehl ehz ree') אלעזרי, in H., "God is my helper";**** and
*Eliezer* (Eh lee eh' zehr) אליעזר, in H., "my God has helped"; in the B.
(Genesis), Abraham's servant and (Exodus) Moses' son. Also spelled
Eleazar.**

**Elchai** (Ehl chahy') אלחי
In H., "God lives."**** Another form is *Elichai* (Eh lee chahy') אליחי,
in H., "my God lives."****

**Elchanan** (Ehl chah nahn') אלחנן
From the H., "God is gracious" or, in H., "God was compassionate";
in the B. (II Samuel), a warrior. Also spelled Elhanan.**

**Eldad** (Ehl dahd') אלדד
From the H., "friend of God"; in the B. (Numbers).***

**Eldar** (Ehl dahr') אלדר
In H., "habitation of God."****

**Eldor** (Ehl dohr') אלדור
In H., "God of the generation."**

**Elez** (Eh' lehz) עלז
In H., "joy."****

**Eli** (Eh lee') עלי
From the H., "uplifted" or, in H., "pestle, condyle"; in the B.
(I Samuel), a high priest. Also the name of a place in Israel in
the Samaria (Shomron).****

**Eliam** (Eh lee ahm') אליעם
In H., "God is my people," meaning "God belongs to my people"; in
the B. (II Samuel).** Another form is *Elami* (Ehl ah mee') אלעמי, in
H., "God of my people" or "to my people, to my nation."****

**Eliav** (Eh lee ahv') אליאב
In H., "my father is God"; in the B. (Numbers).**

**Eliaz** (Eh lee ahz') אליעז
In H., "my God is strong."**

**Elied** (Eh lee ehd') אליעד
In H., "my God is witness."****

**Eliel** (Eh lee ehl') אליאל
In H., "the Lord is my God"; in the B. (I Chronicles).****

**Elifaz** (Eh lee fahz') אליפז

In H., "my God is gold," meaning "my God is pure like gold" or "my God is shining like gold"; in the B. (Job). Also the name of a place (kibbutz) in Israel in the Arava. Also spelled Eliphaz.****

**Elifelet** (Eh lee feh' leht) אליפלט

In H., "God is my deliverance"; in the B. (II Samuel), one of King David's sons. Also the name of a place (moshav) in Israel in the Galilee.****

**Elihu** (Eh lee' hoo) אליהוא

In H., "he is my God"; in the B. (Job).****

**Elihud** (Eh lee hood') אליהוד

In H., "my God is majestic."****

**Elimelech** (Eh lee meh' lehch) אלימלך

In H., "my God is king"; in the B. (Ruth).**

**Elinatan** (Eh lee nah tahn') אלינתן

In H., "my God has given."** Another form is *Elnatan* (Ehl nah tahn') אלנתן, in H., "God has given"; in the B. (II Kings).**

**Elior** (Eh lee ohr') אליאור

In H., "my God is light" or "my light is God."** Another form is *Elor* (Ehl ohr') אלאור, same meaning.**

**Eliram** (Eh lee rahm') אלירם

In H., "my God is lofty."** Another form is *Elrom* (Ehl rohm') אלרום, same meaning. Also the name of a place (kibbutz) in Israel in Ramat Hagolan.**

**Eliran** (Eh lee rahn') אלירן

In H., "my God is joy" or "my God is song."*** Another form is *Eliron* (Eh lee rohn') אלירון, same meaning.**

**Elisha** (Eh lee shah') אלישע

From the H., "God is my salvation"; in the B. (I Kings), a prophet. Also the name of a place in Israel in the Jordan Valley.** Another form is *Elishua* (Eh lee shoo' ah) אלישוע, same meaning, in the B. (II Samuel), one of King David's sons.****

**Elishafat** (Eh lee shah faht') אלישפט

In H., "my God has judged"; in the B. (II Chronicles). Also spelled Elishaphat.****

**Elishama** (Eh lee shah mah') אלישמע

In H., "my God has heard"; in the B. (Numbers). Also the name of a place (moshav) in Israel in the Sharon.****

**Elituv** (Eh lee toov′) אליטוב
In H., "my God is goodness."****

**Elitzedek** (Eh lee tzeh′ dehk) אליצדק
In H., "my God is just."**** Another form is *Eltzedek* (Ehl tzeh′
dehk) אלצדק, in H., "God is righteousness."****

**Elitzur** (Eh lee tzoor′) אליצור
In H., "my God is rock," meaning "my God is strong as a rock"; in the
B. (Numbers). Also spelled Elizur.**

**Eliyahu** (Eh lee yah′ hoo) אליהו
From the H., "the Lord is my God"; in the B. (I Kings), a prophet.
A symbolic name for boys born on Passover. According to Jewish
tradition, Eliyahu never died and will come on the seder night.
During the seder service, a fifth cup—Elijah's cup—is filled with
wine, a door to the outside is opened, and we ask God to bring
wrath on all the enemies of the Jews. The English form is Elijah.
Nickname is *Eli* (Eh′ lee) אלי.**

**Elkana(h)** (Ehl kah nah′) אלקנה
In H., "God bought" or "God is jealous"; in the B. (Exodus), one of
Korach's sons and (I Samuel) the father of Samuel. Also the name of
a place in Israel in the Samaria (Shomron).**

**Elkayam** (Ehl kah yahm′) אלקיים
In H., "God is alive, God exists."**

**Elnadav** (Ehl nah dahv′) אלנדב
In H., "God has donated."****

**Elro'i** (Ehl roh ee′) אלרואי
In H., "God sees me." Also the name of a place in north Israel near
Haifa.** Or in a different H. spelling, אלרועי, in H., "God is my
shepherd."**

**Elul** (Eh lool′) אלול
In H., the name of the sixth month in the Jewish calendar.****

**Elyada** (Ehl yah dah′) אלידע
In H., "God has known"; in the B. (II Samuel), one of King David's
sons. Also spelled Eliada(h).** Other forms are *Elda* (Ehl dah′) אלדע,
in H., "God knows"; **** and *Eli-Yada* (Eh lee′ Yah dah′) אלי-ידע, in H.,
"my God knew."****

**Elyakim** (Ehl yah keem′) אליקים
In H., "God will establish"; in the B. (II Kings). Also the name of a
place (moshav) in central Israel. Also spelled Eliakim.** Another

form is *Elyakum* (Ehl yah koom') אליקום, same meaning. Also spelled Eliakum.\*

**Elyasaf** (Ehl yah sahf') אליסף
In H., "God will increase"; in the B. (Numbers). Also spelled Eliasaf, Eliasaph.\*\* Another form is *Evyasaf* (Ehv yah sahf') אביסף, in H., "Father will increase," referring to God.\*\*

**Elyashiv** (Ehl yah sheev') אלישיב
In H., "God will respond" or "God will bring back." This name is often used in Israel during wars, especially among families of missing soldiers. In the B. (Nehemiah), a high priest. Also the name of a place (moshav) in central Israel. Also spelled Eliashiv.\*\* Another form is *Elyashuv* (Ehl yah shoov') אלישוב, in H., "God will return." Also spelled Eliashuv.\*\*

**Emanuel**
See Imanuel.

**Emek** (Eh' mehk) עמק
In H., "valley." The names of the valleys in Israel start with this word.\*\*

**Enosh** (Eh nosh') אנוש
In H., "man, human being, mankind"; in the B. (Genesis).\*\*

**Eran** (Eh rahn') ערן
From the H., "wakeful" or "singing, happy"; in the B. (Numbers), a grandson of Efrayim.\*\*\*

**Erel** (Ehr ehl') אראל
In H., "angel, messenger" or "I will see God."\*\*

**Erez** (Eh' rehz) ארז
In H., the name of a tree, cedar, or "strong as a cedar tree." Also the name of a place in Israel in the shefelah (coastal plain).\*\*\* Another form is *Erez-Yisrael* (Eh' rehz Yees rah ehl') ארז-ישראל, in H., "cedar of Israel."\*

**Eri** (Eh ree') ערי
In H., "my guardian"; in the B. (Genesis), a son of Gad.\*\*\*\*

**Esav** (Eh' sahv) עשיו
In the B. (Genesis), the twin brother of Jacob.\*

**Eshbol** (Ehsh' bohl) אשבול
In H., "spadix" or "ear of corn." A symbolic name for boys born on Shavuot, the Feast of the Harvest. Also the name of a place (moshav) in Israel in the Negev.\*\*\*\*

**Eshchar** (Ehsh chahr') אשחר
In H., the name of a bush, rhamnus buckthorn. Also the name of a place in Israel in the Galilee, named after the plants in this area.\*\*\*\*

**Eshed** (Eh' shehd) אשד

In H., "waterfall, cascade." Ashdot Yaakov is the name of two kibbutzim in Israel in the Jordan Valley.**

**Eshel** (Eh' shehl) אשל

In H., "tamarisk tree." Several places in Israel contain this word.***

**Eshkol** (Ehsh kohl') אשכול

In H., "cluster," usually "cluster of grapes." In H. literature, a title for a great scholar; a walking encyclopedia; in the B. (Genesis). Eshkolot is the name of a place in central Israel.****

**Etzyon** (Ehtz yohn') עציון

From the H., "tree." Etzyon Gaver was an ancient city in south Israel near Eilat, mentioned in the B. (Numbers). Kfar Etzyon is the name of a place (religious kibbutz) in Israel near Jerusalem.*

**Even** (Eh' vehn) אבן

In H., "stone." Several names of places in Israel contain this word.*

**Evyatar** (Ehv yah tahr') אביתר

From the H., "Father is great, advantageous," referring to God; in the B. (I Samuel), a priest.***

**Eyal** (Eh' yahl) אייל

In H., "power, strength, might, fortitude" or, from the H., "deer." Also the name of a place (kibbutz) in Israel in the Sharon.***

**Ezekiel**

See Yechezkel.

**Ezer** (Eh' zehr) עזר

In H., "help"; in the B. (I Chronicles). Also the name of a place in central Israel.* Other forms are *Eizer* (Ehy' zehr) עיזר, same meaning, in the B. (Nehemiah);* and *Ezri* (Ehz ree') עזרי, in H., "my help"; in the B. (I Chronicles).*

**Ezra** (Ehz rah') עזרא

From the H., "help"; in the B. (Nehemiah), a priest. Also spelled עזרה.**

# F

## THE HEBREW LETTER 'פ

**Feivel** (Fahy' vehl) פייבעל
From the Y., "bright one."*

**Fishel** (Fee' shehl) פישעל
From the Y., "fish."*

# G

## THE HEBREW LETTER 'ג

**Gad** (Gahd) גד
In H., "happiness, luck, fortune"; in the B. (Genesis), one of Jacob's sons. Also the name of a plant, coriander. Nickname is Gadi, Gaddi (Gah' dee) גדי.** Another form is *Gadiel* (Gah dee ehl') גדיאל, from the H., "God is my fortune."****

**Gadish** (Gah deesh') גדיש
In H., "stack of corn." A symbolic name for boys born on Shavuot, known as the Feast of the Harvest. Also in H., "mound of earth on a grave." Also the name of a place (moshav) in north Israel.**

**Gai** (Gahy) גיא
In H., "valley, gorge." Also spelled Guy.***

**Gal** (Gahl) גל
In H., "wave, billow" or "mound." Used also as a girl's name.*** Other forms are *Galon* (Gahl ohn') גלאון, in H., "a wave of strength," also the name of a place (kibbutz) in south Israel;** *Galron* (Gahl rohn') גלרון, in H., "a wave of joy";** *Galel* (Gahl ehl') גלאל, in H., "wave of God."****

**Galil** (Gah leel') גליל
In H., "cylinder" or "rolling hills." Galilee is the name of the northern hilly region in Israel.**** Another form is *Glili* (Glee lee') גלילי, in H., "man from the Galilee."*

**Gamliel** (Gahm lee ehl') גמליאל
From the H., "God is my reward," or "God gave me a reward." In the B. (Numbers), a leader.* Another form is *Gmali* (Gmah lee') גמלי, in H., "my reward"; in the B. (Numbers).*

**Gan** (Gahn) גן
In H., "garden."**** Other forms are *Gani* (Gah nee') גני, in H., "my garden";**** *Ginat(h)* (Gee nath') גינת, from the H., "garden," in the B. (I Kings), also the name of a place in Israel in Samaria (Shomron);**** and *Ganel* (Gan ehl') גנאל, in H., "garden of God."**

**Gavish** (Gah veesh') גביש
In H., "crystal."*****

**Gavriel** (Gahv ree ehl') גבריאל
From the H., "God is my strength"; in the B. (Daniel), an angel. Also the name of a place in Israel in Samaria (Shomron). The English form is Gabriel. Nicknames are *Gabi* (Gah' bee) גבי or *Gavri* (Gahv' ree) גברי.*** Other forms are *Gvaram* (Gvahr ahm') גברעם, from the H., "strength of the nation," also the name of a place (kibbutz) in Israel in the shefelah (coastal plain);** and *Gvarel* (Gvahr ehl') גבראל, from the H., "strength of God."**

**Gdalya** (Gdahl yah') גדליה
From the H., "God is great"; in the B. (Zephaniah), a governor of Judah. Also spelled Gdalia(h). The English forms are Gedalya, Gedalia(h). Tzom Gdalya is a fast day on the day after Rosh Hashanah.* Another form is *Gdalyahu* (Gdahl yah' hoo) גדליהו, same meaning.*

**Gealya** (Geh ahl yah') גאליה
In H., "God redeemed"; also the name of a place (moshav) in Israel in the shefelah (coastal plain).* Other forms are *Geuel* (Geh oo ehl') גאואל, in H., "redeemed by God"; in the B. (Numbers), one of the twelve scouts who explored the Promised Land; **** and *Goel* (Goh ehl') גואל, in H., "redeemer."*

**Gefen** (Geh' fehn) גפן
In H., "vine"; used in the B. as a symbol of peace, "to sit under one's own vine or fig tree." Also the name of a place (moshav) in Israel in the shefelah (coastal plain).** Other forms are *Gafni* (Gahf nee') גפני, in H., "my vineyard";* and *Gfanya* (Gfahn yah') גפניה, in H., "vineyard of God."****

**Geri** (Geh' ree) גרי
From the H., "stranger" or "convert," or a nickname for Gershon. Used especially for those who like a H. name with an English sound.**

**Gershom** (Gehr shohm') גרשום
From the H., "stranger"; in the B. (Exodus), a son of Moshe (Moses).* Another form is *Gershon* (Gehr shohn') גרשון, same meaning, in the B. (Genesis), a son of Levi.*

**Gev** (Gehv) גב
In H., "waterhold, pit, cistern." Gevim is the name of a place (kibbutz) in Israel in the shefelah (coastal plain).**

**Geva** (Geh' vah) גבע
In H., "hill." Also the name of a place (kibbutz) in Israel in the Valley of Esdraelon (Jezreel).**

**Gibor** (Gee bohr') גיבור
In H., "strong person, a hero." Also spelled Gibbor.*

**Gidon** (Geed ohn') גדעון
From the H., "maimed" or "mighty warrior"; in the B. (Judges), one of the judges, a warrior-hero. The English form is Gideon. Nickname is *Gidi* (Gee' dee) גידי.*** Another form is *Gidoni* (Geed oh nee') גדעוני, same meaning.*

**Gidron** (Geed rohn') גידרון
In H., the name of a singing bird, wren.**

**Gil** (Geel) גיל
In H., "joy." Used also as a girl's name.*** Other forms are *Gil-Ad* (Geel Ahd') גיל-עד, in H., "eternal joy";** *Gilam* (Geel ahm') גיל-עם, in H., "joy of the nation";** *Gili* (Gee' lee) גילי or גיל-לי, in H., "my joy";*** and *Gilon* (Gee lohn') גילון, from the H., "joy," also the name of a place in Israel in the Galilee.*

**Gilad** (Geel ahd') גלעד
In H., "hill of testimony, monument"; in the B., a mountainous area east of the Jordan River. The English form is Gilead.*** Another form is *Giladi* (Geel ah dee') גלעדי, in H., "man from Gilad."*

**Gilboa** (Geel boh' ah) גלבוע
The name of a mountain in Israel in the Valley of Esdraelon (Jezreel), where King Saul and his sons were killed (I Samuel).**

**Giora** (Gee yoh' rah) גיורה, גיורא
A symbolic name for boys born on Lag b'Omer, because Shimon Bar Giora was one of the leaders in the war against Rome. Bar Giora is the name of a place (moshav), and also the name of a mountain in Israel near Jerusalem.**

**Gitai** (Gee tahy') גיתי
In H., "one who presses grapes" (in order to make wine).**** Another form is *Giti* (Gee tee').****

**Givon** (Geev ohn') גבעון
From the H., "hill." Also the name of a place in Israel near Jerusalem, named after the ancient city mentioned in the B. Also spelled Gibeon.** Another form is *Givton* (Geev tohn') גבתון, same meaning.****

**Gmarya** (Gmahr yah') גמריה
From the H., "acts of God" or "accomplishment of God"; in the B.
(Jeremiah). Also spelled Gmaria(h).* Other forms are *Gmaryahu*
(Gmahr yah' hoo) גמריהו, in the B. (Jeremiah); same meaning*
and *Gomer* (Goh' mehr) גומר, from the H., "to end, complete"; in the
B. (Genesis).*

**Golan** (Goh lahn') גולן
Ramat Hagolan is the name of the highland in north Israel on the
Syrian border, belonging to Israel since the Six-Day War.*** Another
form is *Golani* (Goh lah' nee) גולני, the name given to the troops of
the Israeli Army Corps that fight in this area.**

**Gonen** (Goh nehn') גונן
In H., "protector." Also the name of a place (kibbutz) in north Israel.**

**Goral** (Goh rahl') גורל
In H., "fate, destiny" or "luck, chance."****

**Goren** (Goh' rehn) גורן
In H., "threshing floor, threshing season, barn, granary." A symbolic
name for both boys and girls born on Shavuot, known as the Feast of
the Harvest. Also the name of a place (moshav) in Israel in the Galilee.***

**Gov** (Gohv) גוב
In H., "pit, lion's den."**

**Gur** (Goor) גור
In H., "cub, whelp, young lion"; in the B. (Genesis), a word used
by Jacob to describe his son Judah.*** Other forms are *Gur-Ari*
(Goor Ah ree') גור־ארי and *Gur-Arye(h)* (Goor Ahr yeh') גור־אריה, in
H., "young lion";** *Guri* (Goo' ree) גורי, in H., "my young lion";**
*Guriel* (Goo ree ehl') גוריאל, from the H., "God is my lion," meaning
"God is my protection";**** and *Guryon* (Goor yohn') גוריון, from
the H., "lion," meaning "strength."*

# H

**Hadar** (Hah dahr') הדר

In H., "splendor, glory, ornament, beauty" or "citrus fruit" or, from the H., "to honor, to respect"; in the B. (Genesis). Also the name of a place in Israel near Tel Aviv. Used also as a girl's name.\*\*\* Other forms are *Hadaram* (Hah dahr ahm') הדר-עם, in H., "glory of the nation," also the name of a place (moshav) in central Israel, because of all the citriculture in the area;\*\* *Hadarezer* (Hah dahr eh' zehr) הדרעזר, in H., "glorious help";\*\*\*\* *Hadriel* (Hahd ree ehl') הדריאל, in H., "splendor of God";\*\*\*\* *Hadur* (Hah door') הדור, in H., "adorned";\* and *Heder* (Heh' dehr) הדר, in H., "beauty, glory, adornment."\*\*\*\*

**Harduf** (Hahr doof') הרדוף

In H., the name of a plant, oleander, that grows on riverbanks. Also the name of a place (kibbutz) in Israel in the Galilee.\*\*\*\*

**Harel** (Hahr ehl') הראל

In H., "mountain of God"; in the B. (Ezekiel), the name of the altar in the Temple. Also the name of a place (kibbutz) in Israel near Jerusalem. Also spelled Harrell.\*\*\*

**Hartov** (Hahr tohv') הרטוב

In H., "mountain of good." Also the name of a railway station in central Israel.\*\*

**Hed** (Hehd) הד

In H., "echo."\*\* Another form is *Hedi* (Heh dee') הדי, in H., "my echo."\*\*\*\*

**Hersh** (Hehrsh) הערש

From the Y., "deer." Other forms are Hersch, Hirsch, Hirsh, Herschel, Hertz, Herz, Herzl, Heschel, Hesh, and Heshel.\*

**Hertzel** (Hehr' tzehl) הרצל

This name became popular because of Theodor (Binyamin-Ze'ev) Herzl, the father of political Zionism, who predicted the establishment of the Jewish state. Therefore it is a symbolic name for boys born on the Israeli Independence Day. It is also the name of a mountain, Har Hertzel, in western Jerusalem, which contains Herzl's grave and graves of other Israeli leaders. The English form is Herzl.\*\*

**Hevel** (Heh' vehl) הבל

In H., "breath, vapor" or "vanity"; in the B. (Genesis), the son of Adam and Eve. The English form is Abel.\*

**Hillel** (Hee lehl′) הילל

From the H., "to praise, glorify" or "to shine"; in the B. (Judges). Hillel the Great was a Talmudic scholar. The nickname is *Hilly* (Hee′ lee) הילי.* Other forms are *Hallel* (Hah lehl′) הלל, in H., "praise, song of praise," also the name of a few psalms in the Book of Psalms recited at the new moon and festivals;** and *Hallelya* (Hah lehl yah′) הלליה, in H., "praise to God."****

**Hitzilya** (Hee tzeel yah′) הציל' יה

In H., "God has saved."* Another form is *Hitzilyahu* (Hee tzeel yah′ hoo) הציליהו, same meaning.*

**Hod** (Hohd) הוד

In H., "glory, splendor, majesty, beauty, grandeur"; in the B. (I Chronicles). Hod Hasharon is the name of a place in Israel near Tel Aviv. Used also as a girl's name.*** Another form is *Hodiya* (Hoh dee yah′) הודיה, in H., "God is my splendor"; in the B. (I Chronicles), also the name of a place (moshav) in Israel in the shefelah (coastal plain). Also spelled Hodia(h).*

**Hoshea** (Hoh sheh′ ah) הושע

From the H., "to deliver, save, help"; in the B. (Hosea), a prophet. The English form is Hosea. Other forms are *Hoshia* (Hoh shee′ ah) הושיע;*** and *Hoshaya* (Hoh shah yah′) הושעיה, in H., "God saves" or "God, please save"; in the B. (Jeremiah). In the Talmud, a scholar. Also the name of a community settlement in Israel in the Galilee.*

---

# I

THE HEBREW LETTERS 'ע, 'א

**Idan** (Ee dahn′) עידן

In H., "time, period, era." Also the name of a place (moshav) in Israel in the Arava. Used also as a girl's name.**

**Ido, Iddo** (Ee doh′) אידו

From the H., "to evaporate, to steam," from the Arabic, "to be strong"; in the B. (Ezra), a leader.* Or (עדוא), from the H., "witness" or "eternally"; in the B. (I Kings, I Chronicles, Zechariah).**

**Ilan** (Ee lahn′) אילן

In H., "tree." A symbolic name for boys born on Tu b'Shvat, the New Year of the Trees, Arbor Day.*** Other forms are *Ilani* (Ee lah nee′) אילני, in H., "my tree";** and *Ilanya* (Ee lahn′ yah) אילניה , in H., "tree of God."\* Ilanot is the name of a plant nursery in Israel in the Sharon.

**Imanuel** (Ee mah noo ehl') עמנואל
In H., "God is with us"; in the B. (Isaiah). Also the name of a place in Israel in the Samaria (Shomron). Also spelled Immanuel, Emanuel, Emmanuel.\*\*

**Imri(e)** (Eem ree') אימרי
In H., "my utterance"; in the B. (I Chronicles).\*

**Ir** (Eer) עיר
In H., "city, town"; in the B. (I Chronicles).\* Another form is *Iram* (Eer ahm') עירעם, in H., "the city of the nation," referring to Jerusalem.\*

**Ira** (Ee rah') עירא
From the H., "young ass"; in the B. (II Samuel).\* Other forms with the same meaning are *Irad* (Ee rahd') עירד, in the B. (Genesis);\* *Iram* (Ee rahm') עירם, in the B. (Genesis);\* *Iran* (Ee rahn') עירן;\* and *Iri* (Ee ree') עירי, in the B. (I Chronicles).\*

**Isaac**
The English form of Yitzchak. See Yitzchak.

**Isaiah**
The English form of Yeshayahu. See Yeshayahu.

**Ishmael**
The English form of Yishmael. See Yishmael.

**Israel**
The English form of Yisrael. See Yisrael.

**Issachar**
The English form of Yisachar. See Yisachar.

**Issar** (Ee sahr') איסר
In H., "vow of abstinence."\*\*

**Itai** (Ee tahy') איתי
From the H., "friendly" or "God is with me"; in the B. (II Samuel), a warrior. Also spelled Ittai.\*\*

**Itamar** (Ee tah mahr') איתמר
In H., "island of palms"; in the B. (Exodus), one of Aaron's sons. Also spelled Ittamar, Ithamar.\*\*\*

**Itiel** (Ee tee ehl') איתיאל
In H., "God is with me"; in the B. (Nehemiah).\*\*\*\*

**Ivri** (Eev ree') עברי
In H., "a Hebrew male," meaning "an Israeli male"; in the B. (Genesis), Abraham (Avraham) was called Ivri, and (I Chronicles) a Levite.\*

**Iyar** (Ee yahr') אייר
From the H., "light." The name of the second month in the Jewish calendar, when the Israeli Independence Day is celebrated (5th Iyar). Also spelled Iyyar.**

**Iyov** (Ee yohv') איוב
From the H., "hated." The English form is Job.*

# J

THE ENGLISH LETTER J

**Jacob**
The English form of Yaakov. See Yaakov.

**Jeremiah**
The English form of Yirmeyahu. See Yirmeyahu.

**Jerusalem**
The English form of Yerushalayim. See Yerushalayim.

**Jethro**
The English form of Yitro. See Yitro.

**Job**
The English form of Iyov. See Iyov.

**Joel**
The English form of Yoel. See Yoel.

**John**
The English form of Yochanan. See Yehochanan.

**Jona(h)**
The English form of Yona. See Yona.

**Jonathan**
The English form of Yonatan. See Yehonatan.

**Jordan**
The English form of Yarden. See Yarden.

**Joseph**
The English form of Yosef. See Yosef.

**Joshua**
The English form of Yehoshua. See Yehoshua.

**Judah**
The English form of Yehuda. See Yehuda.

# K

**Kadmiel** (Kahd mee ehl') קדמיאל
In H., "God is my east" or "my God is ancient"; in the B. (Ezra).*
Another form is *Kedem* (Keh dehm') קדם, in H., "east, front."*

**Kalil** (Kah leel') כליל
In H., "complete, total, perfect."* Other forms are *Klil* (Kleel), in H.,
"crown," also the name of a place in Israel in the Galilee, used also as
a girl's name; see Klil;**** and *Kalul* (Kah lool') כלול, same meaning.*

**Kaniel** (Kah nee ehl') קניאל
From the H., "God is my reed," meaning "God is my support" or "God
had bought me."****

**Karmel, Karmeli**, see Carmel; **Karmi**, see Carmi; **Karmiel, Karmiya**,
see Carmiel.

**Karniel** (Kahr nee ehl') קרניאל
In H., "God is my ray."****

**Katriel** (Kaht ree ehl') כתריאל
In H., "God is my crown."**** Another form is *Keter* (Keh' tehr)
כתר, in H., "crown."*

**Katzir** (Kah tzeer') קציר
In H., "harvest, harvesttime, cut grain." A symbolic name for boys
born on Shavuot, the Feast of the Harvest. Also the name of a place
in Israel in Samaria (Shomron).**

**Kedar** (Kehy dahr') קידר
From the H., "to be darkened, gloomy" or "potter"; in the B. (Genesis),
a son of Ishmael. Also the name of a place in central Israel.****

**Kenan** (Kehy nahn') קינן
From the H., "to acquire, to take possession"; in the B. (Genesis).*

**Keshet** (Keh' sheht) קשת
In H., "rainbow, bow, arch." A symbolic name for boys born on Lag
b'Omer, when Israeli children play with bows and arrows. Also the
name of a place (moshav) in Israel in Ramat Hagolan.** Another
form is *Kashti* (Kahsh tee') קשתי, in H., "my bow" or "my rainbow."*

**Kfir** (Kfeer) כפיר
In H., "young lion," a symbol of a hero.***

**Kochav** (Koh chahv') כוכב
In H., "star" (in the sky and also in an artistic and theatrical sense).

A few names of places in Israel start with this word.* Another form
is *Kochva* (Kohch vah') כוכבא, same meaning, a symbolic name for
boys born on Lag b'Omer, after Bar Kochva (in H., "the son of star"),
a military leader who fought the Romans.*

**Komem** (Koh mehm') קומם
In H., "he reestablished, he restored."*

**Koren** (Koh rehn') קורן
In H., "shining, beaming."**

# L

## THE HEBREW LETTER ל'

**Lahad** (Lah' hahd) להד
In the B. (I Chronicles), a descendant of Judah.****

**Lahat** (Lah' haht) להט
In H., "to burn, glow, blaze up, flame."****

**Lahav** (Lah' hahv) להב
In H., "flame, glitter," a symbolic name for boys born on Hanukkah,
or "blade." Also the name of a place (kibbutz) in south Israel in the
Negev.**

**Lapid** (Lah peed') לפיד
In H., "torch, flame." A symbolic name for boys born on Hanukkah.**
Another form is *Lapidot* (Lah pee doht') לפידות, same meaning, in
the B. (Judges), the husband of Dvora. Also the name of a place
(moshav) in Israel in the Galilee.****

**Larom** (Lah rohm') לרום
In H., "to the height."****

**Lavan** (Lah vahn') לבן
In H., "white"; in the B. (Genesis), the father of Leah and Rachel. The
English form is Laban.*

**Lavi** (Lah vee') לביא
In H., "lion." Also the name of a place (kibbutz) in Israel in the
Galilee.*** The Yiddish forms are Leib,* Leibel,* Label,* Leibus,*
and Loeb.*

**Lazer** (Lahy' zehr) לייזער
The Y. form of Eliezer. See Elazar. Also spelled Lezer.*

**Lee** (Lee) לִי

In H., "me, mine, to me, for myself." Used also as a girl's name. Popular especially among those who like a H. name with an English sound. Also spelled Li.***

**Leeach** (Lee ahch′) לִיאָח

In H., "I have a brother." Also spelled LeeAch; or Liach, LiAch.*

**Leead** (Lee ahd′) לִיעַד

In H., "eternity is mine." Used also as a girl's name. Also spelled LeeAd; or Liad, LiAd.**

**Leeam** (Lee ahm′) לִיעַם

In H., "my nation, my people." Also spelled LeeAm; or Liam, LiAm.** Another form is *Leeami* (Lee ah mee′) לִיעַמִי.*****

**Leeav** (Lee ahv′) לִיאָב

In H., "I have a father," referring to God or to a parent. Used also as a girl's name. Also spelled LeeAv; or Liav, LiAv.**

**Leedon** (Lee dohn′) לִידוֹן

In H., "judgment is mine." Also spelled LeeDon; or Lidon, LiDon.****

**Leedor** (Lee dohr′) לִידוֹר

In H., "my generation." Also spelled LeeDor; or Lidor, LiDor.**

**Leedror** (Lee drohr′) לִידרוֹר

fin H., "freedom is mine" or "I became free." A symbolic name for boys born on Passover, the Feast of Liberation. Also spelled LeeDror; or Lidror, LiDror.****

**Lee El** (Lee Ehl′) לִי־אֵל

In H., "God is mine," or "I belong to God." Also spelled Liel or LiEl.** Another form is *Lael* (Lah ehl′) לָאֵל, same meaning.****

**Leehod** (Lee hohd′) לִיהוֹד

In H., "my beauty, my glory." Also spelled LeeHod; or Lihod, LiHod.**

**Leehu** (Lee hoo′) לִיהוּ(א)

In H., "he is mine." Also spelled Lihu or Li-Hu.*

**Leenur** (Lee noor′) לִינוּר

In H., "I have a fire." A symbolic name for boys born on Hanukkah. Also spelled LeeNour; or Linour, LiNour.*

**Leeon** (Lee ohn′) לִיאוֹן, לִי־אוֹן

In H., "my strength." Also the name of a place in central Israel. Also spelled LeeOn; or Lion, LiOn.**

**Leeor** (Lee ohr′) לִיאוֹר

In H., "my light," or "I have a light." A symbolic name for both boys and girls born on Hanukkah. Also spelled LeeOr; or Lior, LiOr.***

Other forms with the same meaning are *Leeur* (Lee oor') ליאור;****
*Leeori* (Lee oh ree') ליאורי;** and *Leor* (Leh ohr') לאור.****

**Leeoz** (Lee ohz') ליעוז
In H., "my strength, my courage." Also spelled LeeOz; or Lioz, LiOz.**

**Leerom** (Lee rohm') לירום
In H., "I have the height." Also spelled LeeRom; or Lirom, LiRom.**

**Leeron** (Lee rohn') לירון
In H., "my joy, my song." Used also as a girl's name. Also spelled
LeeRon; or Liron, LiRon.*** Another form is *Leeran* (Lee rahn') לירן,
same meaning. Used also as a girl's name. Also spelled LeeRan; or
Liran, LiRan.***

**Leetom** (Lee tohm') ליתום
In H., "my innocence, my purity." Also spelled LeeTom; or Litom,
LiTom.****

**Leetov** (Lee tohv') ליטוב
In H., "I have good fortune"; also spelled LeeTov; or Litov, LiTov.****

**Leshem** (Leh' shehm) לשם
In H., the name of a precious stone, opal.****

**Leumi** (Leh oo mee') לאומי
In H., "national, nationalist."*

**Lev** (Lehv) לב
In H., "heart."****

**Levanon** (Leh vah nohn') לבנון
From the H., "white" or "moon, month." Also the name of a country,
in English, Lebanon.**

**Levi** (Leh vee') לוי
From the H., "joined" or "attendant"; in the B. (Genesis), the son of
Jacob and Leah. The Levites served in the Temple.*

**Livne(h)** (Leev neh') ליבנה
In H., the name of a tree with white flowers, styrax.**

**Lot** (Loht) לוט
In H., "cover, envelope, veil"; in the B. (Genesis), a nephew of Avraham.*

**Lotan** (Loh tahn') לוטן
In the B. (Genesis), a son of Seir. Also the name of a place (kibbutz)
in Israel in the Arava.**

**Lotem** (Loh' tehm) לוטם
In H., the name of a bush with golden yellow flowers, cistus. Also
the name of a place (kibbutz) in Israel in the Galilee. Used also as a
girl's name.**

**Luz** (Looz) לוז
In H., "almond tree." A symbolic name for both boys and girls born
on Tu b'Shvat, Arbor Day.****

# M

THE HEBREW LETTER 'מ

**Maagan** (Mah ah gahn') מעגן
In H., "jetty, anchorage." Also the name of a place (kibbutz) in
Israel on the Kineret beach. A few names of places in Israel contain
this word.****

**Maaseya** (Mah ah seh yah') מעשיה
In H., "God's creation"; in the B. (Jeremiah). Also spelled Maaseyah.*
Other forms are *Maaseyahu* (Mah ah seh yah' hoo) מעשיהו, same
meaning, also the name of a prison in Israel;* and *Maas* (Mah' ahs)
מעש, in H., "deed, action," also the name of a place (moshav) in
Israel in the Sharon.*

**Maayan** (Mah ah yahn') מעיין
In H., "spring, fountain, water well, source." Several names of places
in Israel contain this word. Used also as a girl's name.**

**Macabee** (Mah cah bee') מכבי
In H., an acrostic created by joining the first letters of the words "Mi
Camocha Ba'elim, Adonai!"—"מי כמוך באלים, ה'!"—(in English, "Who
is like unto thee, among the gods, oh Lord!"). This was the battle cry
of the Jews, displayed on their banner when they fought the Greeks.
Judah, the military leader, got the nickname Macabee—some believe
this nickname comes from the battle cry, others think the nickname
is derived from a Hebrew word for hammer, referring to his strength
and his hammerlike blows against the Greeks. Also spelled Maccabee
and Makabi. A symbolic name for boys born on Hanukkah. Macabim
is the name of a place in central Israel.*

**Machseya** (Mahch seh yah') מחסיה
In H., "the shelter of God," meaning "the protection of God"; in
the B. (Jeremiah). Also the name of a place (moshav) in central Israel.*

**Magal** (Mah gahl') מגל
In H., "scythe." A symbolic name for both boys and girls born on
Shavuot, known as the Feast of the Harvest. Also the name of a place
(kibbutz) in Israel in the Samaria (Shomron).**

**Magen** (Mah gehn') מגן
In H., "shield, protector, defender." Also the name of a place (kibbutz) in Israel in the Negev.** Another form is *Megen* (Meh gehn'), in H., "he is protecting," referring to God.*

**Maksim** (Mahk seem') מקסים
In H., "wonderful, enticing, charming, enchanting."*

**Malach** (Mahl ahch') מלאך
In H., "angel, delegate, messenger."* Another form is *Malachi* (Mahl ah chee') מלאכי, in H., "my angel, my messenger" and also the name of a prophet. The English forms are Malachai and Malachy. Kiryat Malachi is the name of a place in south Israel named after the Jewish community of Los Angeles. (Angeles was translated into Hebrew as Angels.)**

**Malki** (Mahl kee') מלכי
In H., "my king."* Other forms are *Malkam* (Mahl kahm') מלכם, in H., "God is their king"; in the B. (I Chronicles), also spelled Malcam;* *Malkiel* (Mahl kee ehl') מלכיאל, in H., "God is my king"; in the B. (Genesis);** *Malkiram* (Mahl kee rahm') מלכירם, in H., "God is mighty"; in the B. (I Chronicles);** *Malkishua* (Mahl kee shoo' ah) מלכישוע, in H., "my king is salvation," referring to God, in the B. (I Samuel), one of King Saul's sons, also the name of a place (kibbutz) in north Israel named after one of King Saul's sons, who died in the battle in this area;* *Malki-Tzedek* (Mahl' kee Tzeh' dehk) מלכי־צדק, in H., "my king is righteousness," referring to God; in the B. (Genesis);* *Malkiya* (Mahl kee yah') מלכיה, in H., "God is my king"; in the B. (Jeremiah), also spelled Malkia(h), also the name of a place (kibbutz) in Israel in the Galilee, used also as a girl's name (see Malka[h]);** *Malkiyahu* (Mahl kee yah' hoo) מלכיהו, in H., "God is my king," in the B. (Jeremiah);* *Mehlech* (Meh' lehch) מלך, in H., "king"; in the B. (I Chronicles);* and *Malkior* (Mahl kee ohr') מלכיאור, in H., "God is my light" or "my God is a light."**

**Manoach** (Mah noh' ahch) מנוח
In H., "resting place, peace, repose, rest"; in the B. (Judges).*

**Manor** (Mah nohr') מנור
In H., "weaver's beam, warp beam" or "boom" (in a boat).****

**Maon** (Mah ohn') מעון
In H., "dwelling, habitation"; in the B. (I Chronicles). Also the name of a place (moshav) in central Israel named after the ancient city mentioned in the B.*

**Maor** (Mah ohr') מאור
In H., "light, brightness." Also the name of a place (moshav) in Israel
in the Sharon. A symbolic name for boys born on Hanukkah, the
Feast of Lights.**

**Maoz** (Mah ohz') מעוז
In H., "strength, force, fortress, shelter, refuge, protection." A symbolic
name for boys born on Hanukkah, because on this holiday we sing
"Maoz Tzur" (Rock of Ages). Maoz Chaim is the name of a place
(kibbutz) in north Israel.** Other forms are *Maozya* (Mah ohz yah')
מעוזיה, in H., "strength of God" or "God's protection";* *Maazya*
(Mah ahz yah') מעזיה, same meaning, in the B. (Nehemiah), a priest,
also spelled Maazia(h);* and *Maazyahu* (Mah ahz yah' hoo) מעזיהו,
same meaning.*

**Marnin** (Mahr neen') מרנין
In H., "gladdening, causing joy, joyful" or the name of a meter used
in Hebrew poetry of medieval Spain.****

**Marom** (Mah rohm') מרום
In H., "height, high place, sky, peak."** Another form is *Merom* (Meh
rohm') מירום, same meaning, in the B. (Joshua). Merom Golan is the
name of a place (kibbutz) in Israel in Ramat Hagolan.**

**Masa** (Mah sah') משא
In H., "burden, load, carrying" or "present, desire, longing"; in the B.
(I Chronicles).*

**Mashiach** (Mah shee' ahch) משיח
In H., "Messiah, the Anointed." Also spelled Mashiah.*

**Maskil** (Mahs keel') משכיל
In H., "intellectual, intelligent, educated."*

**Masos** (Mah sohs') משוש
In H., "joy, gladness."*

**Mata** (Mah tah') מטע
In H., "plantation." Also the name of a place (moshav) in central
Israel. A symbolic name for boys born on Tu b'Shvat, the New Year
of the Trees.****

**Matan** (Mah tahn') מתן
In H., "present, gift"; in the B. (Jeremiah).** Another form is *Matanya*
(Mah tahn yah') מתניה, in H., "gift of God"; in the B. (II Kings), also
spelled Matania(h).** Other forms with the same meaning are
*Matanyahu* (Mah tahn yah' hoo) מתניהו, in the B. (I Chronicles);*
*Matanel* (Mah tahn ehl') מתנאל;** and *Matnan* (Maht nahn') מתנן.****

**Matar** (Mah tahr') מטר

In H., "rain." Also the name of a place in Israel in the Samaria (Shomron).****

**Matitya** (Mah teet yah') מתיתיה

From the H., "gift of God"; in the B. (Ezra). Also spelled Matitia(h).** Another form is *Matityahu* (Mah teet yah' hoo) מתיתיהו, same meaning, a symbolic name for boys born on Hanukkah, because Matityahu (the Greek form is Mattathias) was a Jewish leader, the father of the five Hasmonean brothers who fought the Greeks. Also the name of a place (moshav) in Israel in the shefelah. Nickname is *Mati* (Mah' tee) מתי.**

**Matzliach** (Mahtz lee' ahch) מצליח

In H., "successful." Also the name of a place (moshav) in Israel in the shefelah.*

**Mazor** (Mah zohr') מזור

In H., "bandage, medicine." Also the name of a place (moshav) in Israel near Tel Aviv.****

**Mechubad** (Meh choo bahd') מכובד

In H., "honored, respected."*

**Medad** (Mehy dahd') מידד

From the H., "friend"; in the B. (Numbers), a leader in the time of Moses. Also spelled Meydad.**

**Medan** (Meh dahn') מדן

In H., "quarrel, strife, contention"; in the B. (Genesis), one of Abraham's sons.****

**Meged** (Meh' gehd) מגד

In H., "precious thing, choice fruit, blessing, sweetness." Megadim is the name of a place (moshav) in north Israel.** Another form is *Magdiel* (Mahg dee ehl') מגדיאל, in H., "goodness of God"; in the B. (Genesis). Also the name of a place in Israel near Tel Aviv.****

**Mehulal** (Meh hoo lahl') מהולל

In H., "he is praised, adored."****

**Meir** (Meh eer') מאיר

In H., "he is lighting, shining." Also spelled Meyer, Myer.** Another form is *Meiri* (Meh ee ree') מאירי.**

**Meitar** (Mehy tahr') מיתר

In H., "string, cord, sinew." Used also as a girl's name.****

**Menachem** (Meh nah chehm') מנחם

In H., "comforter, consoler"; in the B. (II Kings), a king. A symbolic name for boys born during the month of Av or on the ninth of Av

(Tishah b'Av), a day of fasting and mourning for the destruction of the Temple. The English form is Menahem. The Yiddish form is Mendel. Menachem Mendel is a symbol of a dreamer, an unrealistic person (the hero in a book by Shalom Aleichem). The nickname is *Meni* (Meh' nee) מני.\* Another form is *Menucham* (Meh noo chahm') מנוחם, in H., "consoled, comforted."\*\*\*\*

**Menashe** (Meh nah sheh') מנשה
In the B. (Genesis), the eldest son of Joseph. The English form is Manasseh. Ramat Menashe is the name of a high area in north Israel. The nickname is *Meni* (Meh' nee) מני.\*

**Meron** (Mehy rohn') מירון
In H., "troops, sheep, soldiers." Also the name of a place (moshav) and a mountain in Israel in the Galilee. A symbolic name for boys born on Lag b'Omer, because Orthodox people in Israel go on that day to this village to the grave of Rabbi Shimeon Bar Yochai (Simeon Bar Yohai), a great sage who started the Jewish mysticism (cabala) and wrote the Zohar for the Hillula (happy festivities). During the night of the Hillula, a unique custom takes place: Three-year-old boys from the Orthodox community get their first haircuts with the blessing of a rabbi, and the newly cut locks are thrown into the bonfire. Also spelled Meiron.\*\*\*

**Meshar** (Mehy shahr') מישר
In H., "straight, upright, horizontal line." Also the name of a place (moshav) in Israel in the shefelah (coastal plain).\*\* Another form is *Mishor* (Mee shohr') מישור, in H., "plain, level land." Mishor Hachof is the name of an area in western Israel, along the sea.\*\*\*\*

**Meshulam** (Meh shoo lahm') משולם
In H., "paid up, wholehearted, genuine"; in the B. (II Kings).\* Another form is *Mishlam* (Meesh lahm') מישלם.\*

**Metav** (Mehy tahv') מיטב
In H., "the best, the choicest, optimum." Also the name of a place (moshav) in Israel in the Valley of Esdraelon (Jezreel). Also spelled Meitav.\*\*\*\* Another form is *Metiv* (Mehy teev') מטיב, in H., "benefactor."\*

**Metushelach** (Meh too sheh' lahch) מתושלח
From the H., "a man who was sent, a messenger"; in the B. (Genesis), the man who lived 969 years, longer than any other human being. A Hebrew idiom says "as old as Metushelach" referring to somebody old, old fashioned, or out of date, and therefore this name has a somewhat bad connotation. The English form is Methuselah.\*

**Mevaser** (Meh vah sehr') מבשר
In H., "herald, messenger of good tidings."* Another form is *Mevaser-Tov* (Meh vah sehr' Tohv) מבשר־טוב, in H., "bearer of good tidings."*

**Mevorach** (Meh voh rahch') מבורך
In H., "blessed."*

**Micha** (Mee chah') מיכה
From the H., "Who is like God?"; in the B. (Micah), one of the twelve Minor Prophets. The English form is Mica(h).** Other forms with the same meaning are *Michaya* (Mee chah yah') מיכיה, in the B. (Nehemiah);* and *Michayahu* (Mee chah yah' hoo) מיכיהו, in the B. (II Chronicles).*

**Michael** (Mee chah ehl') מיכאל
From the H., "Who is like God?"; in the B. (Numbers and Daniel), the prince of God's angels. The English forms are Mitchel and Mitchell. Also spelled Mychael. Nicknames are *Miki* (Mee' kee) מיקי and *Muki* (Moo' kee) מוקי.***

**Migdal** (Meeg dahl') מגדל
In H., "tower." Several names of places in Israel start with this word.*

**Misgav** (Mees gahv') משגב
In H., "fortress, high place, refuge, strength, stronghold." Also the name of a place in Israel in the Galilee.**

**Mishan** (Meesh ahn') משען
In H., "support, staff, rest, buttress."* Another form is *Mashen* (Mahsh ehn'), also the name of a place (moshav) in Israel in the shefelah (coastal plain).*

**Mishlat** (Meesh laht') משלט
In H., "fortified height, commanding ground." Several names of places in Israel start with this word.****

**Mishmar** (Meesh mahr') משמר
In H., "guard, post, prison, division of priests of Levites." Several names of places in Israel start with this word.****

**Mivtach** (Meev tahch') מבטח
In H., "confidence, reliance, trust, faith, secure place, fortress." Mivtachim is the name of a place (moshav) in Israel in the Negev.**** Another form is *Mivtachyahu* (Meev tahch yah' hoo) מבטחיהו, in H., "God is my security."*

**Mivtzar** (Meev tzahr') מבצר
In H., "fortress, stronghold, secure place"; in the B. (Genesis).*

**Mor** (Mohr) מור
In H., the name of a plant, myrrh, used for preparing perfume and incense. Also used as a girl's name. Also spelled Mohr, Moer.***

**Morag** (Moh rahg´) מורג
In H., "threshing sledge." A symbolic name for both boys and girls born on Shavuot, known as the Feast of the Harvest. Also the name of a place (moshav) in Israel, in the Gaza Strip.****

**Moran** (Moh rahn´) מורן
In H., the name of an evergreen plant, viburnum, that grows in thickets. Also the name of a place (kibbutz) in Israel in the Galilee, named after this bush. Used also as a girl's name.***

**Mordechai** (Mohr deh chahy´) מורדכי
From the Persian, "warrior." A symbolic name for boys born on Purim, because Mordechai was the cousin of Queen Ester. The English form is Mordecai. The Yiddish form is Mordche. Yad Mordechai is the name of a place (kibbutz) in Israel in the shefelah (coastal plain). Nicknames are *Moti* (Moh´ tee) מוטי and *Motke* (Moht´ keh) מוטקה.**

**Moriel** (Moh ree ehl´) מוריאל
In H., "God is my teacher, my guide."**** Another form is *Mori* (Moh ree´) מורי, in H., "my teacher."*

**Moshe** (Moh sheh´) משה
From the H., "drawn out of the water"; in the B. (Exodus), the leader who brought the Israeli people out of Egypt and led them to the Promised Land, Canaan. The English form is Moses.**

**Motza** (Moh tzah´) מוצא
In H., "exit, outlet, way out" or "speech, utterance" or "source, fountain"; in the B. (I Chronicles). Also the name of a rural area and a suburb in Israel near Jerusalem.*

# N

**Naaran** (Nah ah rahn') נערן
From the H., "young man, boy, child." Also the name of two places (historic sites) in Israel in the Jordan Valley and in Ramot Haggean.****

**Naarya** (Nah ahr yah') נעריה
In H., "child of God"; in the B. (I Chronicles). Also spelled Naaria(h).****

**Nachal** (Nah' chahl) נחל
In H., "stream, brook, river." All the names of the streams in Israel start with this word.**** Or נח"ל, in H., "pioneering combatant youth" (premilitary cadet corps).****

**Nachliel** (Nahch lee ehl') נחליאל
From the H., "God is my possession"; in the B. (Numbers), the name of a place.* Another form is *Nachlieli* (Nahch lee eh' lee) נחליאלי, in H., also the name of a singing bird, wagtail, that arrives in Israel in the winter.****

**Nachman** (Nahch mahn') נחמן
In H., "comforter."* Other forms are *Nachmani* (Nahch mah nee') נחמני, in H., "my comforter" or "my comfort"; in the B. (Nehemiah), a leader;* *Nacham* (Nah chahm') נחם, in H., "comfort, consolation"; in the B. (I Chronicles), also the name of a place (moshav) in central Israel named after a member of the tribe of Judah;**** *Nocham* (Noh' chahm) נוחם, same meaning;**** *Nachmiel* (Nahch mee ehl') נחמיאל, in H., "God is my comfort";* *Nachum* (Nah choom') נחום, in the B. (Nahum), a Minor Prophet;** and *Nechum* (Neh choom'), in the B. (Nehemiah), a leader of the Babylonian Exile returnees.*

**Nachshol** (Nahch shohl') נחשול
In H., "storm, torrent, wave, surge." Nachsholim is the name of a place (kibbutz) in Israel on Carmel Beach.**

**Nachshon** (Nahch shohn') נחשון
In H., "daring, dashing person." The legend is that Nachshon, chief of the tribe of Judah, was the first to plunge into the Red Sea when Israel left Egypt. Or "adventurous pioneer." Also the name of a place (kibbutz) in Israel in the shefelah. Also the name of a snakebird, darter.**

**Nadav** (Nah dahv') נדב

From the H., "donor, generous, openhanded, noble"; in the B.
(Exodus), the eldest son of Aaron.*** Other forms are *Nadiv*
(Nah deev') נדיב, same meaning;* and *Nedavya* (Neh dahv yah')
נדביה, in H., "generosity of God" or "God's donation"; in the B.
(I Chronicles), also spelled Nedavia(h).*

**Nadir** (Nah deer') נדיר

In H., "rare, scarce" or, from the H., "oath."****

**Naeh** (Nah eh') נאה

In H., "beautiful, handsome, fine."* Another form is *Naot* (Nah oht')
נאות, in H., "suitable, fit, proper, decent." A few names of places in
Israel start with this word.****

**Naftali(e)** (Nahf tah lee') נפתלי

From the H., "meander, struggle, wrestlings"; in the B. (Genesis), the
sixth son of Jacob. Also spelled Naphtali. Ramot Naftali is the name
of a place (moshav) and an area in Israel in the Galilee.*

**Nagid** (Nah geed') נגיד

In H., "governor, ruler, prince, leader."*

**Nahir** (Nah heer') נהיר

In H., "clear, bright."**** Other forms are *Nehor* (Neh hohr') נהור, from
the Aramaic, "light";* *Nahur* (Nah hoor');* and *Nohar* (Noh' hahr)
נוהר, in H., "brightness," used also as a girl's name. See Nehara.**

**Nakdimon** (Nahk dee mohn') נקדימון

From the H., "one who brings dots of light."*

**Namer** (Nah mehr') נמר

In H., "tiger, leopard, panther." This name has bad connotations,
because in H. slang it spells the initials of a first-class nagger.****
Another form is *Namir* (Nah meer') נמיר, same meaning.*

**Naor** (Nah ohr') נאור

In H., "enlightened, cultured, illumined, glorious" or a name of God.**
Another form is *Nehorai* (Neh hoh rahy') נהוראי, same meaning.*

**Nasi** (Nah see') נשיא

In H., "president, chief, prince, king."*

**Natan** (Nah tahn') נתן

In H., "he gave, he granted, he let, he permitted," referring to God; in
the B. (II Samuel), a prophet. The English form is Nathan.** Other
forms that mean in H. "gift of God" are *Netanel* (Neh tahn ehl')
נתנאל, in the B. (I Chronicles); the English form is Nethanel;**
*Netanya* (Neh tahn yah') נתניה, in the B. (II Kings), also the name of

a city in Israel on the Sharon Beach, also spelled Netania(h);**** and
*Netanyahu* (Neh tahn yah' hoo) נתניהו.*

**Nativ** (Nah teev') נתיב
In H., "way, path, track, lane, route, road, direction." Several names
of places in Israel contain this word.**

**Nave** (Nah veh') נווה
In H., "dwelling place, resort, pasture." Many names of places in
Israel start with this word.****

**Navon** (Nah vohn') נבון
In H., "wise, clever, intelligent."*

**Nechemya** (Neh chehm yah') נחמיה
From the H., "comfort of God" or "comforted by God"; in the B.
(Ezra), a governor of Judah. Also spelled Nechemia(h), Nehemiah.**

**Ne'eman** (Neh eh mahn') נאמן
In H., "faithful, trustworthy, loyal, reliable."*

**Negev** (Neh' gehv) נגב
In H., "south, southern region." The Negev is the southern region of
Israel, from below the Dead Sea to Eilat.*

**Nehedar** (Neh heh dahr') נהדר
In H., "splendid, wonderful, superb, glorious."*

**Ner** (Nehr) נר
In H., "candle, light"; in the B. (I Samuel). A symbolic name for boys
born on Hanukkah, the Feast of Lights, or on Friday evening before
the lighting of Sabbath (Shabat) candles.**** Other forms are *Neri*
(Neh ree') נרי, in H., "my candle, my light";** *Neriya* (Neh ree yah')
נריה, in H., "light of God" or "God is my candle, my light"; in the B.
(Jeremiah), also spelled Neria(h), used also as a girl's name (see
Nera);** *Neriyahu* (Neh ree yah' hoo) נריהו;* and *Neriad* (Neh ree
ahd') נריעד, in H., "my candle, light is eternal."**

**Nes(s)** (Nehs) נס
In H., "miracle, wonder" or "flag, standard, signal." A few names of
places in Israel start with this word.* Other forms are *Nisi* (Nee see')
ניסי, in H., "my miracle" or "my sign," also spelled Nissi;* and *Nissim*
(Nee seem') ניסים, in H., "miracles" or "signs."**

**Netael** (Neh tah ehl') נטעאל
In H., "God's seedling, God's plant." A symbolic name for boys born
on Tu b'Shvat, Arbor Day.****

**Netzach** (Neh' tzahch) נצח
In H., "eternity, forever" or, from the H., "victory, triumph, success."****

Other forms are *Netziach* (Neh tzee' ahch) נציח, from the H., "victory";
in the B. (Ezra);* *Natzchan* (Nahtz chahn') נצחן, in H., "victorious,
strong, mighty, debater";**** and *Nitzchi* (Neetz chee') נצחי, in H.,
"my victory" or "everlasting."*

**Netzer** (Neh' tzehr) נצר
In H., "sprout, shoot, branch," a symbolic name for boys born on Tu
b'Shvat, the New Year of the Trees, or "descendant, offspring." A few
names of places in Israel contain this word.**

**Nezer** (Neh' zehr) נזר
In H., "crown, tiara."****

**Nimrod** (Neem rohd') נמרוד
In H., "we will rebel"; in the B. (Genesis). Also a place name in north
Israel in Ramat Hagolan.***

**Nin** (Neen) נין
In H., "great-grandson."****

**Nir** (Neer) ניר
In H., "furrow, plowed field." A symbolic name for boys born on Tu
b'Shvat, the New Year of the Trees, Arbor Day. Many names of places
in Israel contain this word.*** Other forms are *Niran* (Nee rahn')
נירן, also the name of a place (kibbutz) in Israel in the Jordan Valley,
used also as a girl's name (see Nira);** *Niram* (Neer ahm') נירעם, in
H., "cultivated fields of the nation," also the name of a place (kibbutz)
in Israel in the Negev.** Other forms that mean, in H., "cultivated
fields of God" are *Nirel* (Neer ehl') ניראל;** *Niriel* (Nee ree ehl')
ניריאל;**** *Nirya* (Neer yah') ניריה, also spelled Niria(h);** and
*Niriya* (Nee ree yah').****

**Nissan** (Nee sahn') ניסן
From the H., "miracle," the name of the first month in the Jewish
calendar, when we celebrate Passover (Pesach). This is also the first
month of spring. A symbolic name for boys born in this month or
on Passover. Also spelled Nisan.**

**Nitai** (Nee tahy') ניתאי
From the H., "seedling," a symbolic name for boys born on Tu b'Shvat,
Arbor Day. In the Talmud the name of an early scholar.****

**Nitzan** (Nee tzahn') ניצן
In H., "bud." A symbolic name for both boys and girls (see Nitza[h])
born on Tu b'Shvat, Arbor Day.***

**Niv** (Neev) ניב
In H., "expression, phrase, idiom, dialect," or "fang, canine tooth."***
Other forms are *Nivai* (Nee vahy') ניבי, in H., "my expressions"; in

the B. (Nehemiah);** and *Nov* (Nohv) נוב, in H., "to utter, speak" or "to grow, bud, sprout," also the name of a place (moshav) in Israel in Ramat Hagolan, named after an ancient city mentioned in the Talmud.****

**Nivchar** (Neev chahr') נבחר
In H., "chosen, selected, elected."*

**Noach** (Noh' ahch) נוח
From the H., "rest, quiet, peace"; in the B. (Genesis), the man who built an ark to survive the flood. The English form is Noah.* Another form is *Nocha* (Noh' chah) נוחה, same meaning, in the B. (I Chronicles).*

**Noad** (Noh ahd') נועד
In H., "assembled" or "prepared."* Another form is *Noadya* (Noh ahd yah') נועדיה, in H., "assembly of God" or "prepared by God" (to do something); in the B. (Ezra) a Levite, also spelled Noadia(h).*

**Noam** (Noh' ahm) נועם
In H., "loveliness, gracefulness, pleasantness, charm, kindness, tenderness." Also the name of a place (moshav) in south Israel. Used also as a girl's name (see Naama[h]).*** Other forms are *Naam* (Nah ahm') נעם, in H., "to be lovely, pleasant, sweet"; in the B. (I Chronicles);**** *Naaman* (Nah ah mahn') נעמן, same meaning, in the B. (II Kings);** *Naim* (Nah eem') נעים, in H., "pleasant, pleasing, lovely, sweet, agreeable";* and *Naom* (Nah ohm') נעום, same meaning.*

**Noaz** (Noh ahz') נועז
In H., "daring, bold, brave, fearless."*

**Noda** (Noh dah') נודע
In H., "famous, well-known, recognized."*

**Nof** (Nohf) נוף
In H., "panorama, landscape, scene" or "top of tree." Nofim is the name of an urban area in Israel in Samaria (Shomron).** Another form is *Nofi* (Noh fee') נופי, in H., "my scene."**

**Nofech** (Noh' fehch) נופך
In H., the name of a precious stone, turquoise, that was in the breastplate (hoshen) of the high priest. Also the name of a place in Israel in the Sharon.****

**Notea** (Noh teh' ah) נוטע
In H., "a planter," a symbolic name for boys born on Tu b'Shvat, Arbor Day.**** Another form is *Natia* (Nah tee' ah) נטיע, in H., "plant, seedling."****

**Noter** (Noh tehr') נוטר
In H., "watchman, guard."* Another form is *Natur* (Nah toor') נטור,

in H., "a guarded place," also the name of a place (kibbutz) in north Israel, in Ramat Hagolan.****

**Notzer** (Noh tzehr') נוצר
In H., "guard, watchman."*

**Noy** (Nohy) נוי
In H., "beauty, ornament." Used also as a girl's name. Also spelled Noi.**

**Nufar** (Noo fahr') נופר
In H., the name of a water plant, yellow water lily. Also spelled Nuphar. Used also as a girl's name. Another form is *Nofer* (Noh' fehr).****

**Nur** (Noor) נור
From the Aramaic, "fire." A symbolic name for boys born on Hanukkah, the Feast of Lights.** Another form is *Nuri* (Noo' ree) נורי, in H., "my fire."** Other forms that mean, in H., "fire of God" are *Nuriel* (Noo ree ehl') נוריאל;** *Nuriya* (Noo ree yah') נוריה, also spelled Nuria(h);** and *Nurya* (Noor yah') נור־יה.****

# O

THE HEBREW LETTERS ע', א'

**Oded** (Oh dehd') עודד
From the H., "to encourage"; in the B. (II Chronicles), a prophet.***

**Ofek** (Oh' fehk) אופק
In H., "horizon." Ofakim is the name of a small town in Israel in the Negev.**

**Ofer** (Oh' fehr) עופר
In H., "young deer" or "handsome lad" (poetic). Also the name of a place (moshav) in north Israel near Mount Carmel. Also spelled Opher.*** Other forms are *Ofar* (Oh fahr');**** and *Ofri* (Ohf ree') עופרי, in H., "my young deer" or "my handsome lad."****

**Ofir** (Oh feer') אופיר
In H., "gold"; in the B. (Genesis) and, also in the B., the name of a place (I Kings).

**Ogen** (Oh' gehn) עוגן
In H., "anchor."*

**Ohad** (Oh hahd') אוהד
From the H., "love, beloved"; in the B. (Genesis), one of Jacob's

grandsons. Also the name of a place (moshav) in Israel in the Negev.***
Another form is *Ohed* (Oh hehd').*

**Ohel** (Oh' hehl) אוהל

In H., "tent"; in the B. (I Chronicles).* Other forms are *Oholi* (Oh
hoh lee') אוהולי, in H., "my tent";* and *Oholiav* (Oh hoh lee ahv')
אוהוליאב, in H., "Father is my tent," referring to God; in the B.
(Exodus).****

**Omer** (Oh' mehr) עומר

In H., "sheaf of corn, bundle of grain" or an ancient dry measure.
Also the name of an urban area in Israel in the Negev. A symbolic
name for boys born during the period of Counting of the Omer
(forty-nine days between the end of the first day of Passover and
Shavuot) or on Lag b'Omer or on Shavuot, the Feast of the Harvest.***
Another form is *Omri* (Ohm ree') עומרי, in H., "my sheaf"; in the B.
(I Kings), a king of Israel.***

**Ometz** (Oh' mehtz) אומץ

In H., "courage, bravery." Also the name of a place (moshav) in Israel
in the Sharon. Also spelled Omez.*

**On** (Ohn) און

In H., "strength, power, potency, wealth"; in the B. (Numbers), a
leader.*** Other forms are *Oni* (Oh nee') אוני, in H., "my strength";**
and *Onam* (Oh nahm') אונם, in the B. (Genesis).*

**Or** (Ohr) אור

In H., "light, brightness." Several names of places in Israel start with
the word *or*. A symbolic name for both boys and girls born on
Hanukkah, the Feast of Lights.*** Other forms with the same meaning
are *Oran* (Oh rahn') אורן;**** *Oryan* (Ohr yahn') אורריין, also in
Aramaic, "Torah, leaning, scholar";**** *Oryon* (Ohr yohn') אוריון,
also the name of a star;**** *Oron* (Oh rohn') אורון, also the name of
a phosphate project in Israel in the Negev;*** *Ori* (Oh' ree) אורי, in
H., "my light";*** *Or-Chayim* (Ohr' Chah yeem') אור־חיים, in H.,
"light of life," referring to God or to the Torah;* *Or-Tal* (Ohr Tahl')
אורטל or אור־טל, in H., "morning dew," also the name of a place
(kibbutz) in Israel in Ramat Hagolan, used also as a girl's name;***
*Or-Tziyon* (Ohr' Tzee yohn') אור־ציון, in H., "light of Zion" (Israel);*
and *Orad* (Ohr ahd') אורעד, in H., "eternal light."****

**Oren** (Oh' rehn) אורן

In H., the name of a tree, pine; in the B. (I Chronicles).*** Oren-
Yerushalayim (Jerusalem pine) grows widely in Israel's mountains.
Beyth Oren is the name of a place (kibbutz) in Israel in Mount Carmel,

named after the pine woods in the area. Another form is *Orni* (Ohr nee') אורני, in H., "my pine tree."****

**Osher** (Oh' shehr) אושר

In H., "happiness,"* or, in a different H. spelling, עושר, "wealth, richness."* Another form is *Oshri* (Ohsh ree') אושרי, in H., "my good fortune."*

**Otni** (Oht' nee) עותני

From the H., "my strength"; in the B. (I Chronicles), a Levite. Also spelled Othni.* Another form is *Otniel* (Oht nee ehl') עותניאל, in H., "strength of God" or "God is my strength"; in the B. (Joshua). Also the name of a place in central Israel. Also spelled Othniel.*

**Otzar** (Oh tzahr') אוצר

In H., "treasure." Also spelled Ozar.*

**Otzem** (Oh' tzehm) עוצם

In H., "strength, might, force"; in the B. (I Chronicles), a brother of King David. Also the name of a place (moshav) in Israel in the shefelah (coastal plain). Also spelled Ozem.*

**Oved** (Oh vehd') עובד

In H., "workman, servant"; in the B. (Ruth).* Other forms are *Ovad* (Oh vahd');* and *Ovadya* (Oh vahd yah') עובדיה, in H., "servant of God"; in the B. (Obadiah), a prophet. Also spelled Ovadia(h). The English form is Obadiah.**

**Oz** (Ohz) עוז

In H., "strength, power, courage."** Other forms are *Oz-Tziyon* (Ohz' Tzee yohn') עוז־ציון, in H., "the strength of Zion" (Israel);* and *Oz-El* (Ohz Ehl') עוז־אל, in H., "God's strength."*

**Ozer** (Oh zehr') עוזר

In H., "helper," referring to God.* Another form is *Ozeri* (Oh zeh' ree) עוזרי, in H., "my helper."*

# P

**Palti** (Pahl tee') פלטי

In H., "my escape, my deliverance"; in the B. (I Samuel).* Other forms
are *Paltiel* (Pahl tee ehl') פלטיאל, in H., "God is my savior"; in the B.
(Numbers);* *Pelet* (Peh' leht) פלט, in H., "escape, deliverance"; in the
B. (Numbers);* *Platya* (Plaht yah') פלטיה, in H., "the deliverance of
God"; in the B. (I Chronicles);* and *Platyahu* (Plaht yah' hoo) פלטיהו,
in the B. (Ezekiel).*

**Pardes** (Pahr dehs') פרדס

In H., "citrus plantation, orange grove."* Another form is *Pardesya*
(Pahr dehs yah') פרדסיה, in H., "God is my citrus plantation," mean-
ing "my source of wisdom." Also the name of a place in Israel in the
Sharon.*

**Paz** (Pahz) פז

In H., "gold, golden, sparkling." Also the name of the oil distributors in
Israel. Used also as a girl's name.*** Other forms are *Pazi* (Pah' zee)
פזי, in H., "my gold";** and *Pazel* (Pahz ehl') פזאל, in H., "God's gold."****

**Pdatzur** (Pdah' tzoor) פדהצור

From the H., "the Rock has redeemed," referring to God; in the B.
(Numbers), the father of Gamliel. Also spelled Pedatzur.* Another
form is *Pde-Tzur* (Pdeh' Tzoor) פדה־צור, in H., "Rock, redeem me"
(a prayer to God).****

**Pdut** (Pdoot) פדות

In H., "redemption, liberty." A symbolic name for both boys and girls
born on Passover, the Feast of Liberation.** Other forms are *Pdat*
(Pdaht) פדת;* *Pdael* (Pdah ehl') פדהאל, in H., "God's redemption"; in
the B. (Numbers);* *Pdaya* (Pdah yah') פדיה, in H., "God's redemption";
in the B. (II Kings), also the name of a place (moshav) in Israel in the
shefelah (coastal plain);** *Pdayahu* (Pdah yah' hoo) פדיהו, same
meaning, in the B. (I Chronicles);* and *Pduel* (Pdoo ehl') פדואל, same
meaning, also the name of a place in Israel in Samaria (Shomron).**

**Pe'er** (Peh ehr') פאר

In H., "glory, luxury, magnificence." Used also as a girl's name.**

**Peled** (Peh' lehd) פלד

In H., "steel."**

**Peleg** (Peh' lehg) פלג

In H., "brook, stream, rivulet."**

**Pele(h)** (Peh' leh) פלא

In H., "miracle, wonder."* Another form is *Playa* (Plah yah') פלאיה,
in H., "miracle of God"; in the B. (I Chronicles). Also spelled Plaia(h).*

**Peretz** (Peh' rehtz) פרץ

In H., "breach, gap, breakthrough"; in the B. (Genesis). Also spelled
Perez.**

**Peri** (Peh' ree) פרי

From the H., "fruit," meaning, "product, result, offspring, profit, or
gain." Popular especially among those who like a H. name with an
English sound. Used also as a girl's name.**

**Pesach** (Peh' sahch) פסח

From the H., "to pass over." The H. name for Passover. Also spelled
Pesah.* Other forms are *Pesachya* (Peh sahch yah') פסחיה, in H.,
"the Pesach of God," also spelled Pesachia(h);* and *Pesachyahu* (Peh
sahch yah' hoo) פסחיהו, same meaning.*

**Pinchas** (Peen chahs') פינחס

In the B. (Exodus), a high priest, the grandson of Aharon (Aaron).
The English forms are Phineas and Phinehas. The Yiddish form is
Pineh. Nickname is *Pini* (Pee' nee) פיני.**

**Pniel** (Pnee ehl') פניאל

From the H., "face of God" or "light of God."* Another form is *Pnuel*
(Pnoo ehl') פנואל, in the B. (I Chronicles), same meaning.*

**Porat** (Poh raht') פורת

From the H., "fruitful"; in the B. (Genesis), Yaacov (Jacob) described
his son Yosef (Joseph) as a "fruitful son," and it has become the
description of a handsome or clever boy. Also the name of a place
(moshav) in Israel in the Sharon.**

**Priel** (Pree ehl') פריאל

In H., "fruit of God."** Another form is *Poriel* (Poh ree ehl') פוריאל,
in H., "God is my fruitfulness."****

**Ptachya** (Ptahch yah') פתחיה

In H., "open (your heart) to God," or "God, open (your hand) to me";
in the B. (I Chronicles), a priest. Also the name of a place (moshav)
in Israel in the shefelah (coastal plain). Also spelled Petachya,
Petachia(h).* Another form is *Ptachyahu* (Ptahch yah' hoo) פתחיהו,
same meaning.*

# R

**Raam** (Rah' ahm) רעם
In H., "thunder."**** Another form is *Raamya* (Rah ahm yah') רעמיה, in
H., "God's thunder"; in the B. (Nehemiah). Also spelled Ramia(h).****

**Raanan** (Rah ah nahn') רענן
In H., "fresh, green, flourishing" or "invigorated."**

**Rachamim** (Rah chah meem') רחמים
In H., "pity, compassion, mercy." Popular especially among Sephardim.
Also spelled Rahamin.** Other forms with the same meaning are
*Racham* (Rah chahm') רחם;* *Rachman* (Rahch mahn') רחמן, in H.,
"merciful, compassionate, tender-hearted," referring to God;* *Rachim*
(Rah cheem') רחים;* *Rachmiel* (Rahch mee ehl') רחמיאל, in H.,
"God is my comforter"; *Rachum* (Rah choom') רחום;* and *Rechum*
(Reh choom').*

**Ram** (Rahm) רם
In H., "high, lofty, eminent, supreme"; in the B. (I Chronicles).
Nickname is *Rami* (Rah' mee) רמי.** Other forms are *Ramon*
(Rahm ohn') רם־און, in H., "high and strong," also the name of a
place (moshav) in Israel in the Valley of Esdraelon (Jezreel);****
*Ramya* (Rahm yah') רמיה, in H., "God is lofty"; in the B. (Ezra), also
spelled Ramia(h);**** and *Ramiel* (Rah mee ehl') רמיאל, same
meaning.****

**Ran** (Rahn) רן
In H., "he is singing."*** Other forms are *Ranen* (Rah nehn') רנן, in
H., "to sing, to be joyous," also the name of a place (moshav) in Israel
in the Negev;**** *Rani* (Rah' nee) רני, in H., "my song, my joy";***
*Ranon* (Rah nohn') רנון;**** *Ranel* (Rahn ehl') רנאל, in H., "God is
my joy" or "he sings to God";**** *Raniel* (Rah nee ehl') רניאל, same
meaning;**** and *Renen* (Reh' nehn) רנן, in H., "song, exultation,
prayer, chant."***

**Ratzon** (Rah tzohn') רצון
In H., "will, wish, desire." Also spelled Razon.* Another form is
*Retzin* (Reh tzeen') רצין, same meaning, in the B. (II Kings), also
spelled Rezin.*

**Ravid** (Rah veed') רביד
In H., "necklace, chain." Also the name of a place (kibbutz) and a
mountain in Israel in the Galilee. Used also as a girl's name.***

**Raviv** (Rah veev') רביב
In H., "rain, shower, droplet, drizzle." Revivim is the name of a place (kibbutz) in Israel in the Negev.***

**Raz** (Rahz) רז
In H., "secret, mystery." Used also as a girl's name.*** Other forms are *Razi* (Rah' zee) רזי, in H., "my secret";*** and *Raziel* (Rah zee ehl') רזיאל, in H., "secret of God" or "God is my secret."**

**Re'ah** (Reh' ah) רע
In H., "friend, comrade, fellow." Also spelled Reia(h). Reim is the name of a place (kibbutz) in Israel in the Negev.*** Another form is *Re'ei* (Reh ee') רעי, in H., "my friend"; in the B. (I Kings), an officer. Also spelled Rei'i.**

**Rechavam** (Reh chahv ahm') רחבעם
In H., "expanse of the people," as a symbol of freedom or prosperity; in the B. (I Kings), Solomon's son. Also spelled Rehavam. The English form is Rehoboam.* Other forms are *Rechavya* (Reh chahv yah') רחביה, in H., "expanse of God"; in the B. (I Chronicles), also spelled Rechavia(h), Rehavia(h);* and *Rechavyahu* (Reh chahv yah' hoo) רחביהו, same meaning.*

**Re'em** (Reh ehm') ראם
In H., "buffalo."****

**Refael** (Reh fah ehl') רפאל
In H., "God has healed" or "God, please heal." Raphael is the name of the angel of healing. In the B. (I Chronicles), a Levite. Also the name of the Combat Means Development Authority in Israel. Also spelled Rephael. The English form is Raphael. The nickname is *Rafi* (Rah' fee) רפי.*** Another form is *Refaya* (Reh fah yah') רפיה, same meaning, in the B. (I Chronicles). Also spelled Rephaia(h).****

**Regev** (Reh' gehv) רגב
In H., "clod, divot of earth." Regavim is the name of a place (kibbutz) in north Israel.**

**Reichan** (Rehy chahn') ריחן
In H., the name of a fragrant plant, basil. Also the name of a place (moshav) and a wood reserve in Israel in the Samaria (Shomron).****

**Remez** (Reh' mehz) רמז
In H., "hint, sign."****

**Reshef** (Reh' shehf) רשף
In H., "spark, flame, fire, ray of sun, flash"; in the B. (I Chronicles). Also the name of a bird of prey. Reshafim is the name of a place (kibbutz) in north Israel. Also spelled Resheph.**

**Reuel** (Reh oo ehl') רעואל
From the H., "friend of God"; in the B. (Exodus), another name of
Jethro (Yitro), the father-in-law of Moses (Moshe). Also spelled Ruel.****

**Reuven** (Reh oo vehn') ראובן
In H., "Behold, this is a son!"; in the B. (Genesis), Jacob's first son.
The English form is Reuben. Nicknames are *Robi* (Roh' bee) and
*Rubi* (Roo' bee) רובי.**

**Rimon** (Ree mohn') רימון
In H., "pomegranate" (tree and fruit) or "an ornament, finial" (the
two finials on top of the wooden staves on which the Torah scrolls
are rolled are called Rimonim) or "grenade." A symbolic name for
both boys and girls born on Sukkoth, because it is customary to
decorate the sukkah with pomegranates, eat this fruit, and ask God
to bless the world with lots and lots of Jewish people, as many as the
countless kernels in the pomegranate. In the B. (II Samuel), Rimonim
is the name of a place in Israel in Samaria (Shomron).*** Another
form is *Ramon* (Rah mohn') רמון, same meaning, also the name of a
crater (Machtesh) and a place (Mitzpeh-Ramon) in Israel in the
Negev. Used especially among those who like a H. name with an
English sound.***

**Rishon** (Ree shohn') ראשון
In H., "the first one." Sometimes used for the first son in the family.
Rishon Le Tzion is the name of a city in Israel near Tel Aviv.*

**Ro'i** (Roh ee') רועי
In H., "my shepherd," referring to God. Also the name of a place
(moshav) in Israel in the Samaria (Shomron).***

**Rom** (Rohm) רום
In H., "height, altitude."** Another form is *Romem* (Roh mehm')
רומם, in H., "to raise, exalt, glorify, praise."**

**Ron** (Rohn) רון
In H., "song, music" or "joy."*** Other forms are *Ronen* (Roh nehn')
רונן, same meaning;*** *Ronel* (Rohn ehl') רונאל, in H., "song of God"
or "joy of God";**** and *Roni* (Roh' nee) רוני, in H., "my song" or "my
joy," used also as a girl's name.***

**Rotem** (Roh' tehm) רותם
In H., the name of a desert plant, retama. Used also as a girl's name.
Retamim is the name of a place (kibbutz) in Israel in the Negev,
named after the plant.***

**Rozen** (Roh zehn') רוזן
In H., "earl, marquis, baron, ruler."*

# S

**Saad** (Sah' ahd) סעד
In H., "support, assistance, help, aid, welfare." Also the name of a
place (kibbutz) in Israel in the Negev.** Other forms are *Saadya(h)*
(Sah ahd yah') and *Seadya(h)* (Seh ahd yah') סעדיה, in H., "God's
help," also spelled Saadia(h) and Seadia(h);* and *Soed* (Soh ehd')
סועד.*

**Saar** (Sah' ahr) סער
In H., "tempest, storm, gale." Also the name of a place (kibbutz) in
Israel on the Galilee beach.***

**Sade(h)** (Sah deh') שדה
In H., "field" (meaning subject area) or "open country." Many names
of places in Israel start with this word.**

**Sagi(e)** (Sah gee') שגיא
In H., "exalted, lofty, sublime."**

**Sagiv** (Sah geev') שגיב
In H., "strong, mighty, exalted, sublime, great."*** Another form is
*Segev* (Seh' gehv) שגב, same meaning, also the name of a place in
Israel in the Galilee.**

**Sahar** (Sah' hahr) סהר
In H., "moon." Used also as a girl's name.**

**Sapir** (Sah peer') ספיר
In H., the name of a precious stone, sapphire. Also the name of a
place in Israel in the Arava. Used also as a girl's name.**

**Sar** (Sahr) שר
In H., "ruler, commander, noble, prince."* Other forms are *Sar-
Shalom* (Sahr Shah lohm') שר־שלום, in H., "prince of peace"; in the
B. (Isaiah);* *Sriel* (Sree ehl') שריאל, in H., "prince of God";** *Sraya*
(Srah yah') שריה, same meaning, in the B. (II Samuel);** and *Srayahu*
(Srah yah' hoo) שריהו, same meaning, in the B. (Jeremiah).*

**Sarid** (Sah reed') שריד
In H., "remnant, residue, refugee, survivor." Also the name of a place
(kibbutz) in Israel in the Valley of Esdraelon (Jezreel).**

**Sarig** (Sah reeg') שריג
In H., "shoot, branch, twig (especially of vine)."**** Another form is
*Srug* (Sroog) שרוג.*

**Sason** (Sah sohn') שָׂשׂוֹן
In H., "joy, delight, mirth." Nickname is *Sasi* (Sah' see) שָׂשִׂי.*

**Savyon** (Sahv yohn') סַבְיוֹן
In H., the name of a plant, groundsel or yellow-weed. Also the name of a place in Israel in the shefelah named after the flower. Used also as a girl's name.**

**Sela** (Seh' lah) סֶלַע
In H., "rock, cliff," referring to strength. Also the name of an ancient coin.** Another form is *Sal'ee* (Sahl ee') סַלְעִי, in H., "my rock" or "rocky."**

**Shaal** (Shah' ahl) שַׁעַל
In H., "step." Also the name of a place (moshav) in Israel in Ramat Hagolan.****

**Shaanan** (Shah ah nahn') שַׁאֲנָן
In H., "tranquil, carefree, at ease, calm, secure." Also the name of a place (agricultural ranch) in Israel in the shefelah. Neve Shaanan is the name of a neighborhood in Haifa.**

**Shaar** (Shah' ahr) שַׁעַר
In H., "gate" or "chapter, section, front page of a book" or "goal" (in games). Many names of places in Israel contain this word.* Other forms are *Shaarya* (Shah ahr yah') שַׁעֲרִיָּה, in H., "the gate of God," also spelled Shaaria(h);* and *Shearya* (Sheh ahr yah') שְׁעַרְיָה, same meaning, in the B. (I Chronicles), also spelled Shearia(h).*

**Shabat** (Shah baht') שַׁבָּת
From the H., "to rest, stop, come to end." The name of the seventh day of the week, Saturday, which is a day of rest. The English form is Shabbat.*

**Shabtai** (Shahb tahy') שַׁבְּתַאי
In H., the name of a planet, Saturn, or Sabbetaian, the name of a person who belonged to the Sabbetaianism, a sect that believed in the messiahship of Shabbetai Tzvi; in the B. (Ezra), a Levite. Also spelled Shabetai, Shabbetai, or Shabbethai.**

**Shachaf** (Shah' chahf) שַׁחַף
In H., "seagull." Used also as a girl's name.****

**Shachak** (Shah' chahk) שַׁחַק
In H., "clouds, heavens."****

**Shacham** (Shah' chahm) שַׁחַם
In H., "granite."****

**Shachar** (Shah' chahr) שחר

In H., "dawn, morning." Also the name of a place (moshav) in Israel
in the shefelah. Used also as a girl's name.*** Another form is
*Shcharya* (Shchahr yah') שחריה, in H., "God's morning," in the B.
(I Chronicles). Also spelled Shcharia(h).*

**Shadmon** (Shahd mohn') שדמון

The masculine form of Shdema, in H., "field, cornfield" or
"vineyard."****

**Shafat** (Shah faht') שפט

In H., "he judged"; in the B. (I Kings).* Other forms are *Shfatya*
(Shfaht yah') שפטיה, from the H., "judgment of God" or "God is my
judge"; in the B. (II Samuel), also spelled Shfatia(h);* *Shofet* (Shoh
feht') שופט, in H., "judge, referee";* *Shiftan* (Sheef tahn') שיפטן,
same meaning, in the B. (Numbers).*

**Shafir** (Shah feer') שפיר

From the Aramaic, "fine, excellent, good, handsome," or, in H., "sac
of the fetus, amnion." Also the name of a place (moshav) in Israel in
the shefelah, named after an ancient city mentioned in the B. Also
spelled Shaphir.** Other forms with the same meaning are *Shafer*
(Shah fehr') שפר;* *Shefer* (Sheh' fehr) in H., "grace, beauty, loveliness,"
also the name of a place (moshav) in Israel in the Galilee;** *Shapira*
(Shah pee' rah) שפירא, used mainly as a last name;** and *Shifron*
(Sheef rohn') שיפרון.****

**Shafrir** (Shahf reer') שפריר

In H., "canopy," also the former name of Kfar Chabad (Habad—
Hassidic sect).**

**Shai** (Shahy) שי

In H., "gift, present." Used also as a girl's name.***

**Shaked** (Shah kehd') שקד

In H., "almond." A symbolic name for both boys and girls born on Tu
b'Shvat, the New Year of the Trees. The almond trees shed their
leaves toward the end of the summer. All through the fall they are
bare, and they start to blossom by the end of the winter. The Israeli
children sing on that holiday: "The almond trees are white / The sun
is shining bright / Singing birds from every dome / Tell us Tu b'Shvat
has come." Also the name of a place in Israel in Samaria (Shomron)
named after the tree.***

**Shalev** (Shah lehv') שליו

In H., "calm, quiet, at east, restful, secure."**

**Shalman** (Shahl mahn') שלמן
From the H., "to be complete" or "to be rewarded" or "a peacemaker";
in the B. (Hosea).* Other forms are *Shalmon* (Shahl mohn') שלמון,
in H., "bribe," and the name of a plant, Syrian Scabious, or cephalaria;*
and *Shalmoni* (Shahl moh nee') שלמוני, same meaning.*

**Shalom** (Shah lohm') שלום
In H., "peace, quiet, safety, well-being." *Shalom* is the most common
greeting in H.** Other forms are *Shalem* (Shah lehm') שלם, in H.,
"whole, perfect, healthy, peaceful"; Kfar Shalem is the name of a
suburb of Tel Aviv;* *Shalmiya* (Shahl mee yah') שלמיה, from the H.,
"God's peace," also spelled Shalmia(h);* *Shalum* (Shah loom') שלום,
same meaning, in the B. (II Kings, Jeremiah), names of kings; also
spelled Shallum;**** *Shelemya* (Sheh lehm yah') שלמיה, from the H.,
"peace of God"; in the B. (Jeremiah), also spelled Shelemia(h);*
*Shelemyahu* (Sheh lehm yah' hoo) שלמיהו, same meaning;* and
*Shilem* (Shee lehm') שילם, from the H., "to recompense" or "to make
peace," in the B. (Genesis), one of Jacob's grandsons.*

**Shama** (Shah mah') שמע
In H., "he heard"; in the B. (I Chronicles).* Other forms are *Shamua*
(Shah moo' ah) שמוע, in H., "the one who heard, the one who obeyed";
in the B. (II Samuel);* *Shema* (Sheh' mah) שמע, in H., "report, news,
tidings, fame"; in the B. (I Chronicles);* *Shmaya* (Shmah' yah)
שמעיה, in H., "God, please hear, listen!"; in the B. (I Kings), a prophet,
also spelled Shmaia(h);** and *Shmayahu* (Shmah yah' hoo) שמעיהו,
same meaning.*

**Shamash** (Shah mahsh') שמש
In H., "servant, janitor, caretaker." Also the name of the auxiliary
candle for lighting the Hanukkah lamp.* Another form is *Shimshai*
(Sheem shahy') שימשי, same meaning, in the B. (Ezra).*

**Shamir** (Shah meer') שמיר
In H., "emery, flint" (legendary, a worm or a stone created on the
Sabbath eve and capable of cutting stone) or the name of a thorn bush,
thistle, brier, or "conservable, preservable"; in the B. (I Chronicles), a
Levite. Also the name of a place (kibbutz) in north Israel, named after
the strong, hard stone used by Solomon for building the Temple.**
Another form is *Shamur* (Shah moor') שמור, in H., "guarded."*

**Shammai** (Shah mahy') שמאי
In H., "valuer, appraiser, estimator," or, from the H., "name." Kfar
Shammai is the name of a place (moshav) in Israel in the Galilee
named after the Talmudic scholar noted for his disputes with Hillel.
Also spelled Shamia.*

**Shani** (Shah nee') שני

In H., "scarlet, crimson," literally "crimson thread." The principal
motif in a story, the thread that runs through the whole tale. Used
also as a girl's name.**

**Sharir** (Shah reer') שריר

In H., "strong, firm."**

**Sharon** (Shah rohn') שרון

From the H., "plain, flat area." The name of an area in western Israel
from Mount Carmel south to Jaffa. In the B., this area was reputed to
have fertile soil full of woods and flowers. Chavatzelet Hasharon is
the name of a flower (lily) that grows in this area, and also the name
of a place (moshav) in the Sharon named after the flower. Used also
as a girl's name.*** Another form is *Sharoni* (Shah roh nee') שרוני,
same meaning.*

**Shatil** (Shah teel') שתיל

In H., "seedling." A symbolic name for boys born on Tu b'Shvat,
Arbor Day.* Another form is *Shatul* (Shah tool') שתול, in H., "planted."*

**Shaul** (Shah ool') שאול

In H., "borrowed, loaned, taken on loan," or, from the H., "to ask"; in
the B. (I Samuel), the first king of Israel. The English form is Saul.*

**Shavit** (Shah veet') שביט

In H., "comet." Used also as a girl's name.**

**Shaviv** (Shah veev') שביב

In H., "spark, ray of light."**

**Shchanya** (Shchahn yah') שכניה

From the H., "God's abode"; in the B. (I Chronicles). Also the name of
a place in Israel in the Galilee. Also spelled Shchania(h).* Another
form is *Shchanyahu* (Shchahn yah' hoo) שכניהו.*

**Shchem** (Shchehm) שכם

From the H., "shoulder"; in the B. (Genesis). Also the name of a city
in Israel in Samaria (Shomron) mentioned in the B.*

**Shealtiel** (Sheh ahl tee ehl') שאלתיאל

From the H., "I asked from God" or "I borrowed from God"; in the B.
(Haggai). Also spelled Shaltiel שלתיאל.*

**Shear-Yashuv** (Sheh ahr' Yah shuv') שאר-ישוב

In H., "the remnant will return"; in the B. (Isaiah), a symbolic name
given by the prophet to the people who will return to Judah after its
destruction. Also the name of a place (moshav) in north Israel named
after this prophecy.*

**Shefa** (Sheh' fah) שפע
In H., "abundance, plenty, nobility of spirit."**** Another form is
*Shifi* (Sheef ee') שיפעי, in the B. (I Chronicles).*

**Shefi** (Sheh' fee) שפי
In H., "ease, comfort, calm."**

**Shelach** (Sheh' lahch) שלח
In H., "missile, weapon" or "hide of animal" or "ripe olive" or "sprout,
shoot, plant" or the name of a plant, eruca, which is shaped like a
short sword. Also the name of a pioneering combatant youth settlement
in Israel in the Jordan Valley named after the plant.**** Another
form is *Shilchi* (Sheel chee') שילחי, same meaning, in the B. (I Kings).*

**Shelef** (Sheh' lehf) שלף
In H., "field of stubble"; in the B. (Genesis).****

**Shem** (Shehm) שם
In H., "name, noun, designation, reputation"; in the B. (Genesis),
one of Noah's sons.* Other forms are *Shem-Tov* (Shehm' Tohv)
שם־טוב, in H., "good name, good reputation," nickname is *Shemi*
(Sheh' mee) שמי;* and *Shim'i* (Sheem ee') שמעי, in H., "my name,
my reputation"; in the B. (II Samuel).*

**Shemer** (Sheh' mehr) שמר
In H., "watch, preservation"; in the B. (I Kings). Eyn Shemer is the
name of a place (kibbutz) in central Israel.** Other forms are *Shmaram*
(Shmahr ahm') שמרעם, in H., "guardian of the nation";* *Shmarya*
(Shmahr yah') שמריה, in H.,"protection of God";in the B.(II Chronicles),
also spelled Shmaria(h);** *Shmaryahu* (Shmahr yah' hoo) שמריהו,
same meaning;* *Shomer* (Shoh mehr') שומר, in H., "watchman,
guard, keeper"; Hashomer is the name of a Jewish self-defense
organization founded in 1905;* *Shimri* (Sheem ree') שימרי, in H.,
"my guard"; in the B. (I Chronicles);** *Shimron* (Sheem rohn') שימרון,
in the B. (Genesis), same meaning;** and *Shomriel* (Shohm ree ehl')
שומריאל, in H., "God is my guard."**

**Shet** (Sheht) שת
From the H., "appointed"; in the B. (Genesis), one of Adam's sons.
This name is not recommended, because in H. it means "buttocks."
The English form is Seth.*

**Sheva** (Sheh' vah) שבע
From the H., "oath," or, in H., "seven"; in the B. (II Samuel).*

**Shevach** (Sheh' vahch) שבח
In H., "praise, glory, improvement, advantage."**

**Shezaf** (Shehy zahf') שיזף
In H., "jujube."****

**Shikmon** (Sheek mohn') שיקמון
The masculine form of Shikma, in H., the name of a tree, sycamore.**
Another form is *Shakmon* (Shahk mohn') שקמון, same meaning.*

**Shilo(h)** (Shee loh') שילוה
From the H., "his gift"; in the B. (Genesis), the name of a place in
Israel in Samaria (Shomron) named after the ancient city. Used also
as a girl's name.**

**Shimon** (Sheem ohn') שמעון
From the H., "to hear, to be heard" or "reputation"; in the B. (Genesis),
the second son of Jacob. The English form is Simeon. The Greek
form is Simon. Nickname is *Shimi* (Shee' mee) שימי.*

**Shimshon** (Sheem shohn') שמשון
From the H., "to put" or "service" or "sun"; in the B. (Judges), a judge
noted for his long hair, which gave him strength and courage. He
fought the Philistines (Plishtim) until he was betrayed by Delilah,
who cut his hair. Before he died he shouted, "Let me die with the
Philistines," which became a symbol meaning, "to destroy the enemy
even if it costs one's life." Shimshon became a symbol for a strong
person—"Shimshon Hagibor"—"the hero Samson" or "brave as
Samson." "Shualei Shimshon," "Samson's Foxes" was the name of "hit
and run" troops in Israel's War of Independence. Also the name of a
plant, rockrose. The English form is Samson. Nickname is *Shimi*
(Shee' mee) שימי.*

**Shir** (Sheer) שיר
In H., "song, chant, poem." Used mainly as a girl's name.** Another
form is *Shiran* (Shee rahn') שירן, in H., "a happy song."**

**Shlomi** (Shloh mee') שלומי
In H., "my peace"; in the B. (Numbers). Also the name of a place in
north Israel named after the father of a leader of the tribe of Asher.
Used also as a nickname of Shlomo.**

**Shlomo** (Shloh moh') שלמה
From the H., "his peace"; in the B. (II Samuel), a king of Israel, son of
King David and Bathsheba. The English form is Solomon, nickname
is Sol. The Yiddish forms are Zalman, Zalmen, and Zalmon. Nickname
is *Shlomi* (Shloh' mee) שלומי.**

**Shmuel** (Shmoo ehl') שמואל
From the H., "his name is God"; in the B. (I Samuel), a prophet and

judge. The English form is Samuel, nicknames are Sam and Sammy.
The H. nicknames are *Shmulik* (Shmoo' leek) שמוליק and *Shmil*
(Shmeel) שמיל.**

**Shofar** (Shoh fahr') שופר
In H., "horn, ram's horn, trumpet."*

**Shoham** (Shoh' hahm) שוהם
In H., the name of a precious stone, onyx.****

**Shomron** (Shohm rohn') שומרון
From the H., "watch, preservation." Yehuda Ve Shomron is the name
of an area that was in Jordan territory and has belonged to Israel
since the Six-Day War. The English form is Samaria.**

**Shoval** (Shoh vahl') שובל
From the H., "train (of a dress), trail, wake"; in the B. (I Chronicles),
one of Jacob's grandsons. Also the name of a place (kibbutz) in Israel
in the Negev.**

**Shraga** (Shrah' gah) שרגא
From the Aramaic, "candle."*

**Shua** (Shoo' ah) שוע
From the H., "salvation"; in the B. (Genesis).*

**Shvuel** (Shvoo ehl') שבואל
From the H., "returned to God"; in the B. (I Chronicles).* Another form
is *Shavtiel* (Shahv tee ehl') שבתיאל, in H., "I returned to God."****

**Siman-Tov** (See mahn' Tohv) סימן־טוב
In H., "good sign, favorable sign."*

**Simcha** (Seem chah') שמחה
In H., "joy, gladness, mirth, festivity." Used also as a girl's name.*
Other forms with the same meaning are *Simchai* (Seem chahy')
שמחאי;* *Simchon* (Seem chohn') שמחון;* *Simchoni* (Seem choh nee')
שמחוני;* and *Semach* (Seh' mahch) שמח.*

**Sinai** (See nahy') סיני
In the B., the name of the mount on which Moses received the Ten
Commandments, Mount Sinai. In H., it is used figuratively as the
name for an erudite, great scholar, powerful debater.**

**Sion** (See ohn') שיאון
In H., "highest point, climax."**

**Sivan** (See vahn') סיון
The name of the third month in the Jewish calendar, when we celebrate
Shavuot. Used also as a girl's name.**

**Snapir** (Snah peer´) סנפיר
In H., "fin."****

**Sneh** (Sneh) סנה
In H., "bush, thornbush."*

**Snir** (Sneer) שניר
In H., "glacier." Also the name of a place (kibbutz) and a stream in north Israel.****

**Sod** (Sohd) סוד
In H., "secret."** Another form is *Sodya* (Sohd yah´) סודיה, in H., "God's secret."*

**Sofer** (Soh fehr´) סופר
In H., "author, writer, scribe."*

**Somech** (Soh mehch´) סומך
In H., "supporter."* Another form is *Smachyahu* (Smahch yah´ hoo) סמכיהו, from the H., "God's support"; in the B. (I Chronicles), a Levite.*

**Stav** (Stahv) סתיו
In H., "autumn, fall." Used also as a girl's name.**

# ת

THE HEBREW LETTERS ט, 'צ, 'ת.

**Tadmor** (Tahd mohr´) תדמור
In the B. (II Chronicles), the name of a city built by King Solomon. Used also as a girl's name.****

**Tal** (Tahl) טל
In H., "dew." Used also as a girl's name.*** Other forms are *Tal-El* (Tahl Ehl´) טל־אל, in H., "dew of God," also the name of a place in Israel in the Galilee;**** *Tal-Or* (Tahl Ohr´) טל־אור, in H., "dew of light," meaning "morning light," also the name of a place (agricultural ranch) in Israel in the Negev;**** and *Tal-Shachar* (Tahl Shah´ chahr) טל־שחר, in H., "morning dew," also the name of a place (moshav) in central Israel.****

**Talmai** (Tahl mahy´) תלמי
From the H., "mound, hill" or "furrow"; in the B. (II Samuel), father-in-law of King David.* Other forms are *Talmi* (Tahl mee´) תלמי, in H., "my mound" or "my furrow";* *Tel* (Tehl) תל, in H., "mound, hill"; many names of places in Israel start with this word;* and *Telem*

(Teh′ lehm) תלם, in H., "furrow," also the name of a place in Israel in Samaria (Shomron).**

**Talmon** (Tahl mohn′) טלמון
In the B. (Ezra), a Levite.*

**Tam** (Tahm) תם
In H., "innocent, honest, naive."*

**Tamir** (Tah meer′) תמיר
In H., "tall, erect, upstanding, upright like the palm tree."*** Or טמיר, in H., "hidden, secret."** Another form is *Tamur* (Tah moor′) תמור.*

**Tammuz** (Tah mooz′) תמוז
Name of a Babylonian deity in charge of springtime (Ezekiel), and the name of the fourth month in the Jewish calendar. Used also as a girl's name.**

**Tanchum** (Tahn choom′) תנחום
In H., "consolation, comfort, condolence." In the Talmud, a scholar. Also spelled Tanhum.** Another form is *Tanchuma* (Tahn choo′ mah) תנחומא, same meaning.*

**Tanna** (Tah nah′) תנא
From the Aramaic, "teacher."* Another form is *Tanya* (Tahn yah′) תניא, from the Aramaic, "it has been taught."*

**Tarfon** (Tahr fohn′) טרפון
From the H., "to prey upon, tear to pieces" or "declare ritually unfit for food." This name was given to a Talmudic scholar who erroneously declared a slaughtered cow taref (nonkosher). Also spelled Tarphon.*

**Tarshish** (Tahr sheesh′) תרשיש
In H., the name of a precious stone, chrysolite or topaz; in the B. (Jonah), the name of a place.****

**Tavor** (Tah vohr′) תבור
From the Aramaic, "break, fracture, misfortune." The name of a mountain in north Israel in the Galilee.**

**Teman** (Tehy mahn′) תימן
In H., "south" (the right side of a person facing east). Used in Israel for the Jews who arrived from Yemen (Teman). In the B. (Genesis).* Another form is *Temani* (Tehy mah nee′) תימני, in H., "Yemenite"; in the B. (I Chronicles).*

**Teneh** (Teh′ neh) טנא
In H., "wicker basket, fruit basket, pannier." A symbolic name for boys born on Shavuot, known as Hag Ha-Bikurim, meaning "Festival of the First Fruits." During the days of the Temple, farmers went on

that day to Jerusalem to thank God with baskets full of the first
wheat grains, baked loaves of bread, and some of the first ripened
fruits. Today in Israel children celebrate Shavuot by carrying baskets
with fresh fruits, flowers, and leaves. Also the name of a place in
Israel in Samaria (Shomron).**

**Teom** (Teh ohm') תאום
In H., "twin."* Another form is *Teomi* (Teh oh mee') תאומי, in H.,
"my twin."*

**Terach** (Teh' rahch) תרח
In H., this name means "aged imbecile, silly old fool"; in the B.
(Genesis), the father of Abraham.*

**Tidhar** (Teed hahr') תידהר
In H., the name of a tree, elm. Also the name of a place (moshav) in
Israel in the Negev. Used also as a girl's name.****

**Tiran** (Tee rahn') טיראן
This was the name of a place (strait) in south Israel in the Sinai
peninsula before it was returned to Egypt.**

**Tirosh** (Tee rohsh') תירוש
In H., "new wine." Also the name of a place (moshav) in Israel in the
shefelah (coastal plain).**

**Tishrey** (Teesh rehy') תשרי
From the Acadian, "beginning, starting." The name of the seventh
month in the Jewish calendar, and the first month in the civil calendar
when we celebrate Rosh Hashanah.**

**Tivon** (Teev ohn') טבעון
From the H., "natural." Kiryat Tivon is the name of a place in north
Israel near Haifa, named after an ancient city.** Another form is
*Tivoni* (Teev oh nee') טבעוני, in H., "naturist, nature lover, vegetarian."*

**Tom** (Tohm) תום
In H., "innocence" or "wholeness, perfection, purity." Used especially
by those who like a H. name with an English sound.**

**Tomer** (Toh' mehr) תומר
In H., "palm tree, date tree." Also the name of a place (moshav) in
Israel in the Jordan Valley.***

**Tor** (Tohr) תור
In H., "turn, live, era" or the name of a bird, turtle dove, that arrives
in Israel in the spring and is a symbol of the beginning of spring.
"The voice of the turtle is heard in our land" (Song of Songs).**

**Toren** (Toh' rehn) תורן
In H., "mast."**

**Tuval** (Too vahl′) תובל
In the B. (Genesis). Also the name of a place (kibbutz) in Israel in the Galilee.**

**Tuvya** (Toov yah′) טוביה
In H., "goodness of God"; in the B. (Zechariah). Also spelled Tuvia(h). Nickname is *Tuvi* (Too′ vee) טובי.** Other forms are *Tuviyahu* (Too vee yah′ hoo) טוביהו, same meaning, in the B. (II Chronicles), a Levite;* *Tov* (Tohv) טוב, in H., "good, pleasant, kind, well-behaved"; in the B. (II Chronicles);* *Tovi* (Toh vee′) טובי, in H., "my goodness";* *Toviel* (Toh vee ehl′) טוביאל, in H., "my God is goodness";** *Tovim* (Toh veem′) טובים, same meaning;* *Toviya* (Toh vee yah′) טוביה, same meaning, in the B. (Ezra);* and *Toviyahu* (Toh vee yah′ hoo) טוביהו, same meaning.*

**Tzabar** (Tzah bahr′) צבר
In H., "cactus." Tzabar or Sabra is a folk name for an Israeli-born person, referring metaphorically to a prickly exterior and a tender heart. Might be a symbolic name for the first boy in the family born in Israel. Also spelled Zabar.****

**Tzachi** (Tzah′ chee) צחי
From the H. word Tzach, meaning "pure, fresh, clear, bright." Or it might be a modern name derived from Yitzchak (Isaac). Also spelled Zachi.*** Other forms are *Tzach* (Tzahch) צח, same meaning, also spelled Zach;** and *Tzcharya* (Tzchahr yah′) צחריה, in H., "purity of God."*

**Tzadik** (Tzah deek′) צדיק
In H., "righteous person, God-fearing, pious, innocent, honest." Also the name of a Hassidic rabbi. Also spelled Zadik and Zaddik.* Other forms are *Tzadkiel* (Tzahd kee ehl′) צדקיאל, in H., "God is my righteousness," also spelled Zadkiel;* *Tzadok* (Tzah dohk′) צדוק, same meaning, during the days of the Second Temple, the name for a rabbi, also spelled Zadok;** *Tzidkiya* (Tzeed kee yah′) צידקיה, in H., "righteousness of God" or "God is righteousness"; in the B. (II Kings), a king; the English form is Zedekia(h);** and *Tzidkiyahu* (Tzeed kee yah′ hoo) צידקיהו, same meaning.*

**Tzafrir** (Tzahf reer′) צפריר
The name of a morning demon, according to the cabala. In H., "morning light, morning breeze." Tzafririm is the name of a place (moshav) in Israel in the shefelah (coastal plain). Also spelled Zafrir.** Another form is *Tzafriri* (Tzahf ree ree′) צפרירי, same meaning, also spelled Zafriri.*

**Tzahal** (Tzah' hahl) צהל
An acrostic formed from the words צבא הגנה לישראל (Tzva Hagana
Le' Yisrael), meaning "Israel Defense Forces," the name of the Israeli
Army, or, in H., "joy, rejoicing." Also spelled Zahal.* Another form is
*Tzahalon* (Tzah hah lohn') צהלון, also spelled Zahalon.*

**Tzalaf** (Tzah lahf') צלף
In H., the name of a bush, common caperbush, or "marksman"; in
the B. (Nehemiah). Also the name of a place in Israel in Samaria
(Shomron) named after the bush. Also spelled Zalaf.**** Another
form is *Tzlafon* (Tzlah fohn') צלפון, same meaning, also the name of
a place (moshav) in Israel in the shefelah, named after the bush.
Also spelled Zlafon.*

**Tzalmon** (Tzahl mohn') צלמון
In H., "darkness"; in the B. (II Samuel). Also spelled Zalmon.*

**Tzalul** (Tzah lool') צלול
In H., "clear, lucid, pure." Also spelled Zalul.*

**Tzedef** (Tzeh' dehf) צדף
In H., "shell, mother-of-pearl, pearl shell." Also spelled Zedef.****

**Tze'el** (Tzeh ehl') צאל
In H., the name of a tree mentioned in the B. (Some think it is acacia,
others think it is jujube.) Tze'elim is the name of a place (kibbutz) in
Israel in the Negev, named after the acacia trees growing in this area.
Also spelled Ze'el.**** Another form is *Tze'elon* (Tzeh eh lohn')
צאלון, in H., the name of a tree, poinciana. Also spelled Ze'elon.****

**Tzel-El** (Tzehl Ehl') צל־אל
In H., "God's shadow," meaning "under God's protection." Also spelled
Zel-El.****

**Tzemach** (Tzeh' mahch) צמח
In H., "plant, sprout, growth"; in the B. (Zechariah). A symbolic
name for boys born on Tu b'Shvat, Arbor Day. Also the name of a
place in Israel in the Jordan Valley.**

**Tzfanya** (Tzfahn yah') צפניה
From the H., "hidden by God," meaning "protected by God." In the
B. (Tzefanya), one of the Minor Prophets. Also spelled Tzfania(h)
and Zfanya, Zfania(h).** Other forms with the same meaning are
*Tzfanyahu* (Tzfahn yah' hoo) צפניהו;* and *Tzfanel* (Tzfahn ehl')
צפנאל.**

**Tzidon** (Tzee dohn') צידון
In the B., the name of a place, Sidon.**

**Tzion** (Tzee yohn') ציון

In the B., Zion is used as a name for Jerusalem, for the Jewish people, and for the Jewish people's country, Israel. The English form is Zion. Rishon Le Tzion is the name of a city in Israel near Tel Aviv.**

**Tzlafchad** (Tzlahf chahd') צלפחד

From the H., "protection from fear"; in the B. (Numbers), a man who has five daughters and no sons. Also spelled Zlafchad.* Other forms are Tzelafchad and Tzlofchad.*

**Tzlil** (Tzleel) צליל

In H., "tone, sound." Also spelled Zlil.****

**Tzofar** (Tzoh fahr') צופר

In H., "horn, siren, hooter"; in the B. (Job). Also the name of a place (moshav) and a stream in Israel in the Arava. Also spelled Zofar.****

**Tzuf** (Tzoof) צוף

In H., "honeydew" (in plants) or "nectar, drink made from honey" or "to float"; in the B. (I Samuel). Also spelled Zuf and Zuph.****

**Tzuk** (Tzook) צוק

In H., "rock, cliff." Also spelled Zuk.****

**Tzur** (Tzur) צור

In H., "rock, cliff," referring to strength; in the B. (I Chronicles). A few names of places in Israel start with this word. Also spelled Zur.** Other forms are *Tzuri* (Tzoo' ree) צורי, in H., "my rock," meaning "my strength," also spelled Zuri;** *Tzuriel* (Tzoo ree ehl') צוריאל, in H., "God is my rock," meaning "God is my strength"; in the B. (Numbers), also the name of a place (moshav) in Israel in the Galilee, also spelled Zuriel;** *Tzurishadai* (Tzoo ree shah dahy') צורישדי, in H., "God is my rock"; in the B. (Numbers), also spelled Zurishadai;* and *Tzuriya* (Tzoo ree yah') צוריה, in H., "God is my rock," also spelled Zuriya, used also as a girl's name.**

**Tzvi** (Tzvee) צבי

In H., "deer, gazelle." Ma'ayan Tzvi is the name of a place (kibbutz) in north Israel. Tirat Tzvi is the name of a place (kibbutz) in north Israel. Also spelled Tzevi and Zevi, Zvi. Nicknames are *Tzvika* (Tzvee' kah) צביקה and *Tzviki* (Tzvee' kee) צביקי.** Other forms are *Tzviel* (Tzvee ehl') צביאל, in H., "God's gazelle," also spelled Zviel;** and *Tzvieli* (Tzvee eh lee') צביאלי, in H., "God is my gazelle," also spelled Zvieli.*

# U

**Ud** (Ood) אוד

In H., "firebrand, fire stick."\*\*\*\* Other forms are *Udi* (Oo' dee) אודי, in H., "my firebrand," or a nickname of Ehud;\*\* and *Udiel* (Oo dee ehl') אודיאל, in H., "firebrand of God."\*\*\*\* Udim is the name of a place (moshav) in Israel in the Sharon that was built by the Holocaust survivors. In H., "brand snatched from the burning" is an expression of survivors.

**Ur** (Oor) אור

In H., "fire, flame, illumination," or a symbol of wisdom; in the B. (I Chronicles), a man's name and (Genesis) the place where Abraham (Avraham) was born. A symbolic name for boys born on Hanukkah, the Festival of Lights (in H., "Chag Haurim"). Urim is also the name of a collective in Israel, in the Negev.\*\*\*\*

**Uri** (Oo' ree) אורי

In H., "my flame, my light"; in the B. (Exodus), a leader. A symbolic name for boys born on Hanukkah. Also spelled Urie.\*\*\* Other forms are *Uriel* (Oo ree ehl') אוריאל, in H., "God is my flame, God is my light"; in the B. (I Chronicles), a Levite, in the Jewish tradition of God's angels, also the name of a place in Israel near Tel Aviv that started as a village for blind people;\*\*\* *Uriya* (Oo ree yah') אוריה, in H., "God is my flame, light"; in the B. (II Samuel), the husband of Bathsheba (Bat-Sheva), who became King David's wife after Uriel's death, also spelled Uria(h);\*\* *Uriyahu* (Oo ree yah' hoo) אוריהו, same meaning, in the B. (Jeremiah);\* *Uryan* (Oor yahn') אוריין, same meaning, also spelled Urian;\* *Uryon* (Oor yohn') אוריון, same meaning;\* and *Uram* (Oor ahm') אורעם, in H., "the light of the nation,"\* or עורעם, in H., "wake up, people."\*

**Uzi** (Oo' zi) עוזי

In H., "my strength, my power, my courage"; in the B. (II Kings), a king of Judah. Also spelled Uzzi.\*\*\* Other forms are *Uziel* (Oo zee ehl') עוזיאל, in H., "God is my strength"; in the B. (Exodus);\*\* *Uziya* (Oo zee yah') עוזיה, same meaning, in the B. (II Kings), also spelled Usia(h) or Uzzia(h);\* and *Uziyahu* (Oo zee yah' hoo) עוזיהו, same meaning.\*

# V

THE HEBREW LETTER 'ו

**Vardinon** (Vahr dee nohn') ורדינון
In H., "attar of roses" or "essence of roses."* Another form is *Vardimom* (Vahr dee mohn') ורדימון, same meaning.*

**Velvel** (Vehl' vehl) וועלוועל
In Y., "wolf."* Another form is *Volf* (Vohlf) וואלף.*

# Y

THE HEBREW LETTER 'י

**Yaad** (Yah' ahd) יעד
In H., "mission, purpose, aim, target." Also the name of a place (moshav) in Israel in the Galilee.**

**Yaakov** (Yah ah kohv') יעקב
From the H., "to hold by the heel"; in the B. (Genesis), the son of Isaac and Rebeka, the twin brother of Esau. The English form is Jacob. The Yiddish form is Yankel. Nicknames are *Yaki* (Yah' kee) יקי and *Kobi* (Koh' bee) קובי. Also spelled Yaaqov.**

**Yaal** (Yah' ahl) יעל
From the H., "he will ascend."**** Another form is *Yaalon* (Yah ah lohn') יעלון, same meaning. Also the name of a place (kibbutz) and a river in Israel in the Arava.****

**Yaar** (Yah' ahr) יער
In H., "forest." Several names of places in Israel contain this word.**** Another form is *Yaari* (Yah ah ree') יערי, in H., "my forest."****

**Yaasiel** (Yah ah see ehl') יעשיאל
From the H., "God will create me"; in the B. (I Chronicles).* Another form is *Yaasai* (Yah ah sahy') יעשי, same meaning, in the B. (Ezra).*

**Yaazanya** (Yah ah zahn yah') יאזניה
From the H., "God will listen"; in the B. (Jeremiah). Also spelled Yaazania(h).* Another form is *Yaazanyahu* (Yah ah zahn yah' hoo) יאזניהו, same meaning, in the B. (II Kings).*

**Yaaziel** (Yah ah zee ehl') יעזיאל
From the H., "God is my strength" or "God will strengthen me"; in

the B. (I Chronicles).* Other forms are *Yaaziyahu* (Yah ah zee yah' hoo) יעזיהו, same meaning, in the B. (I Chronicles);** *Yaoz* (Yah ohz') יעוז, in H., "he will be strong";** and *Yoaz* (Yoh ahz') יועז, in H., "strength."****

**Yachad** (Yah' chahd) יחד

In H., "together, in unity, jointly, collectively."**** Other forms are *Yachdiel* (Yahch dee ehl') יחדיאל, from the H., "with God" or "God is my only one"; in the B. (I Chronicles);* and *Yachid* (Yah cheed') יחיד, in H., "the only one, single, alone."*

**Yachel** (Yah chehl') יחל

From the H., "to start" or "to wait" or "to hope."* Other forms are *Yachil* (Yah cheel') יחיל;** and *Yachl'el* (Yahch leh ehl') יחלאל, from the H., "waiting for God" or "hoping for God"; in the B. (Genesis).*

**Yachin** (Yah cheen') יכין

In H., "he will prepare, establish" referring to God; in the B. (Genesis), a son of Simeon. Also the name of one of the two pillars in the Temple, and the name of an agricultural development corporation in Israel.** Other forms with the same meaning are *Yehoyachin* (Yeh hoh yah cheen') יהויכין, in the B. (II Kings), a king; the English form is Jehoiachin;* *Yoyachin* (Yoh yah cheen') יויכין;* *Yachini* (Yah chee' nee) יכיני, also the name of a place (moshav) in Israel in the Negev named after Simeon's son;* *Yechanya* (Yeh chahn yah') יכניה;* *Yechanyahu* (Yeh chahn yah' hoo) יכניהו;* and *Yikon* (Yee kohn') יכון, in H., "he will establish," also the name of a place in Israel in the Sharon.***

**Yachon** (Yah chohn') יחון

In H., "he will endow" or "he will pity," referring to God.**

**Yada** (Yah dah') ידע

In H., "he knew"; in the B. (I Chronicles).* Other forms are *Yadua* (Yah doo' ah) ידוע, in H., "known"; in the B. (Nehemiah);* *Yadael* (Yah dah ehl') ידעאל, in H., "God knew";**** *Yedaya* (Yeh dah yah') ידעיה, in H., "knowledge of God"; in the B. (I Chronicles), also spelled Yedaia(h);* *Yediael* (Yeh dee ah ehl') ידיעאל, same meaning, in the B. (I Chronicles);* and *Yehoyada* (Yeh hoh yah dah') יהוידע, in H., "God knew"; in the B. (II Kings), a high priest, also spelled Yehoiada(h).*

**Yadid** (Yah deed') ידיד

In H., "friend, beloved."** Other forms are *Yedid* (Yeh deed'), same meaning;** and *Yedidya* (Yeh deed yah') ידידיה, in H., "friend of God" or "beloved by God"; in the B. (II Samuel), another name for King Solomon, also the name of a place (moshav) in Israel in the Sharon, also spelled Yedidia(h).**

**Yadin** (Yah deen') ידין
From the H., "he will judge."* Other forms are *Yadon* (Yah dohn')
ידון, same meaning, in the B. (Nehemiah);* and *Yadun* (Yah doon').*

**Yafe** (Yah feh') יפה
In H., "beautiful, pretty, handsome, worthy."**** Other forms with the
same meaning are *Yafim* (Yah feem') יפים;* *Yefet* (Yeh feht') יפת, in
the B. (Genesis), one of Noah's sons, also spelled Yafet, Yaphet;*
*Yifad* (Yeef ahd') יפעד, in H., "beautiful forever";**** *Yofi* (Yoh' fee)
יופי;* and *Yofiel* (Yoh fee ehl') יופיאל, in H., "God's beauty."****

**Yagel** (Yah gehl') יגל
In H., "he will rejoice." Also the name of a place (moshav) in Israel
near Tel Aviv.** Another form is *Yagil* (Yah geel') יגיל.**

**Yahahlom** (Yah hah lohm') יהלום
In H., "diamond."**

**Yahav** (Yah' hahv) יהב
In H., "to give" or "gift." Eyn Yahav is the name of a place (moshav)
in Israel in the Arava.**** Another form is *Yahev* (Yah hehv').****

**Yahel** (Yah hehl') יהל
In H., "will build a tent" or "to shine." Also the name of a place (kibbutz) in Israel in the Arava. Used also as a girl's name.** Another
form is *Yahelor* (Yah hehl ohr') יהלאור, in H., "will reflect light."****

**Yair** (Yah eer) יאיר
In H., "he will light up" or "he will enlighten"; in the B. (Deuteronomy),
one of Joseph's grandsons.** Another form is *Yaer* (Yah ehr') יאר.**

**Yakar** (Yah kahr') יקר
In H., "dear, expensive, precious, rare, scarce."* Other forms are *Yakir*
(Yah keer') יקיר, in H., "darling, dear, beloved, respectable, notable";**
and *Yakiram* (Yah kee rahm') יקירם, in H., "precious and mighty."****

**Yakim** (Yah keem') יקים
In H., "he will establish," referring to God; in the B. (I Chronicles), a
priest.* Other forms are *Yakum* (Yah koom') יקום, in H., "will be
established," also the name of a place (kibbutz) in Israel in the Sharon;*
*Yehoyakim* (Yeh hoh yah keem') יהויקים, in H., "God will establish";
in the B. (II Kings), a king; the English form is Jehoiakim;* and
*Yokim* (Yoh keem') יוקים, same meaning, in the B. (I Chronicles).*

**Yamin** (Yah meen') ימין
In H., "the right, right side, right-handed"; in the B. (Genesis), one of
Jacob's grandsons.* Another form is *Yemini* (Yeh mee nee') ימיני, in
H., "my right hand" or a short form of Binyamin (Benjamin).**

**Yanai** (Yah nahy') ינאי
From the H., "to answer"; in the B. (I Chronicles), and, in the Talmud, a Palestinian scholar. Beyth Yanai is the name of a place (moshav) in Israel in the Sharon. The English form is Janai.**

**Yanir** (Yah neer') יניר
In H., "he will plow."**

**Yaniv** (Yah neev') יניב
In H., "he will yield, produce."*** Another form is *Yanuv* (Yah noov') ינוב, same meaning, also the name of a place (moshav) in Israel in the Sharon.**

**Yarden** (Yahr dehn') ירדן
From the H., "to go down." The name of the longest river in Israel that flows from the north to the south, and also the name of a state. The English form is Jordan. Used also as a girl's name.***

**Yariv** (Yah reev') יריב
In H., "opponent, rival, competitor" or "he will quarrel."*** Other forms are *Yarev* (Yah rehv') ירב, same meaning, in the B. (Hosea);* and *Yehoyariv* (Yeh hoh yah reev') יהויריב, in H., "God will quarrel," meaning "God will fight for Israel"; in the B. (I Chronicles), a priest, also the name of a place in central Israel.**

**Yarkon** (Yahr kohn') ירקון
From the H., "green." The name of a river in Israel near Tel Aviv, and also the name of a greenish yellow singing bird, greenfinch, which spends the summers in Israel.**

**Yarom** (Yah rohm') ירום
In H., "he will raise up."** Another form is *Yarum* (Yah room').*

**Yaron** (Yah rohn') ירון
In H., "he will sing, he will be joyous."*** Another form is *Yoran* (Yoh rahn') יורן.****

**Yashar** (Yah shahr') ישר
In H., "honest, fair-dealing, upright, to go straight, to be straight."* Other forms with the same meaning are *Yesher* (Yeh' shehr), in the B. (I Chronicles);* *Yeshurun* (Yeh shoo roon') ישורון, in the B. (Deuteronomy), a poetic name for the Israeli nation; also the name of a synagogue in Jerusalem;** *Yashir* (Yah sheer') ישיר, in H., "direct, directly" or "he will sing";* and *Yosher* (Yoh' shehr) יושר, in H., "honesty."*

**Yashiv** (Yah sheev') ישיב
In H., "he will answer" or "he will bring back."* Other forms are

*Yashuv* (Yah shoov') שוב, in H., "he will return, he will repatriate"; in the B. (I Chronicles);**** *Yeshuvam* (Yeh shoov ahm') ישובעם, in H., "the nation will return";* *Yoshivya* (Yoh sheev yah') יושיביה, in H., "God will return" or "God will bring back"; in the B. (I Chronicles). Also the name of a place (moshav) in Israel in the Negev.*

**Yasis** (Yah sees') ישיש
In H., "he will rejoice."*

**Yas'ur** (Yahs oor') יסעור
In H., the name of a water bird, seawater or puffin. Also the name of a place (kibbutz) in Israel in the Galilee named after the bird. Used also as a girl's name.****

**Yatzliach** (Yahtz lee' ahch) יצליח
In H., "he will succeed."* Another form is *Yitzlach* (Yeetz lahch') יצלח.*

**Yavin** (Yah veen') יבין
In H., "he will understand"; in the B. (Joshua).**

**Yavne'el** (Yahv neh ehl') יבנאל
In H., "God will build"; in the B. (Joshua), the name of a place. Also the name of a place in Israel in the Galilee.** Other forms are *Yavniel* (Yahv nee ehl') יבניאל;** *Yavneh* (Yahv' neh) יבנה, in H., an acrostic for יין, בשמים, נר, הבדלה, in English wine, fragrant plants, and the habdalah candle (used for habdalah after Sabbath is over), also the name of a place in Israel in the shefelah; Kerem Beyavneh is the name of a yeshiva near Yavneh, named after Kerem Deyavneh, the Yavneh College of Rabbi Yohanan Ben Zakkai;** and *Yivneya* (Yeev neh yah') יבניה, in H., "God will build"; in the B. (I Chronicles), one of Benjamin's sons.**

**Yechezkel** (Yeh chehz kehl') יחזקאל
In H., "God will strengthen"; in the B. (Ezekiel), a prophet. Kfar Yechezkel is the name of a place (moshav) in Israel in the Valley of Esdraelon (Jezreel). The English form is Ezekiel. The Yiddish forms are Chaskel and Chatzkel. Nickname is *Chezi* (Cheh' zee) חזי.* Other forms are *Yechizkiya* (Yeh cheez kee yah') יחזקיה, in H., "may God strengthen me!"; in the B. (Ezra);* *Yechizkiyahu* (Yeh cheez kee yah' hoo) יחזקיהו, same meaning, in the B. (I Chronicles);* and *Yachaziel* (Yah chah zee ehl') יחזיאל, in H., "God will see"; in the B. (I Chronicles), a priest.*

**Yechiel** (Yeh chee ehl') יחיאל
In H., "may God live!"; in the B. (Ezra). Nickname is *Chilik* (Chee' leek) חיליק.* Other forms are *Yechieli* (Yeh chee eh' lee) יחיאלי, in H., "may my God live!"; in the B. (I Chronicles);* *Yechiach* (Yeh chee ahch')

יחיאח, in H., "may my brother live!";**** *Yechiam* (Yeh chee ahm')
יחיעם, in H., "may my nation live!" also the name of a place (kibbutz)
in Israel in the Galilee;** *Yechiav* (Yeh chee ahv') יחיאב, in H., "may
my father live!";**** *Yechiya* (Yeh chee yah) יחיה, in H., "may God
live!"; in the B. (I Chronicles), also spelled Yechia(h);* *Yichye* (Yeech
yeh') יחיה, in H., "may he live!" used for a boy who is born sick;****
and *Yechiad* (Yeh chee ahd') יחיעד, in H., "may live forever!"**

**Yedod** (Yeh dohd') ידוד
In H., "spark."****

**Yefune(h)** (Yeh foo neh') יפונה
From the H., "to turn" or "to face"; in the B. (Numbers), the father of
Caleb.*

**Yehalel** (Yeh hah lehl') יהלל
In H., "he will praise."* Another form is *Yehalelel* (Yeh hah lehl ehl')
יהללאל, in H., "he will praise God"; in the B. (I Chronicles).****

**Yehoachaz** (Yeh hoh ah chahz') יהואחז
In H., "God will hold" or "God will support"; in the B. (II Kings), a
king of Israel. The English form is Jehoahaz.* Another form is *Yoachaz*
(Yoh ah chahz') יואחז, same meaning, in the B. (II Kings).*

**Yehoash** (Yeh hoh ahsh') יהואש
From the H., "God is strong"; in the B. (II Kings), a king.* Another
form is *Yoash* (Yoh ahsh') יואש, same meaning, in the B. (Judges).*

**Yehochanan** (Yeh hoh chah nahn') יהוחנן
In H., "God is gracious"; in the B. (Ezra), a high priest. The English
form is Jehohanan.* Another form is *Yochanan* (Yoh chah nahn')
יוחנן, same meaning, in the B. (II Kings). In the Talmud, the name of
many Palestinian scholars. The English forms are Johanan and John.**

**Yehonadav** (Yeh hoh nah dahv') יהונדב
In H., "God is noble"; in the B. (II Samuel), a nephew of King David.*
Another form is *Yonadav* (Yoh nah dahv') יונדב, same meaning, also
the name of a place in central Israel.**

**Yehonatan** (Yeh hoh nah tahn') יהונתן
In H., "God has given"; in the B. (I Samuel), the son of King Saul and
David's best friend. In H., "the love of David and Jonathan" is a symbol
of true fraternal love.*** Another form is *Yonatan* (Yoh nah tahn')
יונתן, also the name of a place (moshav) in Israel in Ramat Hagolan.
The English form is Jonathan. Nickname is *Yoni* (Yoh' nee) יוני.***

**Yehoram** (Yeh hoh rahm') יהורם
In H., "God is exalted"; in the B. (II Kings), the son of King Ahab.

Also the name of a famous singer in Israel (Yehoram Gaon). The English form is Jehoram.** Another form is *Yoram* (Yoh' rahm) יורם, same meaning, in the B. (II Samuel and II Kings). The English form is Joram.**

**Yehoraz** (Yeh hoh rahz') יהורז
In H., "God's secret."****

**Yehoshafat** (Yeh hoh shah faht') יהושפט
In H., "God judged"; in the B. (I Kings), a king. The English form is Jehoshaphat.** Other forms are *Yoshafat* (Yoh shah faht') יושפט, same meaning, in the B. (I Chronicles), a warrior;** and *Yishpot* (Yeesh poht') ישפוט, in H., "he will judge."*

**Yehoshua** (Yeh hoh shoo' ah) יהושוע
In H., "God is my salvation"; in the B. (Exodus), the man who led the children of Israel into the Promised Land. Beth Yehoshua is the name of a place (moshav) in Israel in the shefelah. The English form is Joshua. Nickname is *Shuki* (Shoo' kee) שוקי.**

**Yehotzadak** (Yeh hoh tzah dahk') יהוצדק
In H., "God was right"; in the B. (Haggai).* Another form is *Yotzadak* (Yoh tzah dahk') יוצדק, same meaning, in the B. (Ezra).*

**Yehu** (Yeh hoo') יהוא
From the H., "he is God" or "God lives"; in the B. (I Kings), a king and (I Kings) a prophet. The English form is Jehu.*

**Yehuda(h)** (Yeh hoo dah') יהודה
From the H., "to praise, to thank"; in the B. (Genesis), the fourth son of Jacob. Har Yehuda is the name of a mountainous area in Israel, and Yehuda Ve Shomron is the name of an area in Jordan's territory that belongs to Israel since the Six-Day War. A symbolic name for boys born on Hanukkah after Judas Maccabaeus. The English form is Judah.** Another form is *Yehudi* (Yeh hoo dee') יהודי, in the B. (Jeremiah), in H., "Jew, Jewish, Judaic."*

**Yekamam** (Yeh kahm ahm') יקמעם
In H., "the nation will be established"; in the B. (I Chronicles), a Levite.* Another form is *Yekamya* (Yeh kahm yah') יקמיה, in H., "God will establish"; in the B. (I Chronicles).*

**Yekutiel** (Yeh koo tee ehl') יקותיאל
From the H., "God will nourish"; in the B. (I Chronicles). Nickname is *Kuti* (Koo' tee) קותי.*

**Yeor** (Yeh ohr') יאור
In H., the name of a river, the Nile, and "lake, canal."** Another form is *Yeori* (Yeh oh ree') יאורי, in H., "my river."****

**Yerach** (Yeh' rahch) ירח
In H., "month," a symbolic name for boys born on Rosh Hodesh, the new moon.*

**Yerachmiel** (Yeh rahch mee ehl') ירחמיאל
In H., "God will have mercy on me"; in the B. (Jeremiah).* Other forms are *Yerachm'el* (Yeh rah chehm ehl') ירחמאל, same meaning;* *Yerocham* (Yeh roh chahm') ירוחם, in H., "may he obtain mercy"; in the B. (I Samuel), also the name of a place in Israel in the Negev;** and *Yerucham* (Yeh roo chahm').**

**Yeravam** (Yeh rahv ahm') ירבעם
From the H., "the nation will contend" or "the nation will be increased"; in the B. (I Kings), a king. In the Jewish culture this king became the symbol of one who sins and causes others to sin also. The English form is Jeroboam.*

**Yered** (Yeh' rehd) ירד
From the H., "descendant"; in the B. (Genesis).*

**Yeriel** (Yeh ree ehl') יריאל
From the H., "God has taught me"; in the B. (I Chronicles).* Other forms with the same meaning are *Yeriya* (Yeh ree yah') יריה, in the B. (I Chronicles);* and *Yeriyahu* (Yeh ree yah' hoo) יריהו.*

**Yerushalayim** (Yeh roo shah lah' yeem) ירושלים
From the H., "city of peace." The capital of Israel since biblical times, the holy and spiritual center of Jews, as well as of Christians and Moslems. The English form is Jerusalem.**

**Yeshayahu** (Yeh shah ah yah' hoo) ישעיהו
From the H., "God is salvation"; in the B. (Isaiah), a prophet in the kingdom of Judah. The English form is Isaiah. Also spelled Yeshaiahu. Nickname is *Shaya* (Shah' yah) שעיה.** Other forms with the same meaning are *Yeshaya* (Yeh shah yah') ישעיה, also spelled Yeshaia(h);** *Yesha* (Yeh' shah) ישע, in H., "deliverance, salvation," also the name of a place (moshav) in Israel in the Negev;* *Yeshua* (Yeh shoo ah') ישועה, in H., "salvation, help, rescue"; in the B. (Nehemiah);* *Yishie* (Yeesh ee') ישעי, in H., "my deliverance, my salvation"; in the B. (I Chronicles), also the name of a place (moshav) in central Israel, also spelled Ishi;* *Yoshiyahu* (Yoh shee yah' hoo) יאשיהו, from the H., "God will save"; in the B. (I Kings), a king;* and *Yoshiya* (Yoh shee yah') יאשיה; the English form is Josiah.*

**Yeter** (Yeh' tehr) יתר
In H., "remainder, rest" or "abundance, surplus"; in the B. (Exodus), a nickname of Yitro (Jethro).* Another form is *Yatir* (Yah teer') יתיר,

in H., "he will untie, he will permit," also the name of a place (moshav) in central Israel named after an ancient city mentioned in the B.*

**Yetzer** (Yeh' tzehr) יצר

In H., "instinct, nature, inclination, desire"; in the B. (Genesis).*

**Yevarechya** (Yeh vah rehch yah') יברכיה

In H., "God will bless"* Other forms are *Yevarechyahu* (Yeh vah rehch yah' hoo) יברכיהו, same meaning, in the B. (Isaiah);* and *Yevorach* (Yeh voh rahch') יבורך, in H., "may he be blessed!"**

**Yifdeya** (Yeef deh yah') יפדיה

In H., "God will redeem"; in the B. (I Chronicles).* Another form is *Yifdeh* (Yeef deh') יפדה.*

**Yifrach** (Yeef rahch') יפרח

In H., "he will blossom," meaning "grow" or "may he blossom, grow!"* Another form is *Yifracham* (Yeef rahch ahm') יפרחעם, in H., "the nation will blossom" or "may the nation grow!"****

**Yiftach** (Yeef tahch') יפתח

In H., "he will open"; in the B. (Judges), a judge. Also the name of a place (kibbutz) in Israel in the Galilee. The English form is Jephthah.*** Another form is *Yiftach-El* (Yeef tahch Ehl') יפתח־אל, in H., "God will open."****

**Yigal** (Yeeg ahl') יגאל

In H., "he will redeem"; in the B. (Numbers). Also spelled Igal.** Another form is *Yigael* (Yee gah ehl'), in H., "he will be redeemed."**

**Yigdal** (Yeeg dahl') יגדל

In H., "he will grow, become great."* Another form is *Yigdalyahu* (Yeeg dahl yah' hoo) יגדליהו, in H., "God will exalt"; in the B. (Jeremiah).*

**Yinon** (Yee nohn') ינון

In H., "may he live forever!" A symbolic name for the Messiah. Also the name of a place (moshav) in Israel in the shefelah. Also spelled Yinnon.**

**Yirmeyahu** (Yeer meh yah' hoo) ירמיהו

From the H., "God will raise up"; in the B. (Jeremiah), a prophet. The English form is Jeremiah. Nicknames are *Yirmi* (Yeer' mee) ירמי and Jermi.** Another form is *Yirmeya* (Yeer meh yah') ירמיה, same meaning, in the B. (I Chronicles).**

**Yisachar** (Yee sah chahr') יששכר

From the H., "he will be rewarded"; in the B. (Genesis), one of Jacob's sons. The English form is Issachar.* Another form is *Yisaschar* (Yee sahs chahr') יששכר, same meaning.*

**Yishai** (Yee shahy') ישי
From the H., "gift"; in the B. (I Samuel), the father of King David.
The English form is Jesse.***

**Yishbach** (Yeesh bahch') ישבח
In H., "he will praise" or "he will improve"; in the B. (I Chronicles).*

**Yishmael** (Yeesh mah ehl') ישמעאל
In H., "God will hear"; in the B. (Genesis), son of Abraham. The
English form is Ishmael.* Other forms with the same meaning are
*Yishmaya* (Yeesh mah yah') ישמעיה, in the B. (I Chronicles). Nickname
is *Shmaya* (Shmah' yah) שמעיה;** *Yishmayahu* (Yeesh mah yah' hoo)
ישמעיהו, in the B. (I Chronicles);* and *Yishma* (Yeesh mah') ישמע, in
H., "will hear."*

**Yismach** (Yees mahch') ישמח
In H., "he will be glad, happy" or "may he be glad, happy."* Or יסמך,
in H., "he will support."* Another form is *Yismachyahu* (Yees mahch
yah' hoo) סמכיהו, in H., "God will support"; in the B. (I Chronicles).*

**Yisrael** (Yees rah ehl') ישראל
From the H., "prince of God" or "wrestled with God"; in the B.
(Genesis), this name was given to Jacob (Yaakov) after wrestling
with God's angel. Yisrael is the name of the Jewish nation and the
Jewish state. The English form is Israel. A symbolic name for boys
born on Israeli Independence Day.**

**Yitro** (Yeet roh') יתרו
From the H., "abundance"; in the B. (Exodus), the father-in-law of
Moses. The English form is Jethro. According to a legend he had
seven names, and "Jethro's names" is a H. idiom for someone who
has too many names.*

**Yitzchak** (Yeetz chahk') יצחק
In H., "he will laugh"; in the B. (Genesis), the son who was born to
Abraham and Sara when they were old. Be'erot Yitzchak is the name
of a place (religious kibbutz) in Israel in the shefelah. Also spelled
Yitzhak. The English form is Isaac. Nickname is *Itzik* (Ee' tzeek)
איציק.** Another form is *Yischak* (Yees chahk') ישחק.**

**Yitzhal** (Yeetz hahl') יצהל
In H., "he will be joyous" or "may he be joyous."*

**Yitzhar** (Yeetz hahr') יצהר
In H., "pure oil," a poetic name for scholars ("sons of oil," who "oil"
one another in their discussions) or for an honorable person. Also
the name of a place in Israel in the Samaria (Shomron).**

**Yitzmach** (Yeetz mahch') יצמח
In H., "he will grow."*

**Yivchar** (Yeev chahr') יבחר
In H., "he will choose"; in the B. (II Samuel).*

**Yivsam** (Yeev sahm') יבשם
From the H., "he will be perfumed"; in the B. (I Chronicles).****

**Yizhar** (Yeez hahr') יזהר
In H., "he will shine, he will brighten."***

**Yizrach** (Yeez rahch') יזרח
In H., "he will shine, glow"; in the B. (I Chronicles), an officer.*
Another form is *Yizrachya* (Yeez rahch yah') יזרחיה, in H., "God will shine"; in the B. (Nehemiah), also spelled Yizrachia.*

**Yizr'el** (Yeez reh ehl') יזראל
In H., "God will plant"; in the B. (I Chronicles). Also the name of an area in north Israel, the Valley of Esdraelon (Jezreel) and the name of a place (kibbutz) in this area named after an ancient city.* Other forms are *Yizrael* (Yeez rah ehl');** and *Yizream* (Yeez reh ahm') יזרעם, in H., "the nation will plant," also the name of a place (agricultural farm) in Israel in the Negev.*

**Yoach** (Yoh ahch') יואח
From the H., "God's brother"; in the B. (II Kings).*

**Yoad** (Yoh ahd') יועד
From the H., "God is witness."** Another form is *Yoed* (Yoh ehd'), in the B. (Nehemiah).**

**Yoav** (Yoh ahv') יואב
From the H., "God is father" or "God is willing"; in the B. (II Samuel), the captain of King David's army. The English form is Joab.***

**Yochai** (Yoh chahy') יוחאי
From the H., "God lives." In the Talmud, the father of Simeon. A symbolic name for boys born on Lag b'Omer, when Orthodox Jews go to the grave of Rabbi Shimeon Bar Yochai. Also spelled Yocha'i.*** Another form is *Yocha* (Yoh' chah) יוחא, same meaning, in the B. (I Chronicles).*

**Yoel** (Yoh ehl') יואל
In H., "God will be willing"; in the B. (Joel), one of the Minor Prophets. The English form is Joel.**

**Yoezer** (Yoh eh' zehr) יועזר
In H., "God will help"; in the B. (I Chronicles). Also the name of a place in Israel in Samaria (Shomron).*

**Yogev** (Yoh gehv′) יוגב
In H., "farmer."** Another form is *Yagev* (Yah gehv′) י.גב.*

**Yona(h)** (Yoh nah′) יונה
In H., "dove"; in the B. (Jonah), one of the Minor Prophets. A symbolic name for both boys and girls born on Yom Kippur, the Day of Atonement, when we read the story about Jonah, who was swallowed by a big fish. The English form is Jona(h).** Another form is *Yon* (Yohn) יון, same meaning.****

**Yore(h)** (Yoh reh′) יורה
In H., the name of the first rain, the name of the season of the first rain, or, in H., "shooter" or "he will teach."**

**Yosef** (Yoh sehf′) יוסף
In H., "God will add, increase"; in the B. (Genesis), one of Jacob's twelve sons. The English form is Joseph. Nicknames are *Yossi* (Yoh′ see) יוסי and *Sefi* (Seh′ fee) ספי.** Other forms with the same meaning are *Yosifya* (Yoh seef yah′) יוסיפיה, also the name of a place in Israel in Samaria (Shomron);* *Yehosef* (Yeh hoh sehf) יהוסף;* and *Yosifel* (Yoh seef ehl′) יוסיפאל.****

**Yotam** (Yoh tahm′) יותם
From the H., "God is perfect" or "orphan"; in the B. (Judges), one of Judge Gideon's sons and (II Kings) a king. The English form is Jotham.**

**Yovav** (Yoh vahv′) יובב
From the H., "to cry"; in the B. (Genesis).*

**Yovel** (Yoh vehl′) יובל
In H., "jubilee" (the celebration of certain anniversaries) or "ram's horn."**

**Yuval** (Yoo vahl′) יובל
In H., "river, stream"; in the B. (Genesis). Also the name of a place (moshav) in Israel in the Galilee.***

# Z

**Zach** (Zahch) זך

In H., "pure, clean, clear, innocent."**** Another form is *Zakai* (Zah kahy') זכאי, in H., "innocent"; in the B. (Ezra). Also spelled Zakkai.*

**Zalman** (Zahl' mahn) זלמן

The Y. nickname for Solomon. Other forms are Zalmen, Zalmon.*

**Zamir** (Zah meer') זמיר

In H., the name of a songbird, nightingale, or "song, singing."****

**Zangwill** (Zahng' weel) זאנגוויל

The Y. form of Shmuel (Samuel). See Shmuel. Other forms are Zanvel, Zanvil.*

**Zavad** (Zah vahd') זבד

From the H., "gift, bestowal, bounty"; in the B. (I Chronicles), a warrior. Also spelled Zabad.* Other forms are *Zavdi* (Zahv dee') זבדי, from the H., "my gift"; in the B. (I Chronicles), also spelled Zabdi;* *Zavdiel* (Zahv dee ehl') זבדיאל, from the H., "God is my gift" or "God has endowed me with a good dowry," also the name of a place (moshav) in south Israel;* *Zavud* (Zah vood') זבוד, same meaning, in the B. (I Kings);* *Zvadya* (Zvahd yah') זבדיה, from the H., "God has bestowed"; in the B. (I Chronicles), also spelled Zevadya or Zevadia(h);* *Zvadyahu* (Zvahd yah' hoo) זבדיהו, same meaning, in the B. (I Chronicles), a Levite, also spelled Zevadyahu;* and *Zvid* (Zveed) זביד, same meaning.*

**Zayit** (Zah' yeet) זית

In H., "olive, olive tree."**** Another form is *Zetan* (Zehy tahn') זיתן, in the B. (I Chronicles), a member of Benjamin's tribe. Also the name of a place (moshav) in Israel in the shefelah (coastal plain), because olive trees are plentiful in the area.****

**Zcharya** (Zchahr yah') זכריה

In H., "memory of God, remembrance of God"; in the B., one of the kings of Israel (II Kings). One of the twelve Minor Prophets. Also spelled Zecharya, Zcharia(h), or Zecharia(h). Also the name of a place (moshav) in central Israel. The English pet forms are Zakri and Zeke.** Another form is *Zcharyahu* (Zchahr yah' hoo) זכריהו, same meaning. Also spelled Zecharyahu.*

**Zecher** (Zeh′ chehr) זכר

In H., "memory, remembrance" or "trace, hint"; in the B. (I Chronicles).*
Other forms are *Zichri* (Zeech ree′) זיכרי, in H., "my memory, my
remembrance"; in the B. (Exodus);* and *Zichroni* (Zeech roh′ nee)
זכרוני, same meaning.*

**Ze'ev** (Zeh ehv′) זאב

In H., "wolf"; in the B. (Genesis), Binyamin (Benjamin) is compared
to a wolf.** The Yiddish forms are Seff and Zif(f).* Another form is
*Ze'evi* (Zeh eh vee′) זאבי, in H., "my wolf," or "wolfish."****

**Zehavi** (Zeh hah′ vee) זהבי

In H., "my gold" or "goldsmith."* Another form is *Zahavi* (Zah hah′
vee), same meaning.*

**Zeide** (Zehy′ deh) זיידע

From the Y., "grandfather" or "old man."*

**Zemer** (Zeh′ mehr) זמר

In H., "singing, song, tune, melody."** Another form is *Zmarya*
(Zmahr yah′) זמריה, in H., "melody of God," also spelled Zemarya
and Zemaria(h).* Other forms that mean, in H., "my song, my melody"
are *Zimran* (Zeem rahn′) זימרן, in the B. (Genesis);* *Zimri* (Zeem ree′)
זימרי;* and *Zimroni* (Zeem roh′ nee) זמרוני.*

**Zer** (Zehr) זר

In H., "wreath (bouquet) of flowers."****

**Zerach** (Zeh′ rahch) זרח

From the H., "to shine, glow"; in the B. (Genesis). Also spelled Zerah.*
Other forms are *Zarchi* (Zahr′ chee) זרחי, same meaning;* and
*Zrachya* (Zrahch yah′) זרחיה, in H., "light of God"; in the B. (Ezra), a
son of Pinchas, also the name of a place (moshav) in south Israel;
also spelled Zerachya, Zerachia(h).*

**Zevach** (Zeh′ vahch) זבח

In H., "sacrifice" or "feast"; in the B. (Judges). Also spelled Zevah.*
Another form is *Zvachya* (Zvahch yah′) זבחיה, in H., "sacrifice of
God." Also spelled Zevachya, Zvachia(h), and Zevachia(h).*

**Ziv** (Zeev) זיו

In H., "brilliance, light, splendor, glory." Also a synonym for the
month Iyyar, the second month in the Jewish calendar, when we
celebrate Israel's Independence Day. Used also as a girl's name.***
Other forms with the same meaning are *Zivi* (Zee′ vee) זיווי;**** *Zivan*
(Zee vahn′) זיוון;**** and *Zivel* (Zeev ehl′) זיו-אל, in H., "God's light."**

**Zohar** (Zoh' hahr) זוהר

In H., "brightness, light, splendor, glamour." Used also as a girl's name. Also the name of a place (moshav) in south Israel.*** Other forms are *Zahir* (Zah heer') זהיר; and *Zahur* (Zah hoor') זהור, both mean, in H., "shining, brightening."*

**Zorea** (Zoh reh' ah) זורע

In H., "a farmer, one who plants."*

**Zvulun** (Zvoo loon') זבולון

From the H., "to exalt, to honor" or "palace on high, heavenly mansion"; in the B. (Genesis), the sixth son of Jacob. Also spelled Zevulun. The English form is Zebulun.* Another form is *Zvul* (Zvool) זבול, same meaning, in the B. (Judges). Also spelled Zevul and Zebul.*

# 7.

# Girls' Names

## A

**Abira** (Ah bee' rah) אבירה
The feminine form of Abir, in H., "strong."*

**Achava** (Ah chah vah') אחווה
In H., "friendship." Used also as a boy's name. See Achva.****

**Achinoam** (Ah chee noh' ahm) אחינועם
In H., "my brother is charming, lovely"; in the B. (I Samuel), a wife of King Saul and a wife of King David. Used also as a boy's name.****

**Achishalom** (Ah chee shah lohm') אחישלום
In H., "my brother is peace," meaning "my brother will bring peace." Also a boy's name.****

**Ada(h)** (Ah dah') עדה
In the B. (Genesis), the wife of Lamech and the wife of Esau; from the H., meaning "adorned, beautiful." Also spelled Adda(h).*

**Adara** (Ah dah' rah) אדרה
The feminine form of Adar. From the H., "exalted, praised." Adar is the name of the twelfth month in the Jewish calendar, when we celebrate Purim.**

**Adaya** (Ah dah' yah) עדיה
From the H., "God's jewel" or "God's witness" or a form of Ada.** Another form is *Adiya* (Ah dee' yah), used also as a boy's name.**

**Adel** (Ahd ehl') עדאל
From the H., "God is eternal."

**Adi** (Ah dee') עדי
In H., "a jewel" or "my adornment." Also the name of a place in Israel in the Galilee. Also spelled Addi or Addie. Used also as a boy's name.*** Other forms are *Adiel* (Ah dee el') עדיאל, from the H., "God's ornament";** and *Adielaa* (Ah dee eh' lah) עדיאלה, same meaning.**

**Adina** (Ah dee' nah) עדינה
In H., "noble, delicate, gentle." Also spelled Adena.***

**Adira** (Ah dee rah) אדירה
The feminine form of Adir. In H., "powerful, mighty, splendid."*

**Admonit** (Ahd mo neet') אדמונית
In H., name of a plant, peony.**** Another form is *Admona* (Ahd moh nah') אדמונה, same meaning.****

**Adva** (Ahd vah') אדווה
In H., "ripple, wavelet."***

**Aharona** (Ah hah roh' nah) אהרונה
The feminine form of Aharon (Aaron).** Another form is *Aharonit* (Ah hah ro neet') אהרונית.*

**Ahuva(h)** (Ah hoo' vah) אהובה
In H., "beloved, one who is loved by others."** Another form is *Ahuvit* (Ah hoo veet') אהובית.****

**Aldema(h)** (Ahl deh' mah) אלדמע
From the H., "no tears," meaning, "we wish you a happy life." Used also as a boy's name.****

**Alexandra** (Ah lex ahn' drah) אלכסנדרה
The feminine form of the Greek Alexander. See Alexander.****

**Aliza(h)** (Ah lee' zah) עליזה
In H., "one who is joyful, merry." Also spelled Aleeza.*

**Alma(h)** (Ahl' mah) עלמה
In H., "a young woman, maiden." Also the name of a place (moshav) in the Galilee.**

**Almoga** (Ahl moh gah') אלמוגה
The feminine form of Almog. In H., "coral." Also the name of a tree that grows in India, sandalwood. Almog is also the name of a place (kibbutz) north of the Dead Sea.* Another form is *Almogit* (Ahl moh geet') אלמוגית.**

**Alona** (Ah loh' nah) אלונה
The feminine form of Alon; in H., "oak tree."*** Another form is *Alonit* (Ah loh neet') אלונית.****

**Alte** (Ahl' teh) אלטע
From the Y., meaning "old woman."*

**Alufa** (Ah loo' fah) אלופה
The feminine form of Aluf, meaning "leader."*

**Aluma(h)** (Ah loo mah') עלומה
From the H., "a young woman, maiden" or "hidden secret."**** Or
אלומה, in H., "sheaf, bundle." Popular name for girls who are born on
Shavuot, known as the Feast of the Harvest. Also the name of a place
in south Israel.*** Another form is *Alumit* (Ah loo meet') אלומית,
same meaning.****

**Alva(h)** (Ahl vah') עלווה
In H., "foliage."** Another form is *Alvit* (Ahl veet') עלווית.****

**Amalya** (Ah mahl' yah) עמליה
In H., "work of God" or "industrious." Also spelled Amalia(h).**
Other forms with the same meaning are *Amela* (Ah meh lah') עמלה,*
and *Amelit* (Ah meh leet') עמלית.****

**Amiela** (Ah mee eh' lah) עמיאלה
From the H., "people of God."*

**Amira** (Ah mee' rah) אמירה
In H., "speech, utterance" or the feminine form of Amir, meaning
"treetop."*** Or עמירה, in H., "sheaf of corn." Popular name for girls
who are born on Shavuot, Feast of the Harvest.*** Another form is
*Amirit* (Ah mee reet') עמירית or אמירית.****

**Amiran** (Ah mee rahn') עמירן
In H., "my nation is joyful." Used also as a boy's name.***

**Amit** (Ah meet') עמית
In H., "friend" or "colleague." Used also as a boy's name.*** Another
form is *Amita* (Ah mee tah') עמיתה.*

**Amital** (Ah mee tahl') עמיטל
From the H., "my nation is dew," meaning "my nation has hopes."
Used also as a boy's name.**

**Anafa** (Ah nah fah') אנפה
In H., "heron, egret."****

**Anat** (Ah naht') ענת
From the H., meaning "to sing"; only in the B., used as a boy's name.
Also spelled Anath.***

**Anna** (Ah' nah) אנה
The Greek form of the H. name *Chana(h)* (Hannah), meaning
"gracious." See Chana(h).*

**Anuga(h)** (Ah noo gah') ענוגה
In H., "delicate, tender."****

**Arava** (Ah rah vah') ערבה
In H., "willow, willow branch." One of the Four Species we use on
Sukkoth. A popular name for girls born on Sukkoth, especially on
Hoshanah Rabbah (the seventh day of Sukkoth), also known as the
Seventh Day of the Willow. During the synagogue service on that day,
it is customary to take extra willow twigs and beat them on the
ground until all the leaves fall off. Arava in H. also means "dry land,
desert," and it is the name of an area in southeast Israel.**

**Arda(h)** (Ahr dah') ארדה
The feminine form of Arad. In H., "bronze."**

**Arela, Arella** (Ahr eh' lah) אראלה
The feminine form of Arel. From the H., "angel, messenger."***

**Ariel** (Ah ree ehl') אריאל
In H., "lioness of God." Also the name of a place in Israel in Samaria
(Shomron). Also spelled Arielle.*** Other forms are *Ariela* and
*Ariella* (Ah ree eh' lah) אריאלה, same meaning.***

**Armona** (Ahr mo' nah) ערמונה
The feminine form of the boys' names Armon, in H., "chestnut"
(tree, fruit) (see Armon), or Armoni, in H., "reddish brown."** Another
form is *Armonit* (Ahr mo neet') ערמונית.****

**Arnona** (Ahr noh' nah) ארנונה
The feminine form of Arnon, from the H., "roaring stream."** Another
form is *Arnonit* (Ahr no neet') ארנונית.**

**Arza** (Ahr zah') ארזה
The feminine form of Erez. In H., "cedar." Also the name of a place
(convalescent home) near Jerusalem.** Another form is *Arzit* (Ahr
zeet') ארזית.**

**Ashira** (Ah shee' rah) אשירה
In H., "I will sing."**** Or עשירה, in H., "wealthy."*

**Ashra** (Ahsh rah') אשרה
The feminine form of the biblical name Asher. From the H., means
"blessed, fortunate, happy."** Other forms with the same meaning
are *Ashera* (Ah sheh' rah) (the same Hebrew spelling);* *Asherit*
(Ah sheh reet') אשרית;** *Ashrat* (Ahsh raht') אשרת, also the name
of a place in Israel in Galilee;** and *Ashria* (Ahsh ree yah') אשריה.**

**Astar** (Ahs tahr'), **Aster** (Ahs tehr') אסתר
In H., the name of a plant, starwort.****

**Atalya** (Ah tahl yah') עתליה
From the H., "God is exalted"; in the B. (II Kings). Also spelled
Atalia(h), Athalia(h).****

**Atara** (Ah tah rah') עטרה
In H., "crown" or "wreath"; in the B. (I Chronicles).**

**Ateret** (Ah teh' reht) עטרת
From the name Atara, meaning "crown" or "wreath." Also the name
of a place in Israel in Samaria (Shomron).*** Or עתרת, from the H.,
"prayer."** Other forms are *Atira* (Ah tee' rah) עתירה;**** and *Atura*
(Ah too' rah) עטורה.****

**Atida(h)** (Ah tee' dah) עתידה
The feminine form of Atid; in H., "future, future tense" or "finally,
ready."*

**Atlee** (Aht' lee) אתלי
In H., "you are mine."****

**Atzila(h)** (Ah tzee lah') אצילה
In H., "noble" or "honorable"; also spelled Azila(h).*

**Atzmona(h)** (Ahtz moh' nah) עצמונה
From the H., meaning "strength." Also the name of a place (moshav)
in south Israel in the Gaza Strip.**

**Aviela, Aviella** (Ah vee eh' lah) אביאלה
The feminine form of Aviel; in H., "my father is God."**

**Avigayil** (Ah vee gah' yeel) אביגייל
From the H., "my father is joy"; in the B. (I Samuel), one of King
David's wives. Also spelled Abigail.** Another form is *Avigal*
(Ah vee gahl') אביגל.**

**Avigdora** (Ah veeg doh' rah) אביגדורה
The feminine form of Avigdor, from the H., meaning "father
protector."**

**Avirama** (Ah vee rah' mah) אבירמה
From the H., "my father is strong" or the feminine form of the boys'
names Avraham and Aviram.**

**Avishag** (Ah vee shahg') אבישג
In the B. (I Kings), a servant of King David; also spelled Abishag.**

**Avishav** (Ah vee shahv') אבישב
In H., "my father came back." In Israel used after a father's return
from a war. Used also as a boy's name.**

**Avital** (Ah vee tahl') אביטל
In H., "father of dew," referring to God; in the B. (II Samuel), one of
King David's wives; also the name of a place in north Israel in the
Valley of Esdraelon (Jezreel). Also spelled Abital. Used also as a
boy's name.***

**Aviva(h)** (Ah vee' vah) אביבה
From the H., meaning "spring," "youthfulness, freshness."** Another form is *Avivit* (Ah vee veet') אביבית.***

**Aviya** (Ah vee yah') אביה
In H., "God is my father"; in the B. (II Chronicles). Also spelled Avia(h); used also as a boy's name. See Av.*

**Avuka** (Ah voo kah') אבוקה
In H., "torch." A symbolic name for girls who are born on Hanukkah. Also the name of a place in north Israel.****

**Aya(h)** (Ah' yah) איה
In H., the name of an Israeli bird of prey; in the B. (Genesis).**

**Ayala(h)** (Ah yah lah') איילה
The feminine form of Ayal; in H., "deer, gazelle."*** Other forms are *Ayelet* (Ah yeh' leht) איילת;*** and *Ayelet-Hashachar* (Ah yeh' leht Hah shah' chahr) איילת־השחר, in H., "dawn, morning star, aurora." Also the name of a place (kibbutz) in Israel in the Galilee.****

**Azriela** (Ahz ree eh' lah) עזריאלה
The feminine form of Azriel; in H., "God is my help."* Another form is *Azrielit* (Ahz ree eh leet') עזריאלית.****

# B

### THE HEBREW LETTER ב'

**Bahat** (Bah' haht) בהט
In H., "alabaster" or "porphyry." Used also as a boy's name.**

**Balfouria** (Bahl foor' yah) בלפוריה
The feminine form of Balfour. See Balfour. Also the name of a place (moshav) in Israel in the Valley of Esdraelon (Jezreel).* Another form is *Balfoura* (Bahl foor' rah) בלפורה.*

**Bar** (Bahr) בר
In H., "wheat, grain, corn." A popular name for babies born on Shavuot, known as the Feast of the Harvest. Also means "pure, clean." Used also as a boy's name.***

**Barak** (Bah rahk') ברק
In H., "lightning" or "glitter, spendor, glare, flash, gleam, shine." Also the name of a place (moshav) in north Israel in the Valley of Esdraelon (Jezreel). Used also as a boy's name.***

**Bareket** (Bah reh' keht) ברקת
In H., "emerald" or "agate." Also the name of a place (moshav) in central Israel. Used also as a boy's name.*** Another form is *Barkat* (Bahr kaht') ברקת.****

**Bat** (Baht) בת
In H., "daughter."**

**Bat-Ami** (Baht' Ah mee') בת-עמי
In H., "daughter of my people."** Another form is *Bat-Am* (Baht Ahm') בת-עם, same meaning.*

**Bat-Chen** (Baht Chehn') בת-חן
In H., "daughter of grace," meaning "beautiful, charming girl."****

**Bat-El** (Baht Ehl') בת-אל
In H., "daughter of God."* Other forms with the same meaning are *Batela* (Baht eh' lah) בתאלה;* and *Bat-Eli* (Baht' Eh lee') בת-אלי.*

**Batlee** (Baht' lee) בת-לי, בתלי
In H., "I have a daughter."****

**Bat-Shachar** (Baht Shah' chahr) בת-שחר
In H., "daughter of the dawn."****

**Bat-Sheva** (Baht Sheh' vah) בת-שבע
From the H., "daughter of an oath"; in the B. (II Samuel), the mother of King Solomon. The English form is Bathsheba. The Yiddish forms are Basha and Bashe.**

**Bat-Shir** (Baht Sheer') בת-שיר
In H., "songbird" or "muse."****

**Bat-Tziyon** (Baht' Tzee yohn') בת-ציון
In H., "daughter of Zion."*

**Batya** (Baht' yah) בתיה
In H., "daughter of God." The Yiddish forms are Basha and Bashe.**

**Bdolach** (Bdoh' lach) בדולח
In H., "crystal." Also the name of a place (moshav) in Israel in the Gaza Strip. Used also as a boy's name.**

**Bechora** (Beh choh rah') בכורה
In H., "eldest daughter." Popular among Sephardic families for firstborn daughters. Other forms with the same meaning are *Bechura* (Beh choo' rah) בכורה;* *Bechira* (Beh chee' rah) בכירה;* and *Bikura* (Bee koo' rah) ביכורה.*

**Belah** (Beh' lah) בלה
In Latin, "beautiful one." The French form is Belle; the Yiddish form is Baile.*

**Bilha(h)** (Beel hah') בילהה
From the H., "weak, old"; in the B. (Genesis), the maidservant of
Rachel. The Yiddish form is Baile.*

**Biluya** (Bee loo' yah) בילוייה
The feminine form of Bilu. See Bilu.*

**Bina** (Bee nah') בינה
In H., "understanding, wisdom, intelligence."*

**Binyamina** (Been yah mee' nah) בנימינה
The feminine form of Binyamin. See Binyamin. Also the name of a
place in central Israel in the Sharon.*

**Bluma** (Bloo' mah) בלומה
In Y., "flower."*

**Bosmat** (Bohs maht') בושמת
From the H., "perfumed"; in the B. (Genesis), a wife of Esau and
(I Kings) a daughter of King Solomon.** Other forms with the same
meaning are *Bosem* (Boh' sehm) בושם;**** *Bosma* (Bohs mah')
בושמה; and *Bosmit* (Bohs meet') בושמית.****

**Bracha** (Brah chah') ברכה
In H., "blessing, benediction, luck, profit." Also the name of a place
in Israel in the Samaria (Shomron).** Other forms with the same
meaning are *Brucha* (Broo chah') ברוכה;* and *Bruchiya* (Broo chee
yah') ברוכיה.*

**Brit(t)** (Breet) ברית
In H., "covenant." Used also as a boy's name.**

**Brurya** (Broor yah') ברוריה
From the H., "pure, clean."** Other forms with the same meaning
are *Brura* (Broo rah') ברורה;* and *Brurit* (Broo reet') ברורית.****

**Bsora** (Bsoh rah') בשורה
In H., "good news."*

**Bustan** (Boos tahn') בוסתן
In H., "garden." Used also as a boy's name.****

# C

**Carmel** (Cahr mehl') כרמל

From the H., "vineyard" or, in H., "boiled green grain." The name of a mountain in north Israel. Also spelled Karmel. Used also as a boy's name.*** Other forms with the same meaning are *Carma* (Cahr mah') כרמה, also spelled Karma;* *Carmela* (Cahr meh' lah) כרמלה, also spelled Karmela;** *Carmit* (Cahr meet') כרמית, also spelled Karmit;*** and *Carmi* (Cahr' mee) כרמי, in H., "my vineyard," also spelled Karmi, used also as a boy's name.**

**Carmelit** (Cahr meh leet') כרמלית

In H., "a place which is neither public nor private," "lawn in front of a house," "moving staircase, escalator," or a form of Mount Carmel. Also spelled Karmelit.**

**Carmiya** (Cahr mee yah') כרמיה

From the H., "God is my vineyard," meaning "God is my source of wisdom." Also the name of a place (kibbutz) in Israel in the shefelah (coastal plain). Also spelled Karmia, Karmiya. Used also as a boy's name.* Another form is *Carmiela* (Cahr mee eh' lah) כרמיאלה, same meaning, also spelled Karmiela.*

**Chagit** (Chah geet') חגית

The feminine form of Chagai, from the H., "feast, holiday, celebration." A popular name for girls born on one of the Jewish holidays. In the B. (II Samuel), one of King David's wives. Also spelled Hagit.** Another form is *Chagiya* (Chah gee yah') חגיה, from the H., "God's festival." Also spelled Hagiya, Hagia.*

**Chalutza** (Chah loo tzah') חלוצה

The feminine form of Chalutz, in H., "pioneer." Also spelled Halutza.*

**Chamanit** (Chah mah neet') חמנית

In H., the name of a flower, sunflower. Also spelled Hamanit.****

**Chamutal** (Chah moo tahl') חמוטל

From the H., "dew"; in the B. (II Kings), the wife of King Josiah. Also spelled Hamutal.** Another form is *Chamital* (Chah mee tahl') חמיטל.*

**Chana(h)** (Chah nah') חנה

From the H., "grace, gracious, merciful"; in the B. (I Samuel), the mother of Samuel. Also spelled Hana(h), Hanna(h). The Greek form is Anna. The Yiddish form is Hene(h). See Hene(h). Nickname is

*Chani* (Chah´ nee) חני.** Other forms are *Chanya* (Chahn yah´) חניה, from the H., "grace of God";**** and *Chanana* (Chah nah nah´) חננה, same meaning.****

**Chanita** (Chah nee´ tah) חניתה
From the H., "spear." Also the name of a place (kibbutz) in Israel in the Galilee. Also spelled Hanita.* Another form is *Chanit* (Chah neet´) חנית, also spelled Hanit.*

**Chartzit** (Chahr tzeet´) חרצית
In H., the name of a flower, chrysanthemum. Also spelled Hartzit and Harzit.*

**Chasida** (Chah see dah´) חסידה
In H., "righteous" or "stork." Also spelled Hasida.* Another form is *Chasuda* (Chah soo dah´) חסודה, in H., "pious," also spelled Hasuda.*

**Chasya** (Chahs´ yah) חסיה
From the H., "protected by God." Also spelled Chasia, Hasia, Hasya.*

**Chatzav** (Chah tzahv´) חצב
In H., the name of a plant, squill. Also the name of a place (moshav) in Israel in the shefelah (coastal plain); used also as a boy's name.****

**Chatzeva** (Chah tzeh vah´) חצבה
From the H., "to hew." Also the name of a place (moshav) in Israel in the Arava.****

**Chava** (Chah vah´) חווה
From the H., "life"; in the B. (Genesis), the first woman that God created, Adam's wife. Also spelled Hava. The English form is Eve.*

**Chavatzelet** (Chah vah tzeh´ leht) חבצלת
In H., the name of a flower, lily.* Another form is *Chavatzelet-Hasharon* (Chah vah tzeh´ leht Hah shah rohn´) חבצלת־השרון, in H., the name of a flower growing in Israel in the Sharon, the coastal plain between Mount Carmel and Jaffa. Also the name of a place (moshav) in the Sharon.****

**Chaviva** (Chah vee´ vah) חביבה
The feminine form of Chaviv or Chovav, in H., "lovely, beloved." Also spelled Haviva.* Another form is *Chavuva* (Chah voo´ vah) חבובה, also spelled Havuva.*

**Chaya** (Chah´ yah) חיה
In H., "life, living, alive." It is a custom to give this name as a middle name to a very sick woman, in hopes she will recover. Also spelled Haya.** Another form is *Chayuta* (Chah yoo´ tah) חיותה, also spelled Hayuta.*

**Chedva** (Chehd' vah) חדווה
In H., "joy." Also spelled Hedva.**

**Cheftzi-Ba** (Chehf' tzee Bah') חפצי־בה
From the H., "she is my desire"; in the B. (II Kings and Isaiah), a
nickname for Zion. Also the name of a place (kibbutz) in Israel in
the Valley of Esdraelon (Jezreel). Also spelled Cheftzibah, Hephziba.*
Another form is *Cheftziya* (Chehf' tzee yah') חפציה, from the H.,
"God is my desire."*

**Chelmonit** (Chehl moh neet') חלמונית
In H., the name of a plant, autumn crocus, from the narcissus
family.**** Another form is *Chelmit* (Chehl meet') חלמית.****

**Chemed** (Cheh' mehd) חמד
In H., "grace, charm, beauty, loveliness." Also the name of a place
(moshav) in Israel in the shefelah (coastal plain). Used also as a boy's
name.** Other forms are *Chemda* (Chehm' dah) חמדה, in H., "desire"
or "precious," also spelled Hemda;* *Chemdiya* (Chehm dee yah')
חמדיה, from the H., "God is my desire," also spelled Chemdia(h),
Hemdia(h);**** *Chemdat* (Chehm daht') חמדת, also the name of a
place in Israel in the Jordan Valley.****

**Chen** (Chehn) חן
In H., "gold, charm, loveliness." Also spelled Hen. Used also as a
boy's name.*** Other forms are *Chenya* (Chehn yah') חניה, in H.,
"grace of God," also spelled Chenia, Henia, Henya;**** *Chinanit*
(Chee nah neet') חיננית, same meaning, also the name of a place in
Israel in Samaria (Shomron) and the name of a flower, daisy;**
*Chenli* (Chehn lee') חן־לי, in H., "I have charm."****

**Chermona** (Chehr moh' nah) חרמונה
The feminine form of Chermon. See Chermon.* Another form is
*Chermonit* (Chehr moh neet') חרמונית.****

**Cherut** (Cheh root') חירות
In H., "freedom, liberty." Also the name of a political party in Israel.
Also the name of a place (moshav) in Israel in the Sharon. A symbolic
name for both girls and boys born on Passover, known as the Feast
of Liberation. Also spelled Herut.** Another form is *Cheruta* (Cheh
roo' tah) חירותה.*

**Chiba** (Chee bah') חיבה
In H., "love, liking." Also spelled Hiba.* Another form is *Chibat-
Tziyon* (Chee baht' Tzee yohn') חיבת־ציון, in H., "love of Zion." The
name of a nineteenth-century movement to rebuild the land of
Israel. Also the name of a place (moshav) in Israel in the Sharon.*

**Chochit** (Choh cheet') חוחית
In H., the name of a singing bird, goldfinch.\*\*\*\*

**Chofit** (Choh feet') חופית
The feminine form of Chof, in H., "coast, shore." Also the name of a place in Israel in the Sharon.\*\*

**Chogla** (Chohg lah') חוגלה
In H., the name of a bird, rock partridge; in the B. (Numbers), one of the five daughters of Tzlafchad. Also the name of a place (moshav) in Israel in the Sharon.\*\*\*\*

**Cholit** (Choh leet') חולית
From the H., "sand dune." Also the name of a place in south Israel.\*\*\*\*

**Chulda** (Chool' dah) חולדה
In H., "polecat"; in the B. (II Kings), a prophetess. Also the name of a place in Israel in the shefelah (coastal plain).\*

# D

### THE HEBREW LETTER 'ד

**Dafna** (Dahf nah') דפנה
In H., the name of a plant, "bay, daphne, laurel." Laurel leaves were worn by Greek and Roman victors. Also the name of a place (kibbutz) in Israel in the Galilee. Also spelled Daphna. Pet form is *Dafi* (Dah' fee) דפי.\*\*\* Other forms with the same meaning are *Dafnit* (Dahf neet') דפנית;\*\*\*\* and *Dafnat* (Dahf naht') דפנת.\*

**Dagan** (Dah gahn') דגן
In H., "corn, grain." Popular for both girls and boys born on Shavuot, known as the Feast of the Harvest.\*\*

**Dalya** (Dahl' yah) דליה
In H., "trailing branch, tendril, bough." Also the name of a place (kibbutz) in north Israel. Also spelled Dalia.\*\* Other forms are *Daliya* (Dah lee yah');\* and *Dalit* (Dah leet') דלית.\*\*\*

**Dana** (Dah' nah) דנה
The feminine form of Dan.\*\*\* Another form is *Danit* (Dah neet') דנית.\*\*\*

**Daniel** (Dah nee ehl') דניאל
From the H., "God is my judge." Used also as a boy's name.\*\*\* Another form is *Daniela* (Dah nee el' lah) דניאלה.\*\*\*

**Danya** (Dahn' yah) דניה
From the H., "judgment of God." Also spelled Dania(h).*

**Darit** (Dah reet') דרית
From the H., "to dwell, live in."****

**Dasi** (Dah' see) דסי
A pet form of Hadassa. See Hadassa.**

**Datya** (Daht' yah) דתיה
In H., "faith in God" or "law of God." Also spelled Datia(h).*

**Davida** (Dah vee' dah) דווידה
The feminine form of David. See David.* Another form is *Davidya*
(Dah veed' yah) דווידיה.*

**Daya** (Dah yah') דיה
In H., the name of a bird of prey, kite.****

**Debbi, Debby** (Deh' bee) דבי
Pet forms of Dvora(h). See Dvora(h).*

**Dganya(h)** (Dgahn' yah) דגניה
From the H., "grain." Also the name of a place in north Israel near
Tiberia. Also spelled Deganiah.* Another form is *Dganit* (Dgah neet')
דגנית, same meaning. Popular name for girls born on Shavuot, known
as the Feast of the Harvest.***

**Dikla(h)** (Deek lah') דיקלה
The feminine form of Dekel. In H., "palm tree"; in the B. (Genesis).
Also spelled Dickla.*** Another form is *Diklit* (Deek leet') דיקלית.****

**Dimona** (Dee moh' nah) דימונה
The name of a city in Israel in the Negev.**

**Dina(h)** (Dee' nah) דינה
From the H., "judgment"; in the B. (Genesis), the daughter of Jacob
and Leah. Also spelled Deena. The English forms are Dena, Deanna.**

**Dita** (Dee' tah) דיתה
A pet form of Yehudit (Judith). See Yehudit.*

**Ditza(h)** (Dee' tzah) דיצה
In H., "joy."*

**Dorin** (Doh reen') דורין
From the H., "gift." Used especially by those who like a H. name with
an English sound.**

**Dorit** (Doh reet') דורית
The feminine form of Dor. From the H., "generation." Also spelled
Dorith, Doritt, Dorrit.*** Other forms are *Dorli* (Dohr' lee) דורלי,

in H., "my generation," used also as a boy's name;**** and *Dora*
(Doh' rah) דורה.*

**Dorona** (Doh roh' nah) דורונה
The feminine form of Doron, in H., "gift."* Another form is *Doronit*
(Doh roh neet') דורונית.****

**Dotan** (Doh tahn') דותן
The name of a valley and a place in Israel in Samaria (Shomron). For
more information, see Dotan in the boys' section.***

**Dovra** (Dohv rah') דוברה
In H., "raft."**** Another form is *Dovrit* (Dohv reet') דוברית.****

**Drora(h)** (Droh' rah) דרורה
The feminine form of Dror; in H., "freedom" and the name of a bird,
swallow.* Other forms are *Drorit* (Droh reet') דרורית;** and *Droriya*
(Droh ree yah') דרוריה, from the H., "God gave me freedom."*

**Dvash** (Dvahsh) דבש
In H., "honey."****

**Dvira** (Dvee rah') דבירה
The feminine form of Dvir. In H., "sanctuary, holy place." Also the
name of a place (kibbutz) in Israel in the Negev.*

**Dvora(h)** (Dvoh rah') דבורה
In H., "bee"; in the B. (Genesis), the nurse of Rivka (Rebecca) and
(Judges) the prophetess-judge; "Song of Deborah" was the latter's
poem of victory over Sisra. Also the name of a place (moshav) in Israel
in the Valley of Esdraélon (Jezreel). The English form is Debora(h).
Pet forms for both English and Hebrew are *Debbi, Debby* (Deh' bee)
דבי.* Another form is *Dvorit* (Dvoh reet') דבורית.****

**Dvoranit** (Dvoh rah neet') דבורנית
In H., the name of a flower, ophrys, or a form of Dvora(h).****

# E

**Edna(h)** (Ehd nah') עדנה
In H., "delicacy, tenderness, gentleness" or "rejuvenator."**

**Efrat** (Ehf raht') אפרת
From the word Efrata, in the B. (Genesis), a name for Beth-Lechem where Rachel, the wife of Jacob, died and was buried. Also the name of a place in Israel near Beth-Lechem. Nickname is *Efi* (Eh' fee) אפי.**

**Eilat** (Ehy laht') אילת
The name of a port town in south Israel named after the ancient city mentioned in the B. Also spelled Elat.**

**Einat** (Ehy naht') עינת
From the H., "to sing" or "fountain." Also the name of a place (kibbutz) in Israel in the Sharon. Also spelled Enat.****

**Einav** (Ehy nahv') עינב
In H., "grape." Also the name of a place in Israel in the Samaria (Shomron). Also spelled Enav.***

**Einya** (Ehyn yah') עיניה
In H., "God's eye." Also spelled Enya.* Another form is *Eina* (Ehy nah') עינה.*

**Eitana** (Ehy tah' nah) איתנה
The feminine form of Eitan, in H., "strong, firm."* Another form is *Eitanit* (Ehy tah neet') איתנית.****

**Ela(h)** (Eh lah') אלה
In H., "terebinth tree" or "goddess." Also spelled Eila(h).** Another form is *Elit* (Eh leet') אלית.****

**Eliana** (Eh lee ah' nah) אליענה
In H., "my God has answered." Popular especially among those who like a H. name with an English sound. Also spelled Elianna.**

**Eliava(h)** (Eh lee ah' vah) אליאבה
The feminine form of Eliav, in H., "my father is God" or "my God was willing."****

**Eliezra** (Eh lee ehz' rah) אליעזרה
The feminine form of Eliezer, in H., "my God has helped."*

**Elinoah** (Eh lee noh' ah) אלינוע
From the H., "my God is moving," meaning "my God is everywhere."****

**Elinoar** (Eh lee noh' ahr) אלינוער
In H., "my God is young" or "God of my youth." Popular especially among those who like a H. name with an English sound.**

**Elinor** (Eh lee nohr') אלינור
From the H., "my God is light," meaning "my light is God." Popular especially among those who like a H. name with an English sound.**

**Eliora** (Eh lee oh' rah) אליאורה
The feminine form of Elior. In H., "my God is light," meaning "my light is God."**

**Eliraz** (Eh lee rahz') אלירז
In H., "my God is my secret."**

**Elisheva** (Eh lee sheh' vah) אלישבע
From the H., "my God is my oath" or "God's oath"; in the B. (Exodus), the wife of Aaron (Aharon). The English form is Elisheba and Elizabeth.**

**Eliya** (Eh lee' yah) אליה
In H., "God is my Lord" or the feminine form of Eliyahu. See Eliyahu. Popular among those who like a H. name with an English sound.**

**Elula** (Eh loo' lah) אלולה
The feminine form of Elul. See Elul.*

**Elza** (Ehl zah') עלזה
The feminine form of Elez, in H., "joy."*

**Emanuela**
See Immanuela.

**Emet** (Eh meht') אמת
In H., "truth, honesty, faithfulness."*

**Emuna(h)** (Eh moo nah') אמונה
In H., "faith, confidence, belief, trust." Emunim is the name of a place (moshav) in Israel in the shefelah (coastal plain).*

**Erela** (Ehr eh' lah) אראלה
The feminine form of Erel, in H., "angel, messenger."**

**Erga** (Ehr gah') ערגה
In H., "longing, panting, yearning."****

**Eshda** (Ehsh dah') אשדה
The feminine form of Eshed. In H., "waterfall, cascade."****

**Eshkar** (Ehsh kahr') אשכר
In H., "present, gift, tribute."****

**Ester** (Ehs tehr′) אסתר
From the Persian, "star, bliss." A symbolic name for girls born on
Purim, because Queen Ester is the central character in "Megillat Ester"
(the scroll of Ester) that is read in the synagogue on the eve of Purim
as well as the next morning. The English form is Esther. Nicknames
are *Essi* (Eh′ see) אסי or *Etti* (Eh′ tee) אתי.** Another form is *Esterit*
(Ehs teh reet′) אסתרית.****

**Etzyona** (Ehtz yoh′ nah) עציונה
The feminine form of Etzyon. See Etzyon.*

**Eve**
See Chava.

**Ezraella** (Ehz rah eh′ lah) עזראלה
The feminine form of Ezra. In H., "God is my help."* Another form is
*Ezriella* (Ehz ree eh′ lah) עזריאלה.*

# F

THE HEBREW LETTER פ'

**Feige** (Fehy′ geh) פייגע
From the Y., "fig."*

**Feigel** (Fehy′ gehl) פייגל
From the Y., "bird."*

**Feya** (Feh yah′) פייה
In H., "fairy."****

**Fradel** (Fray′ dehl) פריידל
From the Y., "joy."*

**Frida** (Free′ dah) פרידה
From the German, "peace."*

**Fruma** (Froo′ mah) פרומה
From the Y., "pious one."*

# G

**Gada** (Gah dah') גדה
In H., "bank of a river, shore, brim of a glass." Or, in a different pronunciation (Gah' dah), the feminine form of Gad, in H., "happiness, luck, fortune."* Other forms are *Gadit* (Gah deet') גדית, same meaning;**** *Gadiela* (Gah dee eh' lah) גדיאלה, from the H., "God is my fortune." Also spelled Gadiella.****

**Gafna** (Gahf nah') (גפנה
The feminine form of Gefen, in H., "vine." Also spelled Gaphna.****
Another form is *Gafnit* (Gahf neet') גפנית.****

**Gal** (Gahl) גל
In H., "wave, billow" or "mound." Used also as a boy's name.***
Other forms with the same meaning are *Gala* (Gah' lah) גלה;* *Gali* (Gah' lee) גלי, in H., "my wave";*** *Galya* (Gahl' yah) גליה, in H., "wave of God";*** and *Galiya* (Gah lee yah') גליה.****

**Galila** (Gah lee' lah) גלילה
The feminine form of Galil. See Galil.* Another form is *Glila(h)* (Glee lah') גלילה.*

**Gamliela** (Gahm lee eh' lah) גמליאלה
The feminine form of Gamliel. See Gamliel. Also spelled Gamliella.*
Other forms are *Gamlielit* (Gahm lee eh leet') גמליאלית;* *Gmula(h)* (Gmoo lah') גמולה, in H., "repaid."*

**Gana** (Gah' nah) גנה
The feminine form of Gan, in H., "garden."**** Other forms are *Ganit* (Gah neet') גנית;** and *Ganya* (Gahn' yah) גניה, in H., "garden of God." Also spelled Gania.****

**Gat** (Gaht) גת
In H., "wine press." Also the name of a place (kibbutz) in south Israel, named after the ancient city mentioned in the B.**

**Gavriel(l)a** (Gahv ree eh' lah) גבריאלה
The feminine form of Gavriel, from the H., "God is my strength." The English form is Gabriel(l)a. Nickname is *Gabi* (Gah' bee) גבי.**

**Gazit** (Gah zeet') גזית
In H., "hewn stone." Also the name of a place (kibbutz) in north Israel.****

**Gershona** (Gehr shoh' nah) גרשונה
The feminine form of Gershon. See Gershon, under Gershom.*

**Geula(h)** (Geh oo' lah) גאולה
In H., "redemption".* Another form is *Goelet* (Goh eh' leht) גואלת.*

**Gidona** (Geed oh' nah) גדעונה
The feminine form of Gidon. See Gidon. Also the name of a place (moshav) in Israel in the Valley of Esdraelon (Jezreel).*

**Gil** (Geel) גיל
In H., "joy." Used also as a boy's name.*** Another form is *Gili* (Gee' lee) גילי or גיל־לי, in H., "my joy."**** Other forms meaning "joy" are *Gila(h)* (Gee lah') גילה;** *Gilat* (Gee laht') גילת, also the name of a place (moshav) in Israel in the Negev;*** *Gilit* (Gee leet') גילית;*** and *Giliya(h)* (Gee lee yah') גיליה.*

**Gilada(h)** (Geel ah' dah) גלעדה
The feminine form of Gilad. See Gilad.*

**Gitel** (Gee' tehl) גיטל, גיטעל
From the Y., "good." Also spelled Gitele, Gittel.* Other forms are *Gute* (Goo' teh) גוטע;* and *Gutel* (Goo' tehl) גוטל.*

**Gitit** (Gee teet') גיתית
The name of an ancient musical instrument mentioned in the Book of Psalms. Also the name of a place (moshav) in central Israel.***

**Golana** (Goh lah' nah) גולנה
The feminine form of Golan. See Golan.* Another form is *Golanit* (Goh lah neet') גולנית.****

**Golda** (Gohl' dah) גולדה
From the English and German, "gold, golden."*

**Goren** (Goh' rehn) גורן
In H., "threshing floor, threshing season, barn, granary." A symbolic name for both girls and boys born on Shavuot, known as the Feast of the Harvest. Also the name of a place (moshav) in Israel in the Galilee.*** Other forms are *Garna* (Gahr nah') גרנה;* and *Garnit* (Gahr neet') גרנית.**

**Grofit** (Groh feet') גרופית
In H., "shoot of olive or sycamore." Also the name of a place (kibbutz) in south Israel.****

**Gurit** (Goo reet') גורית
The feminine form of Gur, in H., "cub, whelp, young lion."****

**Gvat** (Gvaht) גבת
From the H., "mound, height." Also the name of a place (kibbutz) in Israel in the Valley of Esdraelon (Jezreel).**

# H

**Hadar** (Hah dahr') הדר
In H., "splendor, glory, ornament, beauty," "citrus fruit," or, from the H.,
"to honor, to respect." Also the name of a place in Israel near Tel Aviv.
Used also as a boy's name.*** Other forms with the same meaning
are *Hadara* (Hah dah' rah) הדרה;* *Hadarit* (Hah dah reet') הדרית;****
and *Hadura* (Hah doo rah') הדורה, in H., "ornamented."*

**Hadas** (Hah dahs') הדס
In H., the name of a plant, myrtle. A symbolic name for girls born on
Sukkoth, because a branch of a myrtle bush, which has a lovely
smell, is one of the Four Species. Also a short form of Hadassa.***

**Hadassa(h)** (Hah dah' sah) הדסה
From the H., "myrtle"; in the B. (Esther), Hadassa is the H. name of
Queen Esther and therefore this is a symbolic name for girls born
on Purim. Also the name of the organization of American Jewish
Women Zionists operating in Israel. A rural boarding school, Hadasim
in Israel, in the Sharon, is named after the organization. Nickname
is *Dasi* (Dah' see) דסי.**

**Hagar** (Hah gahr') הגר
From the H., "emigrant, stranger"; in the B. (Genesis), the concubine
of Abraham (Avraham) and the mother of Ishmael. This name is
sometimes used for adopted girls.***

**Halleli** (Hah leh lee') הללי
The feminine form of Hillel. See Hillel. Or, in H., "you will praise,
glorify."**** Another form is *Halleli-Ya* (Hah leh lee' Yah) הללי־יה,
in H., "praise God."****

**Harela** (Hahr eh' lah) הראלה
The feminine form of Harel. See Harel.**

**Hedi** (Heh' dee) הדי
In H., "my echo." Popular especially among those who like a H. name
with an English sound.** Other forms are *Hedya* (Hehd' yah) הדיה,
in H., "echo of God," also spelled Hedia(h);**** and *Heda* (Heh dah')
הדה, in H., "her echo."*

**Hene(h)** (Heh' neh) הענע
The Y. form of Chana(h) (Hana[h]). See Chana(h).*

**Hertzeliya** (Hehr tzeh lee' yah) הרצליה
The feminine form of Hertzel. See Hertzel. Also the name of a place

(city) in Israel near Tel Aviv. Also spelled Hertzelia(h).* Other forms
are *Hertzela* (Hehr tzeh' lah) הרצלה;* and *Hertzelina* (Hehr tzeh lee'
nah) הרצלינה.*

**Hila** (Hee lah') הילה
In H., "halo, crown, glory, radiance" or the feminine form of Hillel,
from the H., "to praise" or "to shine." Also the name of a community
settlement in Israel in the Galilee. Also spelled Hilla(h).*** Other
forms with the same meaning are *Hilit* (Hee leet') הילית;*** and
*Hili* (Hee' lee) הילי;*** or, in a different H. spelling, היליא, in H.,
"she is mine."****

**Hillela** (Hee leh' lah) היללה
The feminine form of Hillel. See Hillel.*

**Hinda** (Heen' dah) הינדה
A popular Yiddish name from the German "deer." Another form
is Hindel.*

**Hod** (Hohd) הוד
In H., "glory, splendor, majesty, beauty, grandeur." Hod-Hasharon is the
name of a place in Israel near Tel Aviv. Used also as a boy's name.***
Other forms are *Hodi* (Hoh dee') הודי, in H., "my glory" or "you will
praise";**** and *Hoda* (Hoh dah') הודה, in H., "her glory."*

**Hodaya** (Hoh dah yah') הודיה
In H., "praise, eulogy, thanksgiving."*

# I

**Idan** (Ee dahn') עידן
In H., "time, period, era." Also the name of a place (moshav) in
Israel, in the Arava. Used also as a boy's name.** Another form is
*Idanit* (Ee dah neet') עידנית.****

**Idit** (Ee deet') עידית
In H., "good soil" or "elite, best, choicest, finest."***

**Ilana** (Ee lah' nah) אילנה
The feminine form of Ilan, in H., "tree." A symbolic name for girls
born on Tu b'Shvat, the New Year of the Trees, Arbor Day.** Other
forms are *Ilanit* (Ee lah neet') אילנית, same meaning, also the name
of a very popular singer in Israel;*** and *Ilaniya* (Ee lah nee' yah)
אילניה, in H., "tree of God," also the name of a place (moshav) in
Israel in the Galilee.****

**Ilit** (Ee leet') עילית
In H., "elite."**

**Immanuela** (Ee mah noo eh' lah) עמנואלה
The feminine form of Imanuel. See Imanuel. Also spelled Immanuella,
Emanuela, or Emanuella.*

**Inbal** (Een bahl') ענבל
In H., "clapper, tongue of bell." Also the name of an Israeli troupe
specializing in Asian dance and song.***

**Inbar** (Een bahr') ענבר
In H., the name of a tree, amber. Also the name of a place in Israel in
the Samaria (Shomron).****

**Iris** (Ee' rees) איריס
In H., the name of a plant, iris.***

**Irit** (Ee reet') עירית
In H., the name of a plant, asphodel. Also the name of a place in
Israel in the Samaria (Shomron).*** Also spelled אירית, after the
plant, or, from the H., "light."***

**Ivrit** (Eev reet') עברית
In H., "the Hebrew language" or "a Hebrew female," meaning "an
Israeli female."* Other forms with the same meaning are *Ivrita*
(Eev ree tah') עבריתה;* and *Ivriya* (Eev ree yah') עבריה, also
spelled Ivria(h).*

# J

THE ENGLISH LETTER J

**Jacoba**
The English form of Yaakova. See Yaakova.

**Joela**
The English form of Yoela. See Yoela.

**Jona(h)**
The English form of Yona(h). See Yona(h).

**Jordan**
The English form of Yarden. See Yarden.

**Judith**
The English form of Yehudit. See Yehudit.

# K

THE HEBREW LETTERS 'ק, כ

**Kalanit** (Kah lah neet') כלנית
In H., the name of a plant with colorful flowers, anemone. Also the name of a place (moshav) in Israel in the Galilee, named after the plant common in the area.**

**Kama** (Kah mah') קמה
In H., "standing corn, mature grain." A symbolic name for girls born on Shavuot, the Feast of the Harvest.**

**Kana** (Kah nah') כנה
In H., "understock, plant, shoot" or "base, stand, mounting."****

**Kanarit** (Kah nah reet') כנרית
In H., the name of a singing bird, canary.****

**Kanit** (Kah neet') קנית
In H., the name of a songbird, reed warbler.****

**Karkom** (Kahr kohm') כרכום
In H., the name of a plant, saffron, crocus. Also the name of a place in Israel in the Galilee named after the flower.****

**Karmel**, **Karma**, **Karmela**, **Karmit**, **Karmi**, see Carmel; **Karmia**, **Karmiya**, **Karmiela**, see Carmiya; **Karmelit**, see Carmelit.

**Kedma** (Kehd' mah) קדמה
In H., "eastward." Also the name of a place (rural boarding school) in Israel in the shefelah.* Another form is *Kadima* (Kah dee' mah) קדימה, in H., "onward, forward, eastward." Also the name of a place in Israel in the Sharon.*

**Keren** (Keh' rehn) קרן
In H., "ray, beam," "strength, power, might, dignity, glory," "horn, ram's horn," or "fund." Several names of places in Israel contain this word.*** Other forms are *Karni* (Kahr nee') קרני, in H., "my ray";** *Karnit* (Kahr neet') קרנית, in H., "cornea" (of the eye);** *Koranit* (Koh rah neet') קורנית, in H., the name of a plant, thyme, calaminth; also the name of a place in Israel in the Galilee named after the plant;** *Korenet* (Koh reh' neht) קורנת, in H., "shining, beaming";* *Karin* (Kah reen') קארין, used especially by those who like a H. name with an English sound;*** and *Korin* (Koh reen') קורין, used especially by those who like a H. name with an English or French sound.****

**Keret** (Keh' reht) קרת
In H., "town, city, settlement."**** Another form is *Kirya* (Keer yah')
קריה. Many names of places in Israel contain this word. Hakirya is
the name of the seat of government offices in Israel, also spelled
Kiria(h).****

**Kfira** (Kfee rah') כפירה
The feminine form of Kfir, in H., "young lion." Also the name of a place
in central Israel named after an ancient place mentioned in the B.**

**Kinneret** (Kee neh' reht) כינרת
From the H. word *kinor*, "violin." The name of a lake in north Israel
known as Lake Tiberias, Lake Gennesaret, or the Sea of Galilee. Also
the name of two places in Israel on the Kinneret beach.***

**Kitra** (Keet rah') כיתרה
The feminine form of Keter, in H., "crown."* Other forms with the
same meaning are *Kitrit* (Keet reet') כיתרית;** *Kitron* (Keet rohn')
כיתרון;* and *Kitriya* (Keet ree' yah) כיתריה, in H., "God's crown."*

**Klil** (Kleel) כליל
In H., "crown." Also the name of a place (community settlement)
in Israel in the Galilee, used also as a boy's name. See Kalil.****
Another form is *Klila* (Klee lah') כלילה, the feminine form of Kalil, in
H., "complete, total, perfect" or "crown."****

**Kochava** (Koh chah' vah) כוכבה
The feminine form of Kochav, in H., "star" (in the sky and also in an
artistic and theatrical sense).* Other forms with the same meaning
are *Kochavit* (Koh chah veet') כוכבית;** and *Kochevet* (Koh cheh' veht)
כוכבת.*

**Komemiut** (Koh meh mee yoot') קוממיות
In H., "sovereignty, independence, upright." A symbolic name for
girls born on the Israeli Independence Day or November 29, the
beginning of the War of Independence. Also the name of a place
(moshav) in south Israel.**

**Ktura(h)** (Ktoo rah') קטורה
From the H., "incense"; in the B. (Genesis), Abraham's second wife.
Also the name of a place (kibbutz) and a mountain in Israel in the
Arava.****

# L

### THE HEBREW LETTER ל'

**Leah** (Leh ah') לאה
In H., "to be weary"; in the B. (Genesis), the first wife of Jacob. Also spelled Lea or Leia. The Italian form is Lia.**

**Lee** (Lee) לי
In H., "me, mine, to me, for myself." Used also as a boy's name. Popular especially among those who like a H. name with an English sound. Also spelled Li.***

**Leead** (Lee ahd') ליעד
In H., "eternity is mine." Used also as a boy's name. Also spelled LeeAd; or Liad, LiAd.**

**Leeat** (Lee aht') ליאת
In H., "you are mine." Also spelled Liat.***

**Leeav** (Lee ahv') ליאב
In H., "I have a father," referring to God or to a parent. Used also as a boy's name. Also spelled LeeAv; or Liav, LiAv.**

**Leegal** (Lee gahl') ליגל
In H., "my wave," referring to strength. Also spelled LeeGal; or Ligal, LiGal.**

**Leehi** (Lee' hee) לי־היא, ליהיא
In H., "she is mine." Also spelled LeeHi; or Lihi, LiHi.**** Recently became popular in Israel with a different H. spelling, ליהי, because of the English sound.**

**Leemor** (Lee mohr') לימור
From the H., "to exchange," or a form of the name Mohr, in H., the name of a flower, myrrh. Also spelled Limor.***

**Leenoy** (Lee nohy') לינוי
In H., "my beauty, ornament." Also spelled Linoy.***

**Leeona** (Lee oh' nah) ליאונה
The feminine form of Leeon, in H., "my strength." Also spelled Liona.** Another form is Leeonya (Lee ohn' yah) ליאוניה, in H., "I have God's strength."****

**Leeor** (Lee ohr') ליאור
In H., "my light" or "I have a light." A symbolic name for both boys and girls born on Hanukkah. Also spelled LeeOr; or Lior, LiOr.*** Other forms with the same meaning are *Leeora* (Lee oh' rah) ליאורה,

also spelled Liora;** *Leeorit* (Lee oh reet') ליאורית, also spelled
Liorit;**** and *Leeorya* (Lee ohr' yah) ליאוריה, in H., "God's light
is mine."****

**Leeraz** (Lee rahz') לירז
In H., "I have a secret." Also spelled LeeRaz; or Liraz, LiRaz.***

**Leeron** (Lee rohn') לירון
In H., "my joy, my song." Used also as a boy's name. Also spelled
LeeRon; or Liron, LiRon.*** Other forms with the same meaning
are *Leerona* (Lee roh' nah) לירונה, also spelled Lirona;** *Leeran*
(Lee rahn') לירן, used also as a boy's name and also spelled LeeRan;
or Liran, LiRan.***

**Leetal** (Lee tahl') ליטל
In H., "dew is mine." (Dew is a symbol of hope.) Also spelled Lital.***

**Leeya** (Lee' yah) ליה
In H., "I belong to God." Also spelled Liya.*

**Lehava** (Leh hah vah') להבה
In H., "flame, tongue of fire." A symbolic name for girls born on
Hanukkah or on Lag b'Omer.** Another form is *Lehavit* (Leh hah
veet') להבית, same meaning.****

**Leuma** (Leh oo mah') לאומה
The feminine form of Leumi, in H., "nation."* Another form is *Leeuma*
(Lee' oo mah) ליאומה, in H., "I have a nation" or "my nation." A
symbolic name for girls born on Israeli Independence Day. Also
spelled Liuma.****

**Levana** (Leh vah nah') לבנה
In H., "moon," or, from the H., "white."* Other forms are *Lavnona*
(Lahv noh' nah) לבנונה;* and *Lavnina* (Lahv nee' nah) לבנינה.*

**Levia(h)** (Leh vee ah') לביאה
The feminine form of Lavi, in H., "lioness," or "lioness of God,"* or
לוויה, the feminine form of Levi. See Levi.*

**Levona** (Leh voh nah') לבונה
In H., the name of a tree and a white resin, frankincense.**** Another
form is *Levonat* (Leh voh naht') לבונת.****

**Libi** (Lee' bee) ליבי
In H., "my heart." Also spelled Leebi.** Other forms are *Libiya* (Lee
bee yah') ליביה, in H., "my heart belongs to God";* and *Levavit* (Leh
vah veet') לבבית, in H., "hearty, cordial."****

**Lilach** (Lee lahch') לילך
In H., "you are mine." Also the name of a flower, lilac.*** Another
form is *Lila* (Lee' lah) לילה.*

**Lili** (Lee′ lee) לילי
In H., "mine." Also spelled Leeli.**

**Lilit** (Lee leet′) לילית
In H., "night owl," or "queen of the devils." The English form is
Lilith.****

**Lirit** (Lee reet′) לירית
In H., "lyrical, musical." Also spelled Leerit.****

**Livna** (Leev nah′) ליבנה
From the H., "white," or the feminine form of Livne. See Livne. In the
B. (Joshua), the name of an ancient city.**** Another form is *Livnat*
(Leev naht′) ליבנת.****

**Livya** (Leev yah′) לוויה
In H., "crown, wreath."****

**Lotem** (Loh′ tehm) לוטם
In H., the name of a bush with golden yellow flowers, cistus. Also the
name of a place (kibbutz) in Israel in the Galilee. Used also as a
boy's name.***

**Luz** (Looz) לוז
In H., "almond tree." A symbolic name for both girls and boys born on
Tu b'Shvat, Arbor Day.**** Other forms are *Luza* (Loo zah′) לוזה;*
and *Luziya* (Loo zee yah′) לוזיה, in H., "almond tree of God."****

# M

### THE HEBREW LETTER 'מ

**Maayan** (Mah ah yahn′) מעיין
In H., "spring, fountain, water well, source." Several names of places
in Israel contain this word. Used also as a boy's name.*** Another
form is *Maayana* (Mah ah yah′ nah) מעיינה.**

**Magal** (Mah gahl′) מגל
In H., "scythe." A symbolic name for both girls and boys born on
Shavuot, known as the Feast of the Harvest. Also the name of a place
(kibbutz) in Israel in the Samaria (Shomron).**

**Magena** (Mah geh′ nah) מגנה
The feminine form of Magen. See Magen.* Another form is *Megina*
(Meh gee′ nah) מגינה, the feminine form of Megen. See Megen.*

**Makabit** (Mah cah beet′) מכבית
The feminine form of Macabee. See Macabee.*

**Malka(h)** (Mahl kah') מלכה
In H., "queen." Nicknames are *Mali* (Mah' lee) מלי or *Mili* (Mee' lee)
מילי.** Other forms are *Malkit* (Mahl keet') מלכית, same meaning;
*Malkiya* (Mahl kee yah') מלכיה, in H., "queen of God," also spelled
Malkia(h), also the name of a place (kibbutz) in Israel in the Galilee,
used also as a boy's name; see Malki;**** *Milka* (Meel' kah) מילכה,
in the B. (Genesis), also spelled Milca(h);* and *Malkiela* (Mahl kee
eh' lah) מלכיאלה, in H., "queen of God."*

**Margalit** (Mahr gah leet') מרגלית
In H., "pearl." The H. idiom "mouth drips pearls" describes wisdom.
Margaliot is the name of a place (moshav) and a natural reserve in
Israel in the Galilee.** Another form is *Margalita* (Mahr gah lee'
tah) מרגליתה.*

**Marganit** (Mahr gah neet') מרגנית
In H., the name of a plant, pimpernel, with blue or golden red
flowers.** Another form is *Marganita* (Mahr gah nee' tah) מרגניתה.*

**Marnina** (Mahr nee nah') מרנינה
The feminine form of Marnin, in H., "gladdening, causing joy, joyful."**

**Marva** (Mahr vah') מרווה
In H., the name of a plant, sage, salvia, used for preparing medicines
and spices. Also the name of a place in Israel in the Galilee.****

**Masada** (Mah sah' dah) מסדה
From the H., "basis, foundation" or the English form of Metzada. See
Metzada. Also the name of a place in Israel in the Jordan Valley.*

**Maskit** (Mahs keet') משכית
In H., "mosaic, ornament" or "imagination of the heart."**** Another
form is *Maskiya* (Mahs kee yah') משכיה.*

**Masua** (Mah soo ah') משואה
In H., "beacon, fire signal, signal light." A symbolic name for girls born
on Rosh Hodesh, the new moon, because in the past Jews used to light
beacons on the mountains to announce the beginnings of the months.
Also the name of a place (moshav) in Israel in the Jordan Valley.****

**Matana** (Mah tah nah') מתנה
In H., "present, gift."* Another form is *Matat* (Mah taht') מתת, same
meaning. Also the name of a place and a mountain in Israel in the
Galilee.**

**Maya** (Mah' yah) מיה, מאיה
A modern H. name after the month, May, used especially by those
who like a H. name with an English sound. Also spelled Maia.***

**Mazal** (Mah zahl') מזל
In H., "good luck, fortune, fate" or "star, planet."* Other forms with
the same meaning are *Mazala* (Mah zah' lah) מזלה;* and *Mazalit*
(Mah zah leet') מזלית.*

**Mechola** (Mch choh lah') מחולה
In H., "dance." Also the name of a place (moshav) in Israel in the
Jordan Valley, named after the ancient city mentioned in the B.****

**Medina** (Meh dee nah') מדינה
In H., "state, country." A symbolic name for girls born on the Israeli
Independence Day.*

**Meira** (Meh ee' rah) מאירה
The feminine form of Meir, in H., "lighting, shining."** Another form
is *Meirit* (Meh ee reet') מאירית.**

**Meirona** (Mehy roh' nah) מירונה
The feminine form of Meron. See Meron.**

**Meital** (Mehy tahl') מיטל
In H., "dew drops."***

**Meitar** (Mehy tahr') מיתר
In H., "string, cord, sinew." Used also as a boy's name.****

**Menachema** (Meh nah cheh' mah) מנחמה
The feminine form of Menachem. See Menachem.* Other forms are
*Menachemya* (Men nah chehm' yah) מנחמיה, in H., "comfort of God,"
also the name of a place in Israel in the Jordan Valley, also spelled
Menahemia(h);* and *Menachamiya* (Meh nah chah mee' yah) מנחמיה,
same meaning, also spelled Menahamia(h).*

**Menora(h)** (Meh noh rah') מנורה
In H., "lamp, candlestick, candelabrum," a symbolic name for girls
born on Hanukkah. Also the name of a place in Israel in the shefelah
(coastal plain).*

**Menucha** (Meh noo chah') מנוחה
The feminine form of Manoach, in H., "rest, resting place, peace,
quiet, calm." Also the name of a place (moshav) in south Israel.*

**Meora(h)** (Meh oh rah') מאורה
The feminine form of Maor, in H., "light, brightness." A symbolic
name for girls born on Hanukkah, the Feast of Lights.** Another
form is *Meorit* (Meh oh reet') מאורית, same meaning.**

**Merav** (Mehy' rahv) מירב
From the H., "to increase"; in the B. (I Samuel), the eldest daughter
of King Saul. Also the name of a place (kibbutz) in north Israel,
named after King Saul's daughter. Also spelled *Meirau.***

**Merchavya** (Mehr chahv′ yah) מרחביה

In H., "space of God, expanse of God." Also the name of two places (kibbutz and moshav) in Israel in the Valley of Esdraelon (Jezreel). Also spelled Merchavia(h).* Another form is *Merchava* (Mehr chah′ vah) מרחבה.*

**Meroma** (Meh roh mah′) מרומה

The feminine form of Marom, in H., "height, high place." Also spelled Meiroma.**

**Metuka** (Meh too kah′) מתוקה

In H., "sweet."* Another form is *Mitka* (Meet kah′) מיתקה.****

**Metzada** (Meh tzah dah′) מצדה

In H., "fort, stronghold." Metzada is the name of a fortress in Israel on the west shore of the Dead Sea, where the last Jewish fighters held out after the Roman conquest of Jerusalem. Also spelled Mezadah. The English forms are Masada and Massadah.**** Another form is *Metzuda* (Meh tzoo dah′) מצודה. Several names of places in Israel contain this word.****

**Mevorechet** (Meh voh reh′ cheht) מבורכת

The feminine form of Mevorach, in H., "blessed."* Another form is *Mevoracha* (Meh voh rah chah′) מבורכה.*

**Michaela** (Mee chah eh′ lah) מיכאלה

The feminine form of Michael. See Michael. Nickname is *Miki* (Mee′ kee) מיקי.**

**Michal** (Mee chahl′) מיכל

From the H., "who is like God?"; in the B. (II Samuel), the daughter of King Saul, one of King David's wives.*** Another form is *Mika* (Mee′ kah) מיקה, used by those who like a H. name with an English sound.**

**Michmoret** (Meech moh′ reht) מיכמורת

In H., "fishing net." Also the name of a place (moshav) in Israel on the Sharon beach.****

**Mili** (Mee′ lee) מילי

In H., "who is for me?" Also spelled Millie. Used especially by those who like a H. name with an English sound.**

**Mimi** (Mee′ mee) מימי

Nickname for Miryam, see Miryam; or a name without any meaning used especially by those who like a H. name with an English sound.**

**Miryam** (Meer yahm′) מרים

From the H., "sea of bitterness," meaning "a great sorrow"; in the B. (Exodus), the sister of Moses and Aaron. The English spelling is

Miriam. The English form is Mary. The Yiddish forms are Maryasha and Mishke. Nickname is *Miri* (Mee' ree) מירי.* Other forms with the same meaning are *Mira* (Mee' rah) מירה;** *Mirit* (Mee reet') מירית;** and *Marit* (Mah reet') מרית.****

**Mishala** (Meesh ah lah') מישאלה
In H., "request, desire, wish."*****

**Moledet** (Moh leh' deht) מולדת
In H., "birthplace, homeland." A symbolic name for girls born on the Israeli Independence Day. Also the name of a place (moshav) in Israel in the Galilee.**** Another form is *Molada* (Moh lah dah') מולדה.*

**Mor** (Mohr) מור
In H., the name of a plant, myrrh, used for preparing perfume and incense. Used also as a boy's name. Also spelled Mohr, Moer.***

**Morag** (Moh rahg') מורג
In H., "threshing sledge." A symbolic name for both girls and boys born on Shavuot, known as the Feast of the Harvest. Also the name of a place (moshav) in Israel in the Gaza Strip.****

**Moran** (Moh rahn') מורן
In H., the name of an evergreen plant, viburnum, that grows in thickets. Also the name of a place (kibbutz) in Israel in the Galilee named after this bush. Used also as a boy's name.*** Another form is *Moranit* (Moh rah neet') מורנית, in H., also "a spear."****

**Morasha** (Moh rah shah') מורשה
In H., "possession, heritage, legacy."* Another form is *Moreshet* (Moh reh' sheht) מורשת, also the name of a community settlement in Israel in the Galilee.****

**Moriela** (Moh ree eh' lah) מוריאלה
The feminine form of Moriel, in H., "God is my teacher, my guide."*****

**Moriya** (Moh ree yah') מוריה
From the H., "teacher"; in the B. (Genesis), the name of the mountain where God told Abraham to sacrifice his son. Also spelled Moria(h).**

# N

**Na'a(h)** (Nah ah') נאה
In H., "beautiful, good-looking, fine" or "dwelling, pasture, meadow, natural beauty spot."****

**Naama(h)** (Nah ah mah') נעמה
The feminine form of Noam, in H., "loveliness, gracefulness, pleasant-ness, charm, kindness, tenderness"; in the B. (I Kings). Also the name of a place in the Jordan Valley.*** Other forms with the same meanings are *Naamana* (Nah ah mah' nah) נעמנה;* *Naamiya* (Nah ah mee' yah) נעמיה, also spelled Naamia(h);* *Naamit* (Nah ah meet') נעמית, also the name of a bird, ostrich;**** and *Noam* (Noh' ahm) נועם, also the name of a place (moshav) in south Israel, used also as a boy's name.***

**Naara(h)** (Nah ah rah') נערה
In H., "girl, maiden, young woman"; in the B. (I Chronicles).* Another form is *Naarit* (Nah ah reet') נערית.****

**Nachala** (Nah chah lah') נחלה
In H., "estate, property, possession, inheritance." Also the name of a place (moshav) in south Israel.* Another form is *Nachalat* (Nah chah laht') נחלת.*

**Naomi** (Nah oh mee') נעומי
From the H., "beautiful, tender, gentle, lovely"; in the B. (Ruth), the mother-in-law of Ruth. A symbolic name for girls born on Shavuot, when the Bible story of Ruth the Moabitess is read in the synagogue. Nickname is *Nomi* (Noh' mee) נומי.**

**Narkis** (Nahr kees') נרקיס
In H., the name of a flower, narcissus. Also the name of a place in Israel in Samaria (Shomron) named after the plant.**** Another form is *Narkisit* (Nahr kee seet') נרקיסית.****

**Natalie** (Nah tah lee') נטלי
From the H., "he gave me" or a modern name without a meaning, used especially by those who like a H. name with an English or French sound.***

**Natana** (Nah tah' nah) נתנה
The feminine form of Natan, in H., "he gave."* Other forms are *Nataniela* (Nah tah nee eh' lah) נתניאלה, in H., "gift of God," also

spelled Nataniella;* *Netanela* (Neh tahn eh' lah) נתנאלה, the feminine
form of Netanel, also spelled Netanella, also the name of a famous
singer in Israel;** and *Natanya* (Nah tahn yah') נתניה.*

**Nava** (Nah vah') נאווה
In H., "pretty, desirable."** Another form is *Navit* (Nah veet') נאווית.****

**Nechama** (Neh chah' mah) נחמה
In H., "comfort, consolation" or "restoration of Israel."* Other forms
with the same meaning are *Nechamit* (Neh chah meet') נחמית;****
*Nachmaniya* (Nahch mah nee' yah) נחמניה, the feminine form of
Nachman, see Nachman;* *Nachmanit* (Nahch mah neet') נחמנית;****
*Nachuma* (Nah choo mah') נחומה, the feminine form of Nachum, see
Nachman;* and *Nachumit* (Nah choo meet') נחומית.*

**Nedira** (Neh dee rah') נדירה
The feminine form of Nadir. See Nadir.*

**Nediva** (Neh dee vah') נדיבה
The feminine form of Nadav. See Nadav.*

**Neemana** (Neh eh mah nah') נאמנה
The feminine form of Ne'eman. See Ne'eman.* Another form is
*Neemenet* (Neh eh meh' neht) נאמנת.*

**Negba** (Nehg' bah) נגבה
The feminine form of Negev. See Negev. Also the name of a place
(kibbutz) in central Israel.**

**Nehara** (Neh hah rah') נהרה
In H., "light, brightness, daylight" or "a small river."*** Other forms
with the same meaning are *Nehora* (Neh hoh rah') נהורה, also the
name of a place in central Israel;* *Nehira* (Neh hee rah') נהירה;*
*Nehura* (Neh hoo rah') נהורה;* and *Nohar* (Noh' hahr) נוהר, used
also as a boy's name. See Nahir.**

**Neila(h)** (Neh ee lah') נעילה
In H., "locking, shutting, closing." The name of the final service on
Yom Kippur, the Day of Atonement. A symbolic name for girls born
on that day. Also spelled Neilla.*

**Neima** (Neh ee mah') נעימה
In H., "melody, tune" or "pleasant, lovely."****

**Neli** (Neh' lee) נלי
From the girl's name Nili. See Nili. Or a H. name without any meaning,
used by those who look for an English or French sound.** Another
form is *Nela* (Neh' lah) נלה.**

**Neora** (Neh oh rah') נאורה
The feminine form of Naor. See Naor.* Other forms are *Naora* (Nah oh rah'); and *Neira* (Neh ee rah') נאירה.*

**Nera** (Neh rah') נרה
The feminine form of Ner, in H., "candle, light." A symbolic name for girls born on Hanukkah, the Feast of Lights.* Other forms are *Nerit* (Neh reet') נרית, same meaning;** *Neriya* (Neh ree yah') נריה, in H., "light of God" or "God is my candle, my light," used also as a boy's name (see Ner), also spelled Neria(h);** and *Ner-Li* (Nehr' Lee) נר-לי, in H., "I have a candle, I have light" or "the candle, light is mine."****

**Neshama** (Neh shah mah') נשמה
In H., "soul, spirit."*

**Nesicha** (Neh see chah') נסיכה
In H., "princess."****

**Nesya** (Nehs yah') נסיה
In H., "miracle of God," also spelled Nesia(h).* Other forms are *Nessiya* (Neh see yah');* and *Nissit* (Nee seet') ניסית.****

**Neta** (Neh' tah) נטע
In H., "seedling, sapling, plant, plantation." A symbolic name for girls born on Tu b'Shvat, the New Year of the Trees, Arbor Day, when Israeli children plant trees. Also the name of a plantation ranch in Israel in the shefelah (coastal plain).*** Other forms are *Netti* (Neht ee') נטעי, in H., "my plant";* *Netia* (Neh tee ah') נטיעה, in H., "planting";* *Netua* (Neh too ah') נטועה, same meaning, also the name of a place (moshav) in Israel in the Galilee;* and *Netali* (Neh tah lee') נטעלי, in H., "I have a plant," used especially by those who like a H. name with an English or French sound.***

**Netiva** (Neh tee' vah) נתיבה
The feminine form of Nativ. See Nativ.*

**Nevet** (Neh' veht) נבט
In H., "bud," a symbolic name for girls born on Tu b'Shvat, the New Year of the Trees. Nevatim is the name of a place (moshav) in Israel in the Negev.**

**Nevona(h)** (Neh voh nah') נבונה
The feminine form of Navon. See Navon.*

**Nili** (Nee' lee) נילי
An acrostic of the H. words נצח ישראל לא ישקר; in English, "the Everlasting of Israel will not lie," from the B. (I Samuel). This was the

name of a group of Jews in Palestine in World War I who worked for Allied intelligence in the hope of ensuring future Jewish settlement. Also the name of a place in Israel in Samaria (Shomron).\*\*\* Another form is *Nilit* (Nee leet´) נילית.\*\*\*\*

**Nima** (Nee mah´) נימה
In H., "thread, hair, cord, filament, string" or "tune, melody."\* Another form is *Nimi* (Nee´ mee) נימי.\*

**Nina** (Nee nah´) נינה
In H., "great-granddaughter." Also spelled Neena.\*\*\*\*

**Nira** (Nee´ rah) נירה
The feminine form of Nir, in H., "furrow, plowed field." A symbolic name for girls born on Tu b'Shvat, the New Year of the Trees, Arbor Day.\*\* Other forms are *Nirit* (Nee reet´) נירית, in H., the name of a plant, ridolfia, also the name of a place in Israel, in the Sharon, named after the plant;\*\*\* *Nirela* (Neer eh´ lah) ניראלה, the feminine form of Nirel (see Nir), in H., "cultivated field of God," also spelled Nirella;\*\* and *Niran* (Nee rahn´) נירן, same meaning, also the name of a place (kibbutz) in Israel in the Jordan Valley. Used also as a boy's name.\*\*

**Nissana** (Nee sah´ nah) ניסנה
The feminine form of Nissan, from the H., "miracle," the name of the first month of the Jewish calendar, when we celebrate Passover (Pesach). A symbolic name for girls born in this month.\* Another form is *Nissanit* (Nee sah neet´) ניסנית, also the name of a place (moshav) in Israel in the shefelah (coastal plain) named after the Sinai peninsula when it was returned to Egypt.\*\*\*\*

**Nitza(h)** (Nee tzah´) ניצה
In H., "bud," also spelled Niza(h). A symbolic name for girls born on Tu b'Shvat, Arbor Day.\*\* Other forms with the same meaning are *Nitzan* (Nee tzahn´) ניצן, used also as a boy's name;\*\*\* *Nitzana* (Nee tzah´ nah) ניצנה, also the name of a place (moshav) in Israel in the Negev named after an ancient place;\*\* *Nitzanit* (Nee tzah neet´) ניצנית;\*\* *Nitzaniya* (Nee tzah nee´ yah) ניצניה, in H., "bud of God";\* and *Nitzatya* (Nee tzaht´ yah) ניצתיה.\*\*\*\*

**Nitzchiya** (Neetz chee yah´) נצחיה
The feminine form of Netzach, in H., "eternity, forever" or, from the H., "victory."\* Other forms with the same meaning are *Nitzcha* (Neetz chah´) ניצחה;\* *Nitzchit* (Neetz cheet´) נצחית;\*\*\*\* and *Nitzchona* (Neetz choh´ nah) נצחונה.\*

**Niva** (Nee' vah) ניבה
The feminine form of Niv, in H., "expression, phrase, idiom, dialect."
Also the name cf an agricultural ranch in Israel in the shefelah
(coastal plain).*** Other forms are *Nivit* (Nee veet') ניבית, same
meaning;** and *Nivi* (Nee' vee) ניבי, in H., "my expression."**

**Noa** (Noh' ah) נועה
From the H., "movement, motion"; in the B. (Numbers). This name
is very popular in Israel, but it might be confusing in the United
States, because it sounds like Noah, the English form of the masculine
name Noach.***

**Nodeleya** (Noh deh leh yah') נודליה
In H., "we will praise God."****

**Nofit** (Noh feet') נופית
The feminine form of Nof, in H., "panorama, landscape, scene" or
"top of tree." Also spelled Nophit.*** Another form is *Nofiya* (Noh fee
yah') נופיה, in H., "God's landscape," also spelled Nophiya.****

**Noga** (Noh' gah) נוגה
In H., "brightness, light, splendor," and the H. name of the planet
Venus. Also the name of a place (moshav) in south Israel.*** Other
forms with the same meaning are *Nogahat* (Noh gah' haht) נוגהת;****
*Negoha* (Neh goh hah') נגוהה;**** and *Nogit* (Noh geet') נוגית.****

**Noit** (Noh eet') נואית
In H., the name of a plant, noea.****

**Noy** (Nohy) נוי
In H., "beautiful, ornament." Used also as a boy's name. Also spelled
Noi.** Another form is *Noya* (Noy' yah) נויה, in H., "God's beauty."
Also spelled Noia.***

**Nufar** (Noo fahr') נופר
In H., the name of a water plant, yellow water lily. Also spelled Nuphar.
Used also as a boy's name.**** Other forms with the same meaning
are *Nofer* (Noh' fehr);**** and *Nofrit* (Nohf reet') נופרית.****

**Nurit** (Noo reet') נורית
In H., the name of a plant with red or yellow flowers, buttercup, ranun-
culus. Also the name of a place in north Israel named after the plant.***

# O

### THE HEBREW LETTERS 'ע, 'א

**Odeda** (Oh deh' dah) עודדה
The feminine form of Oded, from the H., "to encourage."** Another
form is *Odedya* (Oh dehd' yah) עודדיה, in H., "encouraged by God."*

**Odelya** (Oh dehl' yah) אודליה
In H., "I will thank God, I will praise God." Also spelled Odelia(h).**
Other forms with the same meaning are *Odiya* (Oh dee' yah) אודיה;*
and *Odit* (Oh deet') אודית.****

**Ofira** (Oh fee' rah) אופירה
The feminine form of Ofir, in H., "gold," and the name of a place
mentioned in the B. It was also the name of a place in south Israel
in the Sinai peninsula before it was returned to Egypt. Also spelled
Ophira.***

**Ofra** (Ohf rah') עופרה
The feminine form of Ofer, in H., "young deer." Also the name of a
place in Israel in the Samaria (Shomron) named after the ancient
city mentioned in the B. The name of a famous Israeli singer, Ofra
Haza. Also spelled Ophra.*** Other forms with the same meaning
are *Ofrat* (Ohf raht') עופרת;**** and *Ofrit* (Ohf reet') עופרית.****

**Ogenya** (Oh gehn' yah) עוגניה
In H., "anchor of God" or "God is my anchor," meaning "my helper,
my savior."*

**Ohada** (Oh hah' dah) אוהדה
The feminine form of Ohad, in H., "love, beloved."*

**Ohela** (Oh heh' lah) אוהלה
The feminine form of Ohel, in H., "tent."* Another form is *Ohala*
(Oh hah lah').*

**Omrit** (Ohm reet') עומרית
The feminine form of Omer, in H., "sheaf of corn." A symbolic name
for girls born during the period of Counting the Omer (forty-nine
days between the end of the first day of Passover and Shavuot), on
Lag b'Omer, or on Shavuot, the Feast of the Harvest.**

**Or** (Ohr) אור
In H., "light, brightness." A symbolic name for both girls and boys
born on Hanukkah, the Feast of Lights.** Other forms are *Orah*
(Oh' rah) אורה, same meaning, also the name of a place (moshav) in
Israel near Jerusalem;** *Orya* (Ohr yah') אוריה, in H., "light of God";*

*Orit* (Oh reet') אורית, in H., "light";*** *Orli* (Ohr' lee) אורלי or אור־לי,
in H., "light is mine" or "you are my light," also spelled Or-lee or
Orlee;*** *Orlit* (Ohr leet') אורלית, same meaning;**** *Or-Tal* (Ohr
Tahl') אור־טל or אורטל, in H., "morning dew," also the name of a
place (kibbutz) in Israel in Ramat Hagolan, used also as a boy's
name;*** *Or-Gal* (Ohr Gahl) אורגל, in H., "wave of light";**** and
*Orpaz* (Ohr pahz') אורפז, in H., "sparkling light."****

**Orna** (Ohr' nah) אורנה
The feminine form of Oren, in H., "pine tree."** Other forms with
the same meaning are *Ornat* (Ohr naht') אורנת;**** *Ornina* (Ohr
nee' nah) אורנינה;**** and *Ornit* (Ohr neet') אורנית,** in a different
H. spelling, אורנע, in H., "moving light."****

**Oshra** (Ohsh rah') אושרה
The feminine form of Osher, in H., "happiness, good fortune."**
Another form is *Oshrat* (Ohsh raht') אושרת.**

**Osnat** (Ohs naht') אוסנת
In the B. (Genesis), the wife of Joseph. Also spelled Asnat.**

**Ozera** (Oh zeh' rah) עוזרה
The feminine form of Ozer, in H., "helper."*

# P

### THE HEBREW LETTER פ'

**Paz** (Pahz) פז
In H., "gold, golden, sparkling." Also the name of the oil distributors
in Israel. Used also as a boy's name.*** Other forms with the same
meaning are *Pazit* (Pah zeet') פזית;*** and *Pazya* (Pahz yah') פזיה,
in H., "God's gold."****

**Pdut** (Pdoot) פדות
In H., "redemption, liberty." A symbolic name for both girls and boys
born on Passover, the Feast of Liberation.** Other forms are *Pduya*
(Pdoo yah') פדויה, in H., "redeemed," also spelled Pduia;* and *Poda(h)*
(Poh dah') פודה, in H., "redeemer."*

**Pe'er** (Peh ehr') פאר
In H., "glory, luxury, magnificence." Used also as a boy's name.**
Other forms are *Pe'era* (Peh eh rah') פארה, same meaning;* and
*Pe'er-Lee* (Peh ehr' Lee) פאר־לי, in H., "my glory," or "I am adorned,"
also spelled Pe'er-Li.****

**Perach** (Peh' rahch) פרח

In H., "flower, blossom."**** Other forms are *Pirchit* (Peer cheet')
פרחית, same meaning;**** and *Pirchiya* (Peer chee' yah) פרחיה, in
H., "blossoming of God," meaning "prosperity, blessing of God."*

**Peri** (Peh' ree) פרי

From the H., "fruit," in many meanings: product, result, offspring,
profit, gain. Popular especially among those who like a H. name with
an English sound. Used also as a boy's name.**

**Plia(h)** (Plee ah') פליאה

From the H., "miracle, wonder."* Another form is *Pileet* (Peel eet')
פילאית, in H., "miraculous, wonderful."****

**Pnina(h)** (Pnee nah') פנינה

In H., "pearl" or "coral"; in the B. (I Samuel). Also spelled Penina(h).*
Another form is *Pninit* (Pnee neet') פנינית.**

**Poriya** (Poh ree yah') פוריה

In H., "fruitful, fertile." Also the name of a place and a hospital in
Israel in the Galilee.** Other forms with the same meaning are *Pora*
(Poh rah') פורה;* and *Porit* (Poh reet') פורית.****

**Priela** (Pree eh' lah) פריאלה

The feminine form of Priel, in H., "fruit of God."** Another form is
*Poriela* (Poh ree eh' lah) פוריאלה, the feminine form of Poriel (see
Priel), in H., "God is my fruitfulness."****

**Pua(h)** (Poo ah') פועה

From the H., "to groan, bleat"; in the B. (Exodus), a Hebrew midwife.**

# R

### The Hebrew Letter ר'

**Raanana** (Rah ah nah' nah) רעננה

The feminine form of Raanan. In H., "fresh, green, flourishing" or
"invigorated." Also the name of a city in Israel in the Sharon near Tel
Aviv.* Another form is *Raananit* (Rah ah nah neet') רעננית.****

**Rachel** (Rah chehl') רחל

In H., "ewe, sheep"; in thc B. (Genesis), the sister of Leah and the
wife of Jacob. Nicknames are *Racheli* (Rah cheh' lee) רחלי, *Cheli*
(Cheh' lee) חלי, or *Reli* (Reh' lee) רלי. Also spelled Rahel. The English
form is Rachelle. The English nicknames are Rae, Ray, and Raye.

Rachel is the name of a place (kibbutz) in Israel near Jerusalem,
named after Rachel's grave, which is nearby.** Other forms with
the same meaning are *Rechela* (Reh cheh lah') רחלה; and *Recheiit*
(Reh cheh leet') רחלית.****

**Raizel** (Rahy' zehl) רייזעל
From the Y., "rose." Other forms are Raisa, Raise, Raisel, Raizi,
Rosina(h), Rosita, Ros, and Rosalyn.*

**Rakefet** (Rah keh' feht) רקפת
In H., the name of a plant that grows in rocky places, cyclamen.**

**Rama** (Rah mah') רמה
In H., "height, high place, highlands" or "standard, level, degree";
in the B. (Nehemiah), the name of a place. Many names of settle-
ments in Israel contain the word Ramat or Ramot.** In a different
pronunciation (Rah' mah), the feminine form of Ram. See Ram.**
Other forms with the same meaning are *Ramit* (Rah meet') רמית;***
*Roma* (Roh' mah) רומה;* *Romema* (Roh meh' mah) רוממה, also the
name of a big neighborhood in Jerusalem;* *Romemit* (Roh meh
meet') רוממית;* *Romemiya* (Roh meh mee yah') רוממיה;* *Romit* (Roh
meet') רומית;* *Romiya* (Roh mee yah')*; and *Rumya* (Room yah'),
both spelled רומיה, in H., "heights of God."*

**Rani** (Rah' nee) רני
The feminine form of Ran, in H., "she is singing."** Other forms
with the same meaning are *Ranit* (Rah neet') רנית;*** *Ranita* (Rah
nee' tah) רניתה;* and *Ranya* (Rahn' yah) רניה, in H., "song of God,"
also spelled Rania(h).****

**Ravid** (Rah veed') רביד
In H., "necklace, chain." Also the name of a place (kibbutz) and a
mountain in Israel in the Galilee. Used also as a boy's name.***

**Raya** (Rah' yah) רעיה
In H., "female friend" or "married woman, lady."** Other forms
with the same meaning are *Reah* (Reh ah') רעה;* and *Reit* (Reh
eet') רעית.**

**Raz** (Rahz) רז
In H., "secret, mystery." Used also as a boy's name.*** Another form
is *Razi* (Rah' zee) רזי, in H., "my secret."*** Other forms that mean,
in H., "secret of God" or "God is my secret" are *Razel* (Rahz ehl')
רזאל;** *Raziela* (Rah zee eh' lah) רזיאלה;* and *Raziya* (Rah zee yah')
רזיה;**** *Razli* (Rahz' lee) רזלי;** *Razili* (Rah zee' lee) רזילה, in H.,
"the secret is mine," also spelled Razlee or Razilee;**** and *Razit*
(Rah zeet') רזית, in H., "a small secret".**

**Re'ema** (Reh eh mah') ראמה
The feminine form of Re'em, in H., "buffalo."\* Another form is *Reuma*
(Reh oo mah') ראומה, in the B. (Genesis).\*

**Refaela** (Reh fah eh' lah) רפאלה
The feminine form of Refael. See Refael. Also spelled Rephaela.\*
Another form is *Refiya* (Reh fee yah') רפיה, same meaning.\*

**Regba** (Rehg' bah) רגבה
The feminine form of Regev. See Regev. Also the name of a place
(moshav) in Israel in the Galilee.\*

**Renana** (Reh nah nah') רננה
In H., "song, exultation, prayer, chant."\*\*\* Other forms with the
same meaning are *Renanit* (Reh nah neet') רננית;\*\*\* and *Renina*
(Reh nee' nah) רנינה.\*

**Reut** (Reh oot') רעות
In H., "friendship, companionship." Also spelled Re'ut, Reout.\*\*\*

**Reuvena** (Reh oo veh' nah) ראובנה
The feminine form of Reuven. See Reuven.\* Another form is *Reuvit*
(Reh oo veet') ראובית.\*

**Revaya** (Reh vah yah') רוויה
In H., "saturation." Also the name of a place (moshav) in north Israel
in an area filled with fountains.\*\*\*\* Another form is *Ravit* (Rah
veet') רווית.\*\*

**Revital** (Reh vee tahl') רוויטל
In H., "be saturated with dew."\*\*\* Another form is *Ravital* (Rah vee
tahl') רביטל, in H., "my master is my dew," referring to God.\*\*\*\*

**Reviva** (Reh vee' vah) רביבה
The feminine form of Raviv. See Raviv.\*

**Rimon** (Ree mohn') רימון
In H., "pomegranate." For further explanation, see Rimon in the
boys' section.\*\*\* Other forms are *Rimona* (Ree moh' nah) רימונה,
the feminine form of Rimon;\*\* and *Ramona* (Rah moh' nah) רמונה,
used especially by those who like a H. name with an English sound.\*\*

**Rina** (Ree nah') רינה
In H., "singing, song, joy, exultation." Also spelled Rinna.\*\* Other
forms are *Rinat* (Ree naht') רינת, same meaning;\*\*\* and *Rinatya*
(Ree naht yah') רינתיה, in H., "song of God" or "joy of God," also the
name of a place (moshav) in Israel in the shefelah (coastal plain).\*\*\*\*

**Rishona** (Ree shoh nah′) ראשונה
In H., "the first one." Sometimes used for the first daughter in the family.*

**Riva** (Ree vah′) ריבה
In H., "maiden, lass, damsel, wench." Sometimes used as a modern form of Rivka. Nickname is *Rivi* (Ree′ vee) ריבי.**

**Rivka** (Reev kah′) רבקה
In the B. (Genesis), the wife of Isaac and the mother of Jacob and Esau. Nicknames are *Rivi* (Ree′ vee) ריבי and *Riki* (Ree′ kee) ריקי. Also spelled Rivca or Rivcka. The English form is Rebecca.** Another form is *Rivkit* (Reev keet′) רבקית, same meaning.****

**Roni** (Roh′ nee) רוני
In H., "my song" or "my joy." Used also as a boy's name.*** Other forms are *Rona* (Roh′ nah) רונה, in H., "song, joy," used especially by those who like a H. name with an English sound;*** *Ronela* (Rohn eh′ lah) רונאלה, in H., "song of God" or "joy of God," also spelled Ronella;**** *Ronena* (Roh neh nah′) רוננה, in H., "song" or "prayer";**** *Ronit* (Roh neet′) רונית, in H., "song," also spelled Ronnit;*** *Roniya* (Roh nee yah′) רוניה, in H., "song, joy of God";**** and *Ronli* (Rohn′ lee) רונלי, in H., "joy is mine" or "you are my joy."*****

**Rotem** (Roh′ tehm) רותם
In H., the name of a desert plant, retama. Used also as a boy's name. Retamim is the name of a place (kibbutz) in Israel in the Negev, named after the plant.***

**Ruchama** (Roo chah′ mah) רוחמה
The feminine form of Rachamim, in H., "comfort, compassion"; in the B. (Hosea). Also the name of a place (kibbutz) in Israel in the shefelah (coastal plain). Also spelled Ruhama.** Other forms are *Rachmona* (Rahch moh′ nah) רחמונה, same meaning;* and *Rachmiela* (Rahch mee eh′ lah) רחמיאלה, in H., "God is my comforter."*

**Rut** (Root) רות
From the H., "friendship"; in the B. (Ruth), Rut the Moabitess was not born Jewish, married Naomi's son, became Jewish, and followed the rules of the Torah faithfully even after the death of her husband. A symbolic name for girls born on Shavuot, when the Book of Ruth is read in the synagogues. The English form is Ruth. Nickname is *Ruti* (Roo′ tee) רותי.***

# S

**Sagit** (Sah geet') שגית
From the H., "exalted, lofty, sublime."****

**Sahar** (Sah' hahr) סהר
In H., "moon." Used also as a boy's name.**

**Salit** (Sahl eet') סלעית
The feminine form of Sela, in H., "rock, cliff," and the name of
a singing bird, wheatear, that inhabits south Israel in Samaria
(Shomron).**** Another form is *Silit* (Seel eet') סילעית.****

**Sapir** (Sah peer') ספיר
In H., the name of a precious stone, sapphire. Also the name of a
place in Israel in the Arava. Used also as a boy's name.** Other
forms with the same meaning are *Sapira* (Sah pee rah') ספירה;**
and *Sapirit* (Sah pee reet') ספירית.**

**Sara(h)** (Sah rah') שרה
The feminine form of Sar, in H., "noble, princess"; in the B. (Genesis),
Abraham's wife, the mother of Isaac and Esau. The Yiddish forms are
Sorali, Sorke, Sura, and Tzirel.** Other forms with the same meaning
are *Sarai* (Sah rahy') שרי, in the B. (Genesis), the original name
of Sara;* *Sari* (Sah' ree) שרי;** *Sarit* (Sah reet') שרית;** *Sarita*
(Sah ree' tah) שריתה;* and *Sarali* (Sah rah lee') שרהלי, in H., "my
princess."****

**Sasona** (Sah soh' nah) ששונה
The feminine form of Sason, in H., "joy." Nickname is *Sisi* (See'
see) שישי.*

**Savyon** (Sahv yohn') סביון
In H., the name of a plant, groundsel or yellow-weed. Also the name
of a place in Israel in the shefelah, named after the flower. Used also
as a boy's name.** Other forms with the same meaning are *Savyona*
(Sahv yoh' nah) סביונה;* and *Savyonit* (Sahv yoh neet') סביונית.**

**Shaanana** (Shah ah nah nah') שאננה
The feminine form of Shaanan, in H., "tranquil, peaceful."* Another
form is *Shaananit* (Shah ah nah neet') שאננית.****

**Shachaf** (Shah' chahf) שחף
In H., "seagull." Used also as a boy's name.****

**Shachar** (Shah′ chahr) שחר
In H., "dawn, morning." Also the name of a place (moshav) in Israel in
the shefelah. Used also as a boy's name.*** Another form is *Shacharit*
(Shah chah reet′) שחרית, also the name of the morning prayer.*

**Shafirit** (Shah fee reet′) שפירית
The feminine form of Shafir, in H., "fine, excellent, good."**

**Shafririt** (Shahf ree reet′) שפרירית
Another form of Shafirit, or the feminine form of Shafrir, in H.,
"canopy."**

**Shai** (Shahy) שי
In H., "gift, present." Used mainly as a boy's name.** Another form
is *Shai-Lee* (Shahy′ Lee) שי־לי, in H., "my gift."****

**Shaked** (Shah kehd′) שקד
In H., "almond." A symbolic name for both girls and boys born on Tu
b'Shvat, the New Year of the Trees. For more information, see Shaked
in the boys' section.** Other forms with the same meaning are
*Shkeda* (Shkeh dah′) שקדה;* and *Shkediya* (Shkeh dee yah′) שקדיה.*

**Shalechet** (Shah leh′ cheht) שלכת
In H., "fall of leaves, effoliation."****

**Shalhevet** (Shahl heh′ veht) שלהבת
In H., "flame, blaze."**** Other forms are *Shalhavit* (Shahl hah veet′)
שלהבית, in H., the name of a plant with big yellow flowers, phlox;
also the name of a community settlement in Israel in the Negev
named after the flower;**** and *Shalhevetya* (Shahl heh veht yah′)
שלהבתיה, in H., "God's flame."****

**Shalva(h)** (Shahl vah′) שלווה
In H., "calmness, tranquility, security, peace." Also the name of a
place (moshav) in Israel in the shefelah.** Other forms are *Shalvit*
(Shahl veet′) שלווית, same meaning;**** and *Shalviya* (Shahl vee yah′)
שלוויה, in H., "God's calmness."****

**Shani** (Shah nee′) שני
In H., "scarlet, crimson." Literally "crimson thread" is the principal
motif of a story, the thread that runs through the whole tale. Used
also as a boy's name.** Another form is *Shanit* (Shah neet′) שנית, in
H., "scarletina" and also the name of a plant, lythrum.**

**Sharon** (Shah rohn′) שרון
From the H., "plain, flat area." The name of an area in west Israel,
from Mount Carmel south to Jaffa. In the B., this area was reputed to
be fertile soil, filled with woods and flowers. Chavatzelet Hasharon is

the name of a flower (lily) growing in this area, and also the name of
a place (moshav) in the Sharon named after the flower. Used also as
a boy's name.*** Other forms with the same meaning are *Sharona*
(Shah roh' nah) שרונה, also the name of a place (moshav) in Israel in
the Galilee;*** and *Sharonit* (Shah roh neet') שרונית.**

**Shaula** (Shah oo' lah) שאולה
The feminine form of Shaul (Saul), see Shaul.* Another form is
*Shaulit* (Shah oo leet') שאולית.*

**Shavit** (Shah veet') שביט
In H., "comet." Used also as a boy's name.**

**Shchina** (Shchee nah') שכינה
In H., "Divine Presence."*

**Shdema** (Shdeh mah') שדמה
In H., "field, cornfield." A symbolic name for girls born on Shavuot,
the Feast of the Harvest. Also the name of a place (moshav) in Israel
in the shefelah.*** Another form is *Shadmit* (Shahd meet') שדמית.****

**Sheina** (Shehy' neh) שיינא
From the Y., "beautiful." Other forms are Shaina, Shayna, and Sheindel.*

**Sheli** (Sheh' lee) שלי
In H., "mine, belong to me." Also spelled Shelli.**

**Shenhav** (Shehn hahv') שנהב
In H., "ivory."****

**Shfi** (Shfee) שפי
In H., "bare hill."****

**Shibolet** (Shee boh' leht) שיבולת
In H., "ear of corn, grain stalk" or "current of a river." A symbolic
name for girls born on Shavuot, the Feast of the Harvest. Shibolim is
the name of a place (moshav) in Israel in the Negev.** Another form
is *Shibolit* (Shee boh leet') שיבולית.****

**Shifra(h)** (Sheef rah') שיפרה
From the H., "good, fine, beautiful" or "to improve"; in the B. (Exodus),
a midwife.*

**Shikma** (Sheek mah') שיקמה
In H., the name of a tree, sycamore, that grows in Israel in the Shefelah
and in the Negev.** Another form is *Shikmona* (Sheek moh' nah)
שיקמונה, also the name of an ancient city in Israel.*

**Shilo(h)** (Shee loh') שילוה
From the H., "his gift"; in the B. (Genesis), the name of a place. The
name of a community settlement in Israel in Samaria (Shomron)

named after this ancient city. Used also as a boy's name.**** Another
form is *Shilat* (Shee laht') שילת, also the name of a place (moshav) in
central Israel.****

**Shimona** (Sheem oh' nah) שמעונה
The feminine form of Shimon (Simeon), see Shimon.* Another form
is *Shimat* (Sheem aht') שימעת, in the B. (II Kings).*

**Shimrit** (Sheem reet') שימרית
From the H., "guard, keeper, protector"; in the B. (I Chronicles).***
Other forms with the same meaning are *Shimra* (Sheem rah') שימרה;*
*Shimrat* (Sheem raht') שימרת;**** *Shimriya* (Sheem ree yah') שימריה,
in H., "God is my protector," also spelled Shimria(h);** *Shomera*
(Shoh meh rah') שומרה, in H., "watchman's hut," also the name of a
place (moshav) in Israel in the Galilee;* *Shomriya* (Shohm ree yah')
שומריה, same meaning, also spelled Shomria(h), also the name of a
place (kibbutz) in central Israel;* *Shomrat* (Shohm raht') שומרת,
from the H., "guard," also the name of a place (kibbutz) in Israel in
the Galilee;** and *Shmura* (Shmoo rah') שמורה, in H., "reserve" or
"eyelash"; many names of places in Israel start with this word.****

**Shir** (Sheer) שיר
In H., "song, chant, poem." Used also as a boy's name.*** Other forms
are *Shiri* (Shee' ree) שירי, in H., "my song" or "you will sing";***
*Shira(h)* (Shee rah') שירה, in H., "poetry";** *Shirel* (Sheer ehl') שיראל,
in H., "God's song";**** *Shir-Lee* and *Shirly* (Sheer' Lee) שירלי,
in H., "the song is mine";*** *Shirili* (Shee ree lee') שירילי, in H., "sing
to me";**** *Shirit* (Shee reet') שירית, in H., "a small song";** *Shiran*
(Shee rahn') שירן, in H., "a happy song," used also as a boy's name
(see Shir);** and *Shiraz* (Shee rahz') שירז, in H., "a secret song."**

**Shita** (Shee tah') שיטה
In H., the name of a tree, acacia. Beyth Hashita is the name of a place
(kibbutz) in Israel in the Valley of Esdraelon (Jezreel). Shitim is the
name of a place in Israel in the Negev, named after the tree.**

**Shlomit** (Shloh meet') שלומית
From the H., "peace, peaceful"; in the B. (Leviticus).***

**Shlom-Tziyon** (Shlohm' Tzee yohn') שלום־ציון
In H., "peace of Zion." Another name for Salome Alexandra, who was
a ruler of Judea.*

**Shmuela** (Shmoo eh' lah) שמואלה
The feminine form of Shmuel (Samuel). See Shmuel.*

**Shomrona** (Shohm roh' nah) שומרונה
The feminine form of Shomron. See Shomron.**

**Shoshana(h)** (Shoh shah nah') שושנה
In H., "lily, rose." Shoshanat Haamakim is the name of a flower, lily of the valley, and the name of a place in Israel in the Sharon, named after the flower. Also spelled Shoshanna(h). The English form is Susannah. Nickname is *Shoshi* (Shoh' shee) שושי.** Another form is *Shoshan* (Shoh shahn') שושן, same meaning, also the name of a musical instrument mentioned in the B.****

**Shtila** (Shtee lah') שתילה
In H., "planting." A symbolic name for girls born on Tu b'Shvat, Arbor Day.* Another form is *Shtula* (Shtoo lah') שתולה, also the name of a place (moshav) in Israel in the Galilee.*

**Shulamit** (Shoo lah meet') שולמית
From the H., "peace, peaceful"; in the B. (Song of Songs). Nicknames are *Shula* (Shoo' lah) שולה and *Shuli* (Shoo' lee) שולי.**

**Shunamit** (Shoo nah meet') שונמית
In H., "from Shunam"; in the B. (II Kings), the name of a city. Avishag Hashunamit was reputed in the B. (I Kings) to be the most beautiful young woman in Israel, and "warmed" King David in his old age.****

**Shunit** (Shoo neet') שונית
In H., "cliff, reef in the seacoast."**** Another form is *Shuni* (Shoo' nee) שוני, only in the B. (Genesis) used as a boy's name.*

**Si** (See) סי
The name of the seventh note in music. Also, the name of a famous Israeli singer, Si Heiman.****

**Sigal** (See gahl') סיגל
From the H., the color violet; the name of a flower, viola tricolor; or "treasure."*** Other forms are *Sigalit* (See gah leet') סיגלית, same meanings, nickname *Sigi* (See' gee) סיגי;*** *Sigaliya* (See gah lee yah') and *Sigliya* (Seeg lee yah') סיגליה, from the H., "God's treasure";* and *Sgula* (Sgoo lah') סגולה, in H., "treasure, tract, remedy," also the name of a place (moshav) in Israel in the shefelah.*

**Sima** (See' mah) סימה
From the Aramaic, "treasure."* Another form is *Simona* (See moh' nah) סימונה.*

**Simcha** (Seem chah') שמחה
In H., "joy, gladness, mirth, festivity." Used also as a boy's name.* Other forms with the same meanings are *Simchit* (Seem cheet') שמחית;**** *Simchona* (Seem choh' nah) שמחונה;* *Simchonit* (Seem choh neet') שמחונית;**** and *Smecha* (Smeh chah') שמחה, in H., "she is glad, happy."*

**Sinaya** (See nahy' yah) סיניה
The feminine form of Sinai. See Sinai.**

**Siona** (See oh' nah) שיאונה
The feminine form of Sion, in H., "highest point, climax."** Another
form is *Sionit* (See oh neet') שיאונית.****

**Sivan** (See vahn') סיוון
The name of the third month in the Jewish calendar, when we celebrate Shavuot. Used also as a boy's name.*** Other forms with the
same meaning are *Sivana* (See vah' nah) סיוונה;** and *Sivanit* (See
vah neet') סיוונית.***

**Smadar** (Smah dahr') סמדר
In H., "bud, blossom"; in the B. (Song of Songs), this word is used for
the sign of spring. Also the name of a place (moshav) in Israel in
the Galilee.***

**Snunit** (Snoo neet') סנונית
In H., the name of a bird, swallow.****

**Stav** (Stahv) סתיו
In H., "autumn, fall." Used also as a boy's name.** Other forms are
*Stavit* (Stah veet') סתווית, in H., "autumnal";** and *Sitvanit* (Seet vah
neet') סיתוונית, in H., the name of a plant, colchicum, that starts to
bloom in Israel in the fall after the first rain.****

**Sufa** (Soo fah') סופה
In H., "storm." Also the name of a place (kibbutz) in south Israel.****

## ת

THE HEBREW LETTERS 'ת, 'צ, 'ט

**Tadmor** (Tahd mohr') תדמור
In the B. (II Chronicles), the name of a city built by King Solomon.
Used also as a boy's name.****

**Tal** (Tahl) טל
In H., "dew." Used also as a boy's name.*** Other forms are *Tali* (Tah'
lee) טלי;*** *Tal-Li* (Tahl' Lee) טל־לי, in H., "my dew";**** *Talila* (Tah
lee' lah) טלילה;** *Tal-Ora* (Tahl Oh' rah) טל־אורה, the feminine form
of Tal-Or (see Tal), in H., "dew of light," meaning "morning light";**
*Tlalit* (Tlah leet') טללית, in H., the name of a plant, "sundew";****
*Talya* (Tahl' yah) טליה, in H., also "young lambs";*** *Tal-Chemed*

(Tahl Cheh' mehd) טל־חמד, in H., "dew of grace, charm, beauty";****
and *Tal-Chen* (Tahl Chehn') טל־חן, in H., "dew of charm."****

**Talma** (Tahl' mah) תלמה
The feminine form of Tel, in H., "mound, hill." Or the feminine form
of Telem, see Telem under Talmai, in H., "furrow."** Another form is
*Talmit* (Tahl meet') תלמית, same meanings.****

**Tamah** (Tah mah') תמה
The feminine form of Tam, in H., "innocent, honest" or "to be surprised,
to wonder."**** Another form is *Tmima* (Tmee mah') תמימה.*

**Tamar** (Tah mahr') תמר
In H., "palm tree, date tree." A symbolic name for girls born on
Sukkoth, because the branches of this tree are used for the roof of the
Sukkah. In the B. (Genesis), the granddaughter of Judah. Nickname
is *Tami* (Tah' mee) תמי. The English nickname is Tammy.*** Other
forms with the same meanings are *Tamarah* (Tah mah' rah) תמרה;**
*Tmarah* (Tmah rah') תמרה;** and *Timrat* (Teem raht') תימרת, also
the name of a community settlement in Israel in the Galilee.****

**Tammuz** (Tah mooz') תמוז
Name of a Babylonian deity in charge of springtime (Ezekiel) and
the name of the fourth month in the Jewish calendar. Used also as
a boy's name.**

**Tavora** (Tah voh' rah) תבורה
The feminine form of Tavor. See Tavor.*

**Tchiya** (Tchee yah') תחיה
In H., "revival, resurrection, rebirth, renewal." Also spelled Tchia(h).*

**Tchula** (Tchoo lah') תכולה
In H., "blue."****

**Te'ena** (Teh eh nah') תאנה
In H., "fig, fig tree." A symbol of peace, "to sit under one's vine and fig
tree." Also a symbolic name for girls born on Tu b'Shvat, because on
this day we eat fruits which grow in Israel (the seven kinds), and figs
are one of them. Te'enim is the name of a place in Israel in Samaria
(Shomron).****

**Tehila** (Teh hee lah') תהילה
In H., "praise, song of praise, psalm" or "glory, fame." Also spelled
Tehilla.**

**Temana** (Tehy mah' na) תימנה
The feminine form of Teman. See Teman.*

**Tidhar** (Teed hahr') תידהר
In H., the name of a tree, elm. Also the name of a place (moshav) in Israel in the Negev. Used also as a boy's name.****

**Tifara** (Teef ah rah') תפארה
In H., "beauty, splendor, glory."* Another form is *Tiferet* (Teef eh' reht) תפארת.*

**Tifrachat** (Teef rah' chaht) תפרחת
In H., "blossoming, flourishing."*

**Tikva** (Teek vah') תקווה
In H., "hope." Hatikva is the Jewish national anthem. Only in the B., used as a boy's name. Nickname is *Tiki* (Tee' kee) תיקי.**

**Tiltan** (Teel tahn') תלתן
In H., "clover, trefoil."****

**Timna** (Teem' nah) תמנע
From the H., "to parry, withhold, to deny, prevent"; only in B., used as a boy's name. Also the name of a place (copper mine) in south Israel.**** Another form is *Timnat* (Teem naht') תמנת.****

**Tira** (Tee rah') טירה
In H., "villa, palace, small village." A few names of places in Israel contain this word.*

**Tirtza** (Teer tzah') תרצה
From the H., "to please" or "to explain"; in the B. (Numbers).*

**Tirza** (Teer zah') תירזה
In H., the name of a tree, holm oak (in biblical times), linden (currently).****

**Tivona** (Teev oh' nah) טבעונה
The feminine form of Tivon, in H., "naturist, nature lover."**** Another form is *Tivonit* (Teev oh neet') טבעונית, in H., "vegetarian."****

**Tkuma(h)** (Tkoo mah') תקומה
In H., "resistance, recovery, revival." Also the name of a place (moshav) in Israel in the shefelah.*

**Tmira(h)** (Tmee rah') תמירה
The feminine form of Tamir, in H., "tall, erect, upstanding, upright like the palm tree."** Or טמירה, in H., "hidden, secret."** Other forms are *Timora* (Tee moh' rah) תימורה, in H., "palmette" (ornament);** and טימורה, from the H., "hidden."**

**Tmura(h)** (Tmoo rah') תמורה
In H., "exchange, value, substitution."*

**Tnuva(h)** (Tnoo vah') תנובה
In H., "produce, product, yield." Also the name of the workers cooperative in Israel for marketing and distributing farm produce. Tnuvot is the name of a place (moshav) in Israel in the Sharon.****

**Tochelet** (Toh cheh' leht) תוחלת
In H., "hope, expectation." Also the name of a place in Israel in the shefelah.*

**Tova(h)** (Toh vah') טובה
In H., "good."** Other forms with the same meaning are *Tovit* (Toh veet') טובית;** and *Tuvit* (Too veet') טובית.****

**Truma(h)** (Troo mah') תרומה
In H., "offering, gift, donation, contribution."*

**Tshura(h)** (Tshoo rah') תשורה
In H., "gift, present."****

**Tshuva(h)** (Tshoo vah') תשובה
In H., "reply, answer, return, repentance." A symbolic name for girls born during the Ten Days of Penitence (in H., Asseret Yemey Tshuva) between Rosh Hashanah and Yom Kippur.*

**Tushiya** (Too shee yah') תושיה
In H., "advice, wisdom, understanding." Also the name of a place in Israel in the Negev.*

**Tut** (Toot) תות
In H., "strawberry, mulberry."****

**Tvuna(h)** (Tvoo nah') תבונה
In H., "intelligence, understanding, wisdom."*

**Tzabarit** (Tzah bah reet') צברית
The feminine form of Tzabar. See Tzabar. Also spelled Zabarit.*

**Tzadika** (Tzah dee kah') צדיקה
The feminine form of Tzadik, in H., "pious." Also spelled Zudika.* Another form is *Tzadeket* (Tzah deh' keht) צדקת, same meaning, also spelled Zadeket.*

**Tzafnat** (Tzahf naht') צפנת
From the H., "secret"; in the B. (Genesis), Zzafnat Pa'aneach was the Egyptian name of Joseph, meaning "revealer of secrets." Also spelled Zafnat.****

**Tzafrira** (Tzahf ree rah') צפרירה
The feminine form of Tzafrir, in H., "morning light, morning breeze." Also spelled Zafrira.** Other forms are *Tzafra* (Tzahf' rah) צפרה, from the Aramaic, "morning," also spelled Zafra;* and *Tzafrit* (Tzahf

reet') צפרית, in H., "aubade, morning music," also spelled Zafrit.**
Other forms with the same meaning are *Tzafririt* (Tzahf ree reet')
צפרירית, also spelled Zafririt;** and *Tzfira* (Tzfee' rah) צפירה, also
spelled Zfira.*

**Tzahala** (Tzah hah lah') צהלה
In H., "joy, rejoicing." Also the name of a suburb of Tel Aviv. Also
spelled Zahala.*

**Tzameret** (Tzah meh' reht) צמרת
In H., "tree top" and "upper class, upper part, leadership." Also spelled
Zameret.****

**Tzchora** (Tzchoh rah') צחורה
In H., "white." Also spelled Zchora.* Another form is *Tzchorit*
(Tzchoh reet') צחורית, also spelled Zchorit, same meaning.****

**Tzidona** (Tzee doh' nah) צידונה
The feminine form of Tzidon. See Tzidon. Nickname is *Tzidi* (Tzee'
dee) צידי.*

**Tzifriya** (Tzeef ree yah') צפריה
From the H., "ornithologist." Also spelled Zifriya. Also the name of a
place (moshav) in central Israel.**** Another form is *Tzifrona* (Tzeef
roh' nah) צפרונה, also spelled Zifrona, same meaning.****

**Tzila** (Tzee lah') צילה
From the H., "shadow, shade." Also spelled Zilu. In the B. (Genesis),
one of Lamech's wives.** Other forms are *Tzili* (Tzee' lee) צילי, in
H., "my shadow," also spelled Zili;** and *Tzelya* (Tzehl yah') צליה, in
H., "God's shadow," meaning "God's protection."****

**Tzipiya** (Tzee pee yah') ציפיה
In H., "expectation, anticipation." Also spelled Zipiya.*

**Tzipora(h)** (Tzee poh' rah) ציפורה
In H., "bird"; in the B. (Exodus), the wife of Moses. Also spelled
Zipora(h), Zippora(h). The Yiddish forms are Tzeitl and Tzertel.
Nickname is *Tzipi* (Tzee' pee) ציפי.** Other forms are *Tzipor* (Tzee
pohr') ציפור, same meaning, also spelled Zipor;**** *Tzipori* (Tzee
poh ree') ציפורי, in H., "my bird," also the name of a place (moshav)
in Israel in the Galilee, also spelled Zipori;* and *Tziporit* (Tzee poh
reet') ציפורית, in H., "small bird," also spelled Ziporit.****

**Tziporen** (Tzee poh' rehn) ציפורן
In H., "nail" and the name of a plant with colorful flowers, carnation.
Also spelled Ziporen.****

**Tzira** (Tzee rah′) צירה
From the H., "messenger." Also spelled Zira.*

**Tziyona** (Tzee yoh′ nah) ציונה
The feminine form of Tzion. See Tzion. Nes Tziyona is the name of a place in Israel near Tel Aviv. Also spelled Ziona.* Another form is *Tzionit* (Tzee yoh neet′) ציונית, also spelled Zionit.*

**Tzlila** (Tzlee′ lah) צלילה
The feminine form of Tzlil, in H., "tone, sound." Also spelled Zlila.* Other forms are *Tzlili* (Tzleel′ lee) צלילי, in H., "my tone," also spelled Zlili;**** and *Tzlilit* (Tzlee leet′) צלילית, from the H., "tone," also spelled Zlilit.****

**Tzofit** (Tzoh feet′) צופית
From the H., "scout, guard." Also the name of a place (moshav) in Israel in the Sharon. Also spelled Zofit.** Another form is *Tzofiya* (Tzoh fee yah′) צופיה, in H., "she is watching," also spelled Zofiya.*

**Tzruya** (Tzroo yah′) צרויה
In H., "pointed with tzere" (vowel). Also spelled Zruya.****

**Tzufit** (Tzoo feet′) צופית
In H., the name of a small singing bird, honeysucker or sunbird, that lives only in Israel. Also spelled Zufit.****

**Tzukit** (Tzoo keet′) צוקית
In H., the name of a singing bird, thrush, that lives in the mountains.****

**Tzurit** (Tzoo reet′) צורית
In H., the name of a plant, sedum. Also the name of a community settlement in Israel in the Galilee named after the flower. Or the feminine form of Tzur, in H., "rock, cliff," referring to strength. Also spelled Zurit.**** Other forms are *Tzuriela* (Tzoo ree eh′ lah) צוריאלה, the feminine form of Tzuriel (see Tzur), in H., "God is my rock," meaning "God is my strength," also spelled Zuriela;**** and *Tzuriya* (Tzoo ree yah′) צוריה, in H., "God is my rock," also spelled Zuriya, used also as a boy's name (see Tzur).**

**Tzviya** (Tzvee yah′) צביה
The feminine form of Tzvi, in H., "deer, gazelle." Also the name of a place (kibbutz) in Israel in the Galilee. Also spelled Zviya. Nickname is *Tzivi* (Tzee′ vee) ציבי.** Other forms are *Tzivya* (Tzeev yah′) ציביה, in H., "God's gazelle," in the B. (II Kings), the mother of King Yehoash, also spelled Tzivia and Zivia;* and *Tzviela* (Tzvee eh′ lah) צביאלה, the feminine form of Tzviel (see Tzvi), in H., "God's gazelle," also spelled Zviela.*

# U

**Udit** (Oo deet') אודית
The feminine form of Ud. See Ud.**** Another form is *Udiya* (Oo dee yah') אודיה, in H., "fire of God." Also spelled Udia(h).****

**Uma** (Oo mah') אומה
In H., "nation." A symbolic name for girls born on the Israeli Independence Day.*

**Uriela** (Oo ree eh' lah) אוריאלה
In H., "flame of God, light of God." A symbolic name for girls born on Hanukkah. Also spelled Uriella.***

**Urit** (Oo reet') אורית
The feminine form of Ur, in H., "flame, fire, light." Also spelled Urith.**** Another form is *Uranit* (Oo rah neet') אורנית, same meaning.****

**Uzit** (Oo zeet') עוזית
The feminine form of Uzi, in H., "strength."**** Another form is *Uziela* (Oo zee eh' lah) עוזיאלה, in H., "God is my strength." Also spelled Uziella.**

# V

**Varda** (Vahr' dah) ורדה
From the H., "rose" or "pink" (the color).*** Other forms with the same meaning are *Vardina* (Vahr dee' nah) ורדינה;** and *Vardit* (Vahr deet') ורדית.*** Other forms that mean, from the H., "rose of God," are *Vardiya* (Vahr dee yah') ורדיה;* and *Vardiel(l)a* (Vahr dee eh' lah) ורדיאלה.****

**Vered** (Veh' rehd) ורד
In H., "rose." Vered Hagalil is the name of a place in Israel in Galilee.*** Another form is *Veredya* (Veh rehd yah') ורדיה, in H., "rose of God."*****

# Y

**Ya'a** (Yah ah') יאה
In H., "beautiful" or "to fit."*

**Yaakova** (Yah ah koh' vah) יעקובה
The feminine form of Yaakov (Jacob). See Yaakov. The English form
is Jacoba.* Other forms with the same meaning are *Yaakovina* (Yah
ah koh vee' nah) יעקובינה;* and *Yaakovit* (Yah ah koh veet') יעקובית.*

**Yaara** (Yah ah rah') יערה
The feminine form of Yaar, in H., "forest" or "honeycomb" or the
name of a plant, honeysuckle. Also the name of a place (moshav) in
Israel in the Galilee named after the forests in this area.** Another
form is *Yaarit* (Yah ah reet') יערית, same meaning, also the name of
a place in Samaria (Shomron).***

**Yael** (Yah ehl') יעל
In H., "mountain goat"; in the B. (Judges), the woman who killed Sisra.
Also the name of a place in north Israel.*** Other forms with the same
meaning are *Yaala* (Yah ah lah') יעלה, in H., the symbol of a graceful
woman;* *Yaalat* (Yah ah laht') יעלת;**** *Yaalat-Chen* (Yah ah laht'
Chehn) יעלת־חן, in H., "beautiful, charming woman";**** *Yaalit* (Yah
ah leet') יעלית;**** *Yeela* (Yeh eh lah') יעלה;** and *Ye'elit* (Yeh eh
leet') יעלית.****

**Yaen** (Yah ehn') יען
In H., "ostrich."** Another form is *Yaanit* (Yah ah neet') יענית.****

**Yafa** (Yah fah') יפה
In H., "beautiful, pretty, lovely" or "worthy."* Other forms with the
same meaning are *Yafit* (Yah feet') יפית, also the name of a place
(moshav) in Israel in the Jordan Valley;*** and *Yofit* (Yoh feet')
יופית.****

**Yahaloma** (Yah hah loh' mah) יהלומה
The feminine form of Yahahlom, in H., "diamond."* Another form is
*Yahalomit* (Yah hah loh meet') יהלומית.****

**Yahel** (Yah hehl') יהל
In H., "will build a tent" or "will shine." Also the name of a place
(kibbutz) in Israel in the Arava. Used also as a boy's name.*** Other
forms with the same meaning are *Yahala* (Yah hah lah') יהלה;** and
*Yahali* (Yah hah lee') יהלי.**

**Yaira** (Yah ee' rah) יאירה
The feminine form of Yair, in H., "to light, to shine, to enlighten."**
Another form is *Yeira(h)* (Yeh ee' rah) יאירה.**

**Yakinton** (Yah keen tohn') יקינתון
In H., the name of a plant, hyacinth.****

**Yakira** (Yah kee rah') יקירה
The feminine form of Yakar, in H., "dear, expensive, precious."*
Another form is *Yekara(h)* (Yeh kah rah') יקרה.*

**Yama** (Yah mah') ימה
In H., "lake, closed sea."** Or, in a different pronunciation (Yah' mah),
in H., "westward."* Another form is *Yamit* (Yah meet') ימית, same
meaning, the name of a place in south Israel in the Sinai peninsula,
before it was returned to Egypt.**

**Yarden** (Yahr dehn') ירדן
From the H., "to go down." The name of the longest river in Israel
that flows from the north to the south. Also the name of a state. The
English form is Jordan. Used also as a boy's name.*** Other forms
with the same meaning are *Yardena* (Yahr deh' nah) ירדנה, also the
name of a very popular Israeli singer, Yardena Arazi;*** *Yardenya*
(Yahr deh nee yah') ירדניה, in H., "Jordan of God," also spelled
Yardenia(h);* *Yarden-Li* (Yahr dehn Lee') ירדן-לי, in H., "my
Jordan";**** and *Yardenit* (Yahr deh neet') ירדנית, same meaning.**

**Yarkona** (Yahr koh' nah) ירקונה
The feminine form of Yarkon. See Yarkon.*

**Yarona** (Yah roh' nah) ירונה
The feminine form of Yaron, in H., "she will sing, she will be joyous."**

**Yasmin** (Yahs meen') יסמין
In H., the name of a plant, jasmine.**** Another form is *Yasmina*
(Yahs mee' nah) יסמינה.*

**Yas'ur** (Yahs oor') יסעור
In H., the name of a water bird, seawater or puffin. Also the name of a
place (kibbutz) in Israel in the Galilee. Used also as a boy's name.****

**Yavn'ela** (Yahv neh eh' lah) יבנאלה
The feminine form of Yavne'el. See Yavne'el.*

**Yechezkela** (Yeh chehz keh' lah) יחזקאלה
The feminine form of Yechezkel (Ezekiel). See Yechezkel.*

**Yechiela** (Yeh chee eh' lah) יחיאלה
The feminine form of Yechiel. See Yechiel. Also spelled Yechiella.*

**Yedida(h)** (Yeh dee dah') ידידה
In H., "female friend, beloved"; in the B. (II Kings), the mother of
Josiah. Also the name of a place in central Israel. Nickname is *Didi*
(Dee' dee) דידי.**

**Yehava** (Yeh hah vah') יהבה
The feminine form of Yahav, in H., "to give" or "gift."**** Other forms
with the same meaning are *Yahava* (Yah hah vah');**** and *Yahavit*
(Yah hah veet') יהבית.****

**Yehoadan** (Yeh hoh ah dahn') יהועדן
From the H., "God has adorned"; in the B. (II Kings), the wife of
King Yoash.****

**Yehosheva** (Yeh hoh sheh' vah) יהושבע
From the H., "God's oath"; in the B. (II Kings), a daughter of Yoram.*
Another form is *Yehoshavat* (Yeh hoh shahv aht') יהושבעת.*

**Yehudit** (Yeh hoo deet') יהודית
The feminine form of Yehuda(h), from the H., "to praise, to thank" or
"Jewish woman"; in the B. (Genesis), the wife of Esau. The English
form is Judith. Nickname is *Yudit* (Yoo' deet) יודית.**

**Yemima** (Yeh mee' mah) ימימה
From the H., "one who lived many days, an old one"; in the B. (Job).*

**Yentel** (Yehn' tehl) יענטל
A Yiddish name. Other forms are Yenta, Yente, and Yentil.*

**Yeruchama** (Yeh roo chah' mah) ירוחמה
The feminine form of Yerucham. See Yerucham under Yerachmiel.
Another form is *Yerachmiela* (Yeh rahch mee eh' lah) ירחמיאלה, the
feminine form of Yerachmiel. See Yerachmiel.*

**Yerusha** (Yeh roo shah') ירושה
In H., "inheritance"; in the B. (II Chronicles), the mother of King
Jotham.*

**Yifat** (Yeef aht') יפעת
From the H., "beauty, brightness, brilliance, splendor." Also spelled
Yif'at. Also the name of a place (kibbutz) in Israel in the Valley of
Esdraelon (Jezreel).*** Another form is *Yifa* (Yeef ah') יפעה, also
spelled Yif'a, same meaning.****

**Yigaela** (Yee gah eh' lah) יגאלה
The feminine form of Yigal. See Yigal.*

**Yisraela** (Yees rah eh' lah) ישראלה
The feminine form of Yisrael, the name that was given to Jacob
(Yaakov) after wrestling with God's angel. The name of the Jewish

nation and the Jewish state (Israel). A symbolic name for girls born on the Israeli Independence Day.** Another form is *Yisraelit* (Yees rah eh leet') ישראלית, in H., "female Israeli."*

**Yizr'ela** (Yeez reh eh' lah) יזרעאלה
The feminine form of Yizr'el. See Yizr'el.*

**Yochana** (Yoh chah' nah) יוחנה
The feminine form of Yochanan. See Yochanan under Yehochanan.*

**Yocheved** (Yoh cheh' vehd) יוכבד
From the H., "God's glory, God's respect"; in the B. (Exodus), the mother of Moses, Aaron, and Miriam. Nickname is *Yochi* (Yoh' chee) יוכי.*

**Yodfat** (Yohd faht') יודפת
The name of a place (moshav) in Israel in the Galilee named after an ancient place.****

**Yoela** (Yoh eh' lah) יואלה
The feminine form of Yoel, in H., "God will be willing." The English form is Joela.** Another form is *Yoelit* (Yoh eh leet') יואלית, same meaning.****

**Yona(h)** (Yoh nah') יונה
In H., "dove." A symbolic name for both girls and boys born on Yom Kippur, the Day of Atonement, when we read the story about Yonah, the prophet who was swallowed by a big fish. The English form is Jona(h).* Other forms with the same meaning are *Yonat* (Yoh naht') יונת;**** *Yonati* (Yoh nah tee') יונתי, in H., "my dove";**** *Yonina* (Yoh nee' nah) יונינה;* and *Yonit* (Yoh neet') יונית, from the H., "small dove."**

**Yosefa** (Yoh seh' fah) יוספה
The feminine form of Yosef (Joseph). See Yosef. Nickname is *Sefi* (Seh' fee) ספי.*

**Yotvat** (Yoht vaht') יוטבת
From the H., "good." Yotvata is the name of a place (kibbutz) in Israel in the Arava.**** Another form is *Yatva* (Yaht vah') יטבה, same meaning, in the B. (II Kings), the name of a place.*

**Yovela** (Yoh veh' lah) יובלה
The feminine form of Yovel. See Yovel.*

**Yuli** (Yoo' lee) יולי
The H. name for the month of July. Used especially by those who like a H. name with an English sound.**** Another form is *Yulit* (Yoo leet') יולית, no meaning in H.****

# Z

**Zaha(h)** (Zah kah') זכה
The feminine form of Zach, in H., "pure, clean, clear, innocent."* Other forms with the same meaning are *Zakit* (Zah keet') זכית;* and *Zakiya* (Zah kee yah') זכיה, also spelled Zakia(h).*

**Zeeva** (Zeh eh vah') זאבה
The feminine form of Ze'ev, in H., "wolf."* Another form is *Zeevit* (Zeh eh veet') זאבית.*

**Zehava** (Zeh hah' vah) זהבה
In H., "gold, golden."** The Y. forms are Golda or Zlate.* Other forms with the same meaning are *Zahava* (Zah hah' vah);* *Zehavit* (Zeh hah veet') זהבית;** *Zehovit* (Zeh hoh veet') זהובית;**** *Zehuva* (Zeh hoo vah') זהובה;**** *Zehuvit* (Zeh hoo veet') זהובית;**** and *Zehavya* (Zeh hahv' yah) זהביה, in H., "God's gold."****

**Zichriya** (Zeech ree' yah) זיכריה
The feminine form of Zcharya, in H., "remembrance."* Other forms are *Zichrini* (Zeech ree' nee) זיכריני, in H., "remember me," also the name of a plant with blue flowers (forget-me-not);**** and *Zichrona* (Zeech roh' nah) זיכרונה, in H., "my memory."*

**Zilpa(h)** (Zeel pah') זילפה
From the H., "dripping, sprinkling"; in the B. (Genesis), one of Jacob's wives.*

**Zimra** (Zeem rah') זימרה
In H., "choice fruit, choice produce, object of praise," or "singing, music, chant."** Other forms are *Zimrat* (Zeem raht') זימרת, same meaning, also the name of a place (moshav) in Israel in the Negev;** *Zimriya* (Zeem ree yah') זימריה, in H., "singing festival";**** and *Zmira* (Zmee' rah) זמירה, in H., "song, singing, hymn."**

**Ziv** (Zeev) זיו
In H., "brilliance, light, splendor, glory." Also a synonym for the month Iyar, the second month in the Jewish calendar, when we celebrate Israel's Independence Day. Used also as a boy's name.*** Other forms with the same meaning are *Ziva* (Zee' vah) זיווה;*** *Zivi* (Zee' vee) זיווי, used also as a boy's name (see Ziv);** *Zivit* (Zee veet') זיווית;*** and *Zivanit* (Zee vah neet') זיוונית, also the name of a flower, mayflower.***

**Zmora(h)** (Zmoh rah′) זמורה
In H., "branch, shoot, vine, twig."****

**Zohar** (Zoh′ hahr) זוהר
In H., "brightness, light, splendor, glamour." Used also as a boy's name. Also the name of a place (moshav) in south Israel.*** Other forms with the same meaning are *Zahara* (Zah hah′ rah) זהרה;* *Zohara* (Zoh hah′ rah) זוהרה;** *Zoheret* (Zoh heh′ reht) זוהרת, in H., "she shines";**** and *Zaharira* (Zah hah ree′ rah) זהרירה.*

# APPENDIXES

# Appendix I:

# Names from the
# Jewish Calendar

Many names are related to Jewish holidays. If you know the baby's due date, you can plan ahead and choose a name reflecting the season, month, or the Jewish holiday of the birthday.

Boys' Names

*Names of Months:*

Adar, Av, Cheshvan, Elul, Iyar, Nissan, Sivan, Tammuz, Tishrey, and Ziv (a synonym for the month Iyar)

*Names of Seasons:*

Aviv (and its variations) and Stav

*Symbolic Name for Boys Born on Yom Kippur:*

Yona(h)

*Symbolic Names for Boys Born on Sukkoth:*

Asaf, Dekel, and Rimon

*Symbolic Names for Boys Born on Hanukkah:*

Achiner, Chanoch, Lahav, Lapid, Leenur, Leeor (and its variations), Macabee, Maor, Maoz, Matityahu (see under Matitya), Ner (and its variations), Nur (and its variations), Or (and its variations), Shamash, Ur, Uri (and its variations), and Yehuda(h)

*Symbolic Names for Boys Born on Tu b'Shvat:*

Alon, Dekel, Eilon, Elon (see under Eilon), Ilan (and its variations), Luz, Mata, Netael, Netzer, Nir (and its variations), Nitzan, Notea, Shaked, Shatil, Tomer, and Tzemach

*Symbolic Names for Boys Born on Purim:*

Adar, Avichayil, and Mordechai

*Symbolic Names for Boys Born on Passover:*

Amichur, Amidror, Ben-Chorin, Cherut, Dror, Eliyahu, Leedror, Nissan, Pesach (and its variations), and Pdut (and its variations)

*Symbolic Names for Boys Born on the Israeli Independence Day:*

Amichur, Artzi, Binyamin-Ze'ev, Hertzel, and Yisrael

*Symbolic Names for Boys Born on Lag b'Omer:*

Akiva, Bar-Kochva, Chetz, Giora, Keshet, Meron, Omer, and Yochai

*Symbolic Names for Boys Born on Shavuot:*

Amir, Asif (see under Asaf), Bar, Boaz, Dagan, Eshbol, Gadish, Goren, Katzir, Magal, Morag, Omer, Sinai, Sivan, and Teneh

*Symbolic Name for Boys Born on Tishah b'Av:*

Menachem

*Symbolic Names for Boys Born on Shabbat:*

Ner (and its variations) and Shabbat

*Symbolic Names for Boys Born on Rosh Hodesh:*

Sahar and Yerach

*A Symbolic Name for All the Jewish Holidays:*

Chagai (and its variations)

GIRLS' NAMES

*Names of Months:*

Adara, Elula, Nissana, Sivan (and its variations), Tammuz, and Ziv (and its variations)

*Names of Seasons:*

Aviva(h) (and its variations) and Stav (and its variations)

*Symbolic Name for Girls Born on Rosh Hashanah:*

Tshuva(h)

*Symbolic Names for Girls Born on Yom Kippur:*

Neila(h), Yona(h) (and its variations)

*Symbolic Names for Girls Born on Sukkoth:*

Arava, Hadas, Rimon (and its variations), and Tamar (and its variations)

*Symbolic Names for Girls Born on Hanukkah:*

Avuka, Lehava, Makabit, Menora(h), Meora, Nera(h) (and its variations), Or (and its variations), Uriela, and Urit

*Symbolic Names for Girls Born on Tu b'Shvat:*

Alona, Ilana (and its variations), Luz, Neta (and its variations), Nevet, Nira (and its variations), Nitza(h) (and its variations), Shaked (and its variations), Shtila, and Te'ena

*Symbolic Names for Girls Born on Purim:*

Ester and Hadassa(h)

*Symbolic Names for Girls Born on Passover:*

Cherut, Drora(h) (and its variations), Nissana, and Pdut (and its variations)

*Symbolic Names for Girls Born on the Israeli Independence Day:*

Komemiut, Leuma, Medina, Moledet, Uma, and Yisraela

*Symbolic Names for Girls Born on Lag b'Omer:*

Meirona and Omrit

*Symbolic Names for Girls Born on Shavuot:*

Aluma(h), Amira, Bar, Dagan, Dganit (see under Dganya[h]), Goren (and its variations), Kama, Magal, Morag, Naomi, Omrit, Rut, Shdema, Shibolet, and Sivan (and its variations)

*Symbolic Names for Girls Born on Rosh Hodesh:*

Masua and Sahar

*A Symbolic Name for All the Jewish Holidays:*

Chagit (and its variations)

# *Appendix II:*

# "Double Names"

Many biblical names sound fine in both Hebrew and English, but during the past ten years, more and more Israelis have been looking for modern names that have an international (English or French) sound. Some of these names have a meaning in Hebrew; others have no Hebrew meaning but are still popular.

Even if you have no plans to visit or move to Israel, you might want a Hebrew name for your child that will sound nice in both languages. It is less confusing for a child to have only one name.

### Boys' Names

Adam, Ben, Dan, Din, Don, Edi, Geri, Lee (and its variation), Peri, Ramon (see under Rimon), Ron (and its variations), and Tom

### Girls' Names

Dana, Dina(h), Dorin, Eliana, Elinor, Elinoar, Eliya, Karin and Korin (see both under Keren), Lee (and its variation), Leehi, Libi, Maya, Natalie, Neli, Netali (see under Neta), Peri, Ramona (see under Rimon), Rona (see under Roni), Sharon, Sheli, Shirly, Si, Yuli (and its variation)

# *Appendix III:*

# Names for Multiple Births

As a mother of twins, I am aware of the special dilemma involved in naming them. Some people like to give twins rhymed names, and others believe that rhymed names keep them from developing their own personalities. The decision is yours.

Here you'll find some suggestions for rhymed names and for names with the same meaning.

### TWIN BOYS

Eldad and Medad
Gur and Ari
Ami and Chai
Ami and Yisrael
Dor and Idan
Gil and Ron
Gal and Tal
Raz and Paz
Omer and Tomer
Golan and Dotan

Hillel and Shammai
Ram and Hadar
Yuval and Peleg
Ravid and Raviv
Tal and Shachar
David and Yonatan (see
    Yehonatan)
Amos and Amotz
Ilan and Alon

### TWIN GIRLS

Shir and Rina
Tal and Shachar
Amit and Reut
Ravid and Atara
Rina and Shira (see Shir)
Leeor and Leemor

Zohar and Hila
Gali (see Gal) and Tali (see Tal)
Raz and Paz
Nili and Lili
Ayelet (see Ayala) and Shachar
Moran and Shiran (see Shir)

Keren and Or                     Mor and Levona
Avital and Revital               Idit and Irit
Inbal and Inbar                  Dorit and Orit (see Or)


## TWIN BOYS AND GIRLS

Doron and Dorit                  Dror and Drorit (see Drora[h])
Amnon and Tamar                  Leeor and Leeora (see Leeor)
Ofer and Ofra                    Ben and Bat
Ilan and Ilanit (see Ilana)      Yisrael and Yisraela
Gal and Adva                     Yona(h) and Yonit (see Yona[h])
Alon and Alona                   Ron and Ronit (see Roni)
Dekel and Dikla(h)               Aviv and Avivit (see Aviva[h])
Ori (see Or) and Orit (see Or)   Shalom and Shlomit


## NAMES FOR TRIPLETS

Are you expecting triplets? It's not easy—and it's also not necessary—to find three rhymed names.

I know Israeli parents who named their three boys Am (a short form of Ami), Yisrael, and Chai, which means "the nation of Israel is alive." It's a nice combination, and all three names are modern and popular.

I know Israeli parents who named their three daughters Leeron, Leemor, and Leeraz. Here again, it's a nice combination, but because all the names begin with Lee, they can't give their daughters nicknames.

If you are expecting a multiple birth, the best suggestion is to go through the book *now* (before they arrive in the world) and look for names with a similar meaning but not a similar sound. This will minimize confusion.